The Theory of Poetry

By Lascelles Abercrombie

New York
Harcourt, Brace and Company

PREFACE

THIS volume consists of two distinct treatises, each
of which is meant to be complete in itself. They
are, however, closely related, not only in subject, but
also in the nature and conduct of their argument.
Both, in fact, are attempts to substantiate and illustrate
a general theory of art in the facts of a particular art.
But, while the first treatise, *The Theory of Poetry*,
organises the data of poetical criticism at large, the
second, *The Idea of Great Poetry*, is concerned with a
peculiar and recognisable variety of poetical achievement, and discusses this in order to show how actual
critical judgement (and not merely the methods of
criticism) may be derived from æsthetic theory. That
there are limits to the validity of intellectual criticism in art, I hope I have shown myself properly
aware: temperament and feeling are no more to be
denied here than anywhere else. But where they come
in, criticism, in any strict sense of the word, must stand
aside. Enjoyment, no question, is the main thing; but
the case for criticism is just this, that enjoyment varies
directly with understanding. Now criticism is precisely an attempt to improve and secure understanding; and if criticism must stand aside to let temperament and feeling pass, it does so in order to allow
them to pass *forward*, on the path its pioneering has
cleared; and intelligence is its hatchet.

5

Preface

I know very well that both treatises have deficiencies for which some apology may be expected. In the first, the grounds of criticism are in some places but cursorily surveyed; in the second, many obvious instances of great poetry are but casually mentioned, and many more are not mentioned at all. My plea is, in both cases, that I am printing lectures; and a lecturer's powers of expatiation must accommodate themselves to his audience's powers of endurance. There are advantages in this which, I think, are worth transferring from the platform to the printed page, even at the risk of leaving unsatisfied those readers whose appetites are exacting. Accordingly, I have kept the lectures substantially in the form in which they were delivered; though here and there I have fortified their texture. *The Theory of Poetry* consists of public lectures given in the Universities of Liverpool and of Leeds; *The Idea of Great Poetry* of the Clark lectures in Trinity College, Cambridge, revised and condensed to suit the requirements of the Ballard Mathews lectures in the University College of North Wales, Bangor. I must record my sense of the privilege these institutions have conferred on me.

When I was honoured with the suggestion that these lectures might be put forth in an American edition, I readily acquiesced in the proposal that the two series should be allowed to assist each other by appearing side by side in one volume. But this makes it necessary, after apologising for faults of deficiency, to apologise also for faults of superfluity. Inevitably, there is some repetition, both of argument and of results. A radical correction of this would have meant a complete re-writing, and indeed a complete re-conception, of the two treatises, for which I had neither the time nor the inclination. Some tinkering might have been possible; a paragraph or two might have been struck out or modified, but I could find no place where this could be done without leaving hiatus in the immediate argument. Rather than break the continuity of each chain of reasoning, I preferred to duplicate several of the links.

I do not think there is any need for me to give an abstract of the æsthetic philosophy (I use the term with a good deal of diffidence) which this book assumes. Its tenor will be sufficiently discerned in the course of the concrete arguments which are here set out. What it owes to Croce will be evident enough; and also, I hope, what it declines to owe to that stimulating and persuasive thinker. At any rate, a theory which makes so much of the thing he so serenely disregards—*technique*—could hardly seem to him anything more than a bastard slip which cannot thrive. No one, of course, can escape Croce's influence nowadays; but I should like to point out that, so far at least as my own reckoning goes, my debt to Aristotle is a good deal greater. In æsthetic theory, Aristotle, it seems to me, is still what he was to Dante—"the master of those who know"; and I doubt if there is anything of permanent value in Croce's *Estetica* which does not make explicit (and that means, at the hands of such a writer, irre-

Preface

sistibly explicit) something which was already implicit in Aristotle. But, if it were a question of the parentage of my theory, what I should chiefly like to point out, had I any hopes that such audacity would be allowed, would be its claims to an ancestry even more illustrious: I should like, in fact, to point out the claims of my philosophy to direct descent from Common Sense. If anyone wishes to examine them, they may be found in *An Essay Towards a Theory of Art*, which was published in England several years ago.

L. A.

THE UNIVERSITY,
LEEDS.

CONTENTS

THE THEORY OF POETRY

THE IDEA OF GREAT POETRY

The Theory of Poetry

I

INTRODUCTORY

GENERAL observations on the art of poetry are common enough. Critics, for example, are apt to back their particular judgments by asserting broadly that "Poetry should do this" or "Poetry cannot do that." If a critic is sufficiently lavish of such remarks we say that he has a *theory of poetry:* his theory being nothing but a conviction of what poetry *ought* to do. Thus Matthew Arnold, as everybody knows, had a theory that poetry should be a criticism of life.

It is not in this sense that I am taking the theory of poetry as my topic. If it were, there would be many of you, I hope, whose minds would be busy with demands for my authority: and what authority could I give you? There is no one who can say what poetry *ought* to be on any better grounds than his own personal preference. But if I simply attempt to say what poetry is in fact—the things it does and the way it does them—you will always know the authority I am building on: poetry itself.

Let me make another disclaimer. I shall try to describe—very sketchily, as you will find—how poetry does its business; but I have no notion of telling any one how to write poetry. This has been attempted. Baudelaire undertook to turn any one into a poet in so

13

many lessons; but I never heard that he succeeded. No one can be taught how to be an artist; but it is nevertheless quite true that no one can be an artist who has not learned his medium. You must know your perspective or your counterpoint—the grammar of your art—if you do not want to be like a high-minded foreigner labouring his inefficient discourse in broken English. But once you have learnt the grammar, then there is no one who can help you but yourself. The person who wishes to write poetry, however, has already arrived at that stage. He has no perspective or counterpoint to learn, because he has been learning command of his medium ever since he was a baby; if he has not got hold of it now, no one can teach him. And for the use that he is to make of his medium—of language, that is—he can only consult his own talent.

What is left, then, if we are not to dogmatise on the duties of poetry, nor to prescribe for its composition? More than enough, at any rate, to occupy this course of lectures. Poetry has usually been regarded as one of the notable facts in the life of man; and a general analysis of its nature and methods cannot but improve our knowledge of ourselves—of what we are and what we would like to be. There is a feeling that it is dangerous to examine too nicely into the way poetry works. It may be like taking a watch to pieces; you may not be able to put it together again, or if you do, it may not go as well as it did before. I think, on the contrary, that the closer you look into poetry, the more you have to discover, and to *enjoy*.

Introductory

At any rate, theory of this kind—theory which, without pretending to legislate for poetry, tries to understand the nature of its power—has had many devotees, and not only among the philosophers. Some of the greatest minds in the history of thought have, indeed, had their say in the theory of poetry—Aristotle, Plato, Kant. Bacon summed up one aspect of it in a few profound and majestic sentences. But the poets themselves have certainly not been unwilling to theorise their art. We have such considered treatises as those of Dante, Sidney, du Bellay, Wordsworth, Shelley; we have contributions scarcely less valuable in such flashes of lightning penetration as Coleridge's distinction between Milton's genius and Shakespeare's, or Sophocles' distinction between himself and Euripides: "My kind of poetry represents men as they should be, Euripides' kind men as they are." The poets even introduce sometimes a thread of poetic theory into the texture of their art. Shakespeare's speech about the poet's eye "in a fine frenzy rolling" is perhaps so familiar that we do not always realise what a sound piece of theory it is. The image, the shaped and concrete *thing*—that is what poetry deals in; the abstract of thought and the intangible of fantasy, poetry translates into forms, into vividly actual definition—what Shakespeare, practising his theory while he enounces it, calls "a local habitation and a name." Landor even made poetic use of the pangs of composition. The intimacies of technique are curiously revealed in his account of the youthful queen's difficulties with the

unruly energy of words, when she was drawing up a
diplomatic speech:

> She formed them, and reformed them, with regret
> That there was somewhat lost in every change:
> She could replace them—what would that avail?—
> Moved from their order they have lost their charm.

There you have strikingly expressed the fact, common
to all usages of language, but of supreme importance
in poetry, that the meaning of a word depends not
simply on the word itself, but on the other words
round about it.

It would be easy to go on enumerating casual or
deliberate contributions to the theory of poetry. And
yet, in spite of their plenty, the whole ground has
never been mapped out; still less has anything like a
consistent and accepted body of doctrine resulted. I
am not now proposing to supply that deficiency; but
so long as the deficiency exists, it may excuse any attempt at a broad and connected account of the main
facts of poetry.

I begin by limiting my subject. This is clearly required. The nature of poetry, thoroughly searched
out, would take me through all the departments of
human knowledge and illusion. It would be like that
heaven-high, hell-deep journey Wordsworth describes
as his exploration of the secrets of man's mind:

> For I must tread on shadowy ground, must sink
> Deep—and aloft ascending breathe in worlds
> To which the heaven of heavens is but a veil.

Introductory

All strength—all terror, single or in bands,
That ever was put forth in personal form,
Jehovah, with His thunder, and the choir
Of shouting Angels, and the empyreal thrones—
I pass them unalarmed. Not chaos, not
The darkest pit of lowest Erebus
Nor aught of blinder vacancy scooped out
By help of dreams—can breed such fear and awe
As fall upon us often when we look
Into our Minds, into the Mind of Man.

Yes, and all the Mind of Man comes, or may come, within the scope of poetry; and,

Had we but world enough and time,

all of it might, under one colour or another, be ransacked for our theory of poetry.

But at my back I always hear
Time's winged chariot hurrying near.

Limitation is decidedly required. I shall not, as the great philosopher did, start by asking, *is* there such a thing as my subject? And if there is, by what possibility and by what right does it exist?—I shall assume that poetry exists. I shall assume that it is, on the whole, desirable. I shall not reach out into the psychology of that; and I shall not be daunted by the apparition of the man who says: "But honestly, I don't like poetry." I shall not trace his affliction back to its source in some obscure mental deformity. I leave him to the alienists.

Besides, there are laws of trespass in this region as

in others. Psychology, for instance, is a great land-owner hereabouts. I have no permit which would excuse my rambling over his property; and I fear the noise of my floundering in the watery soil he cultivates would unpleasantly attract his notice. Metaphysics, too, has some thorny preserves marching with our pleasant grasslands; and metaphysics is a notoriously litigious creature. We shall find we have range enough without such risks as these.

But there is another neighbouring science, of whom we must be even more careful. This is the science of Æsthetics; and now it is not resentment we must avoid, but friendliness. For Æsthetics, not being quite sure of his dignity, is only too anxious to do the neigh-bourly thing and put his whole property at our dis-posal. The danger is, that if we accept his invitation, he assumes the right to walk about our estate and to have some say in its management; and several previous cultivators of our ground have been quite taken in by his specious advice. In order then that we may keep safely to our own ground, and be able to warn off the officious friendship of this busybody, we must be sure of our boundary.

We are to study the art of poetry. Now art, if it is successful, is judged to be beautiful; and æsthetics can certainly be described as the science of everything that may be brought up for judgment as beautiful or the reverse: it is too narrow a description, but it will do for the present. This apparently gives æsthetics a claim to be considered as the landlord of our territory;

Introductory

but we have just as good a claim to an absolute autonomy, if not independence.

If I contemplate Nature with delight, I am certainly providing material for the science of æsthetics, and I may consider myself to be in a poetical state of mind; but what is to be noted now is, that the experience is wholly *my own*. If, however, I contemplate with delight a work of art—a poem, say—the experience is not wholly my own: another man's experience is involved with mine: namely, the poet's. This may not seem a very great difference; but in fact it is crucial: it is the vitally characteristic thing in poetry: for it is this that makes poetry one of the Arts. The theory of poetry, then, must take account not only of the quality of certain remarkable kinds of experience, but also of the no less remarkable Art by which the poet has communicated his experience and enabled it to become ours as well. However nicely we examine into poetical states of mind, their study will never give us what is characteristic of poetry—namely, the conveying of these states of mind, whatever they may be, by the methodical use of language. Poetry must be studied as a deliberately designed activity leading up to a foreordained end; and solely because it is this is it capable of its peculiar spiritual function.

And this is the reason why the theory of poetry should be kept decisively apart from the general science of æsthetics. For outside poetry anything like the *art* to which poetry owes its existence is utterly unknown—the art or system of contrivances whereby experience

The Theory of Poetry

can be transferred whole and unimpaired, in all its subtlety and complexity, from one mind to another. This gives us our boundary: we need nothing beyond it, and we shall assume our right to independence within it. Unless we do so, there is no end to the possibilities of irrelevance and error; for it is evident that general æsthetics must regard an aspect of innumerable things which belong in their substance to every sort of intellectual compartment. These may not only be quite irrelevant to the study of an art; they may endanger it; since under the colour of their æsthetic value they will always be ready to offer themselves as explanations of the art. Thus we have been told that the highest art, in poetry as elsewhere, is known by the physiological disturbance it causes; especially by a certain thrilling shudder down the spine, or a chilly tingle over the skin of arms and legs: in fact what is vulgarly called gooseflesh. Accordingly, it is at gooseflesh that poetry should aim. Whether it should or not, there is no doubt about the fact that, at least as an occasional occurrence, gooseflesh accompanies poetry. I find it quite an interesting fact; and it at once raises a question which is almost exciting—the question whether poetry proceeds through gooseflesh to the mind or through the mind to gooseflesh. But how does this æsthetic fact enrich the study of poetic *art?* It depends, for one thing, on the mere chance of my physical condition; I gooseflesh one day, but another day I do not, at the same passage; but I am just as clear that the art of the passage is good on the one day as on the other.

Introductory

What is more, I gooseflesh not only at art exquisitely good, but with precisely the same thrill at art excruciatingly bad.

Again: the discovery has been announced that the finest poetry, by its nice assembly of vowels and consonants, will always cause an increased secretion of saliva; further, it is alleged that from this comes a sense of well-being, and that the poetry is then judged to have succeeded in its art. According to this, the deficiency of the man who does not relish poetry lies not in his mind but in his mucous membrane.

I am not so sure of this physiological fact as I am of the gooseflesh; and I am doubtful whether an increased flow of saliva really would give me any notable sense of well-being. There are, of course, here and there, lines which do make one's mouth water:

> And still she slept an azure-lidded sleep
> In blanched linen smooth and lavender'd,
> While he from forth the closet brought a heap
> Of candied apple, quince and plum and gourd,
> With jellies soother than the creamy curd,
> And lucent syrops tinct with cinnamon;
> Manna and dates, in argosy transferr'd
> From Fez; and spiced dainties, every one
> From silken Samarkand to cedar'd Lebanon.

That, of course, is one of the stock miracles of diction—the way the articulation of those words makes your mouth work as though it were savouring the very gust of all those sweets. But in the case of inedible imagery, even in a line as superbly vowelled as

> In cedar, marble, ivory or gold—

the resulting salivation, in my case, would require very delicate hygrometry to reveal it; certainly my appreciation does not depend on it. And it is hard to see how the *art* of poetry is to be better understood for being equated with a cooking partridge.

"Not here, O Apollo!"—Enough of these whimsies, these *papillons noirs*, of aberrant poetics. They will at least serve as instances of the sort of stuff I want to keep *out* of our discussion. Our theory will move about the art of poetry as though in a quiet ordered cosmos, a self-contained globe suspended in the midst of what, for these present purposes, I shall regard as chaos. Out of that cosmos I shall make no excursions; though I may sometimes put my head out. When I come to the question of beauty, for example, I shall not go looking outside this prescribed sphere for a definition of beauty in general; all I shall try to determine is how, inside our art, the specific kind of beauty which occurs only in poetry can arise. So with rhythm. Whence comes rhythm into poetry? Some derive it from heart-beats, some from respiration, some from the quantum theory and the insinuations of molecules, some from Hottentots and tom-toms. All this belongs to chaos. Rhythm came from somewhere; our concern is, that we have it in our cosmos. What *sort* of rhythm poetry *uses*—what poetry uses rhythm *for*—these are our questions.

In short, I intend no heroic synthesis of poetry out of its multitudinous elements. I shall take the fact of poetry for granted, and merely analyse its more

Introductory

important qualities. What is the good of this? For analysis cannot extend knowledge. True: but it can clarify apprehension, and clarified apprehension should surely mean a sharpened enjoyment. The gain we can fairly look for in the theoretic study of poetry is, besides its intellectual satisfaction, a certain distinction in our pleasures: the confused pell-mell delight in the many devices of poetry should become a texture of keener feelings, distinctly answering to each separate element of the complex art. I cannot believe that versification, for example, can be enjoyed in the highest degree without we are exactly conscious of the way it works. Here, now, is the movement of Shakespeare's early verse:

> These are the forgeries of jealousy:
> And never, since the middle summer's spring,
> Met we on hill, in dale, forest, or mead,
> By paved fountain or by rushing brook,
> Or in the beached margent of the sea
> To dance our ringlets to the whistling wind,
> But with thy brawls thou hast disturbed our sport.

And this is how Shakespeare's later verse moves:

> Dost think I am so muddy, so unsettled,
> To appoint myself in this vexation; sully
> The purity and whiteness of my sheets,
> Which to preserve is sleep, which being spotted
> Is goads, thorns, nettles, tails of wasps?

Compare with that Milton's final development of the same measure:

The Theory of Poetry

Oh how comely it is and how reviving
To the Spirits of just men long opprest!
When God into the hands of thir deliverer
Puts invincible might . . .

No one, I am sure, who does not perceive—and understand—the huge technical differences in these three quotations, can get the full enjoyment out of any of them. It is just the same with diction. When we can see pretty clearly what it is that governs a poet's choice of words, we can then begin the enjoyment of his nicety.

However, I shall not have time to do much with the details of technique; I can only indicate their place in the whole process of poetic activity. And our survey would not be complete unless I said something about the purpose of that process. For poetry does not only give us enjoyment. It will be part of our theory that poetry, with varying intensity, reveals to us a world which answers to the deepest and gravest requirements of the mind; a world ideal in its harmony and its permanence, in its security and, above all, in its significance, but nevertheless a world real in its substance. That is to say, we must raise our speculation of this art until we can see every poem as the capture and preservation of some perfection of experience. Let me illustrate this; and let me do so, for more cogency, in quite a humble instance. Here is a song translated from the Australian blackfellow:

The Kangaroo ran very fast,
But I ran faster.

24

Introductory

The Kangaroo was very fat:
I ate him.
Kangaroo! Kangaroo!

A legitimate triumph, we must all agree: the blackfellow did well to celebrate it. But in the mere
fact of celebrating it in a song, what has happened?
Kangaroo-hunting has become an affair of the ideal
world. The blackfellow only has to sing his song, and
at once his mind is in a world where kangaroos always
know their duty. They do not always know it in the
everyday reality of things. They are not always to
be run down there; and when they are, they are not
always fat. But hunt them in poetry, and they are
everything they should be. True, these are kangaroos
you cannot eat; but nevertheless they have not been
idealised into unreality. They have not changed their
nature. You still must chase them. The thing is,
the exhilaration of the chase can never be disappointed;
and though you cannot physically eat your quarry, you
can and must enjoy it.

And thereby thrive more remarkably than by any
nourishment the digestive tract can provide. For properly the blackfellow has not idealised kangaroos at
all; he has idealised the experience of hunting them—
simply by making permanent the sense of its success.
Thereby he has created a world which is altogether *his
own:* he has made it *belong* to him and to his desires.
He is the master: he has but to sing his song, and he
will know it. What is much more important, any one
at all can possess himself of the poet's delighted

mastery of things, simply by singing the poet's song.

Look where you will in poetry, that is what, at bottom, you find; it is what I called the perfection of experience. We are always trying to possess the world; but the world does not always seem to want us: it goes its own way in a very troublesome manner. It will even inflict evil on us, and altogether behave as though we did not greatly matter. We correct all that in poetry. Our possession of this world is absolute there. Not by cancelling its evil: this inconvenient world need not change its nature in order to become, in poetry, our very own. If poetry were to ignore the evil of the world, then indeed it would be no better than an amusing fiction. But poetry ignores nothing. It takes the evil of things, and makes that, too, *mean* something: even evil must obey its master, the mind, and be known as an element necessary to the final harmony of things. This is the height of the understanding of poetry which its theory should give us: a reasoned sense of its constant invigoration of our minds by creating for us a world in which our ownership is at last complete; so complete that, in its largest revelation, evil itself ceases to be a meaningless incoherence, and falls in with what we most profoundly desire—some assurance that everything we can experience must somehow be significant to us.

How are we to set out for this eminence? Two courses are open to us. We can collect all the outward signs of poetry—rhythm, rime, imagery, metaphor, euphony, unexpected power of words, and whatever

26

else we may light on: we may then add them all together, and note the result. Against this course the
first thing to be said is, that you can never be sure
that your catalogue of qualities is complete; and unless
it is, the summation of them must be inconclusive.
Moreover, even when all the accepted indications of
poetry are present, it is notorious that poetry itself may
be absent: its place may be taken by a spurious and
repulsive phantom, the more disgusting the more it
imitates the habits and manners of the true presence.
These outward qualities, in fact, are only the signs
of poetry when they serve to reveal a certain dominating purpose working through them; this is what
gives the nature of poetry, though it is true that without embodiment in these outward qualities the nature
of poetry can never be realised. We shall, then, start
our inquiry at the core, and work outwards.

There is nothing abstruse in this. On the contrary,
it is, I suppose, in any discussion of these matters, the
commonest and easiest assumption in the world, that
every poem, big or little, if it is to have the slightest
value for us, must have been, as we say, *inspired*.

That is just the spring-board we require to set us
going in our study of the art of poetry. And to start
off with, we apparently plunge right into a notable
antithesis—Inspiration and Art. Evidently we must
take care to know just what this assumption means by
Inspiration. It is a word, of course, of several meanings. It has a technical meaning in theology, which is
sometimes vaguely used of art to add a flourish to large

27

Poetic inspiration
What?

and rhetorical compliment. But without any super-natural suggestion, inspiration may mean some access of unusual energy—unaccountable, uninvited, and apparently uncontrolled—which invades the poet's mind and makes it then a mind more potent than others, more potent than itself at other times. But this is not confined to poets or to the men of any art. It may happen to scientists, mathematicians, soldiers, business men—to any one whose work comes from the depths of his nature, and is therefore liable to be invaded by this superior energy.

All we can say is, that it is something incalculable and that some lucky natures are open to it. Conscious endeavour has little to do with it. The poets are by no means the only men who have been visited by it in the form of dreams and visions. It was a dream that immortalised the chemist Kekulé. He dreamt a dance of the atoms: and suddenly this atomic dance arranged itself in the formula which he instantly recognised as solving the problem every one else had vainly puzzled over; Kekulé, we say, was *inspired* to make this invaluable contribution to chemical theory. Waking moments can be just as inexplicable. The great mathematician Poincaré describes how, after vainly trying to elucidate some baffling matter, he had to go on a journey. "The incidents of the journey," he says, "made me forget my mathematical work. When we arrived at Coutances we got into a break to go for a drive, and *just as I put my foot on the step*, the idea came to me, though nothing in my former thoughts seemed to have prepared me for it." This was the very idea he had vainly tried to find with all the resources of *conscious* effort; and he goes on to mention several other occasions, when mathematical ideas long sought for shot into his brain from nowhere, in the midst of totally unrelated actions; and always, as he says, "with the same characteristics of conciseness, suddenness, and immediate certainty."

Well, that, as plainly as anywhere in poetry, is inspiration. In its most fortunate manifestation, it comes *at need*, just in the nick: it instantly tells a man the right thing to say, think, do, precisely as the occasion requires, and with absolute precision and authority. Perhaps this is what is meant when we say a man has genius. I suppose every reader of poetry has his favourite instances of it: some piercing insight into human nature, some magical bridge between one thing and another, some vivid touch which makes fantasy gleam more real than everyday fact, some towering flight of vision. Few people could resist quoting Keats' nightingale, singing

Genius = the possession of timely inspiration.

> Perhaps the selfsame song that found a path
> Through the sad heart of Ruth, when sick for home
> She stood in tears amid the alien corn;

to say nothing of the "magic casements" later on. How did Keats manage to think of Ruth—out of the whole world of legend and story, the one figure inexplicably right in this context? It was an *inspiration* to make the Hampstead nightingale call to the fields of Boaz. Or, as an instance of genius at a somewhat lower stage, I might mention that stroke in one of Chatterton's poems, when a giant tears up "a ragged mountain from the ground" and hurls it at his enemy: an obviously borrowed extravagance. But as Chatterton tells it, the thing seems actually to happen, as momentary matter of observed fact. For as the mountain, with all its forests, is rushing through the air, the poet notices how

> The flying wolfins sent a yelling cry;

and the addition of that quite unexpected *noise* to our vision gives sheer fantasy the air of the unquestionably real. *Inspired realisation* of this kind is perhaps the commonest, as it is also perhaps the most useful, of the workings of genius in poetry. There is a fine example in the beautiful Indian drama *Sakuntala*: the chariot of the god Indra driving through heaven passes over a cloud, and at once the wetted rims of the wheels begin to spin moisture off in sparkling showers. Of course! That is just what would happen. Keats has the very same thing in *Endymion*—but he may have looked into Sir William Jones' version of Kalidasa:

> A silver car, air-borne,
> Whose silent wheels, fresh wet from clouds of morn,
> Spun off a drizzling dew.

But this sort of thing pales beside the vision which utterly transcends reality: which, disdaining to imitate our customary experience, nevertheless can assume as

Introductory

convincing an assurance. Dante's *Paradiso* is the great
treasure house of it: think only of the River of Light,
or the White Rose made of the multitudes of the
blest. Impossible to understand where such imagery
comes from! I think I would take for its type that
amazing passage in the *Paradiso* where the sparkling
souls in the heaven of Jove group themselves first into
mystic letters, and thence into a fiery eagle; and the
eagle immediately becomes alive, and speaks. But it
is an experience just as amazing, when we share those
flashes of clairvoyance into the secrets of human nature,
for which we naturally turn to Shakespeare. Think,
for example, of Pericles' recognition of Marina, his
daughter, whom he supposed dead long ago. The in-
credible thing has been gradually turning into an over-
whelming bliss of certainty:

> O Helicanus, strike me, honour'd Sir:
> Give me a gash, put me to present pain;
> Lest this great sea of joys rushing upon me
> O'erbear the shores of my mortality,
> And drown me with their sweetness.

The whole process up to this has been the work of a
poet supremely accomplished: what can he possibly
have to add to it? But now comes the spark from
Heaven. Pericles, from sheer joy, not metaphorically
but exactly, passes into ecstasy. How does Shakespeare
make him reveal it?

> Give me my robes. I am wild in my beholding.
> O Heavens bless my girl!—*But, hark, what music?*

The Theory of Poetry

Tell Helicanus, my Marina, tell him
O'er, point by point, for yet he seems to doubt,
How sure you are my daughter.—*But, what music?*
   HELICANUS. My lord, I hear none.
   PERICLES. None!
The Music of the Spheres!

This, truly, is inspiration coming at need.

Or, finally, take from Shakespeare a case of inspiration in sheer craftsmanship; take the turning point of the tragedy of Othello. Desdemona has been pleading for Cassio, and is piqued at Othello's hesitation; and when Othello, surrendering to what she herself calls her "mammering," at last says, "I will deny thee nothing," he demands in exchange a boon from her: she is "to leave me but a little to myself." So, having won her point, she goes, deliciously rebuking him with her mock submission: "Shall I deny *you?* . . . Whate'er you be, I am obedient." The scene shows most delicately, underneath the slight, half-serious bickering, the perfect confidence these two have in each other: and immediately after its climax, when Othello, captivated by Desdemona's innocent mischief, says, looking after her:

Excellent wretch: Perdition catch my soul
But I do love thee! and when I love thee not
Chaos is come again,

Iago sees his moment. With his artless question

Did Michael Cassio, when you woo'd my lady,
Know of your love?

32

instantly the mood of the scene turns sinister. Evil takes charge; we see Othello, at the top of his confident delight, suddenly at its mercy. Iago, with the exquisite simplicity of a fine artist, needs but a few bare broken phrases to fix his poison deep in his victim's mind:

OTH. O yes, and went between us very oft.
IAG. Indeed!
OTH. Indeed! ay, indeed: discern'st thou aught in that? Is he
    not honest?
IAG. Honest, my lord!
OTH. Honest! ay, honest.
IAG. My lord, for aught I know.
OTH. What dost thou think?
IAG. Think, my lord!
OTH. Think, my lord! By heaven, he echoes me
    As if there were some monster in his thought
    Too hideous to be shewn.

And with that exclamation, we know that Desdemona is as good as murdered.

I suppose it is usually in this sense that inspiration is held to make art unnecessary; sometimes even held to be injured or nullified by art. The notion is, that art, a calculated affair of devices and conventions, is the exact antithesis of the spontaneous heaven-sent energies of genius. But it is a notion clean against all common sense. Of course, if a poet, though his imagination is flaming with splendour, is so unpractical with his art that he has nothing but mechanical dodges to rely on, he will certainly kill his inspiration. But that is through defective art. The poet who can compel us to feel his inspiration as a living force is obviously the poet who can summon the art necessary to exhibit it: and the greater his inspiration, the more art he would require. That extraordinary enabling of the poet's mind which we have been calling inspiration will only be effective when he has the art which can receive it and transmit it; and that must mean, that his technique has, through long practice and much deliberate skill, become second nature to him. It is just possible, even, that inspiration might be *confined* to his art; the spark from heaven might simply light on his technique and kindle it into some strange subtlety and eagerness with no very remarkable imagination behind it. There is, at any rate, no saying what the result of inspiration will be in art. It may be an unusual directness and simplicity, as in that passage from *Othello;* but it may just as well be an unusual elaboration and complexity, as in that famous stanza from Keats' *Nightingale.* What we can say is, that genius, so far from enabling a poet to do without art, enables him to do with his art things we could never have expected it was capable of doing.

But this sort of inspiration has really nothing to do with the theory of poetry. We can but notice it, and pass on. If it is there, we bless our good luck; but it is an occasional visitor, and poetry can exist without it: even Homer, Dante and Shakespeare cannot always command it. Further, it is not peculiar to poetry; and the closest examination of it would not therefore help us to account for the special nature of the poetic ac-

Introductory

tivity. Finally, we do not yet know what it is; speculation about it must belong to studies which at present we leave to the chaos outside our boundaries.

But the word inspiration has another sense, of great theoretical importance: this is the sense in which henceforward I shall use the word. We are now to consider what it means when we say that certain things, persons, or events *inspired* a poet to write. We say that Emilia Viviani inspired Shelley to write *Epipsychidion;* or that the massacre of the Vaudois inspired Milton to write "Avenge, O Lord, thy slaughter'd saints." The other meaning may be there as well, as no doubt it is in the case of these two poems: but we are now regarding something much more precise and seizable. We need no allusions to the unaccountable here. Few people would say that Pope in his *Essay on Man* was inspired in any miraculous fashion; but every one would agree that Pope was inspired by Bolingbroke's philosophy.

Now it is in this sense of the word that we must assume for every poem an inspiration; we mean that every poem has a unique motive of its own, working itself out into the general shape of the poem and into all details of the technique: an individual life organising round itself its necessary and peculiar embodiment. With the recognition of this and with some determination of its nature, the theory of poetry begins its business.

Two things are clear at least. The inspiration, in this latter sense, is what the poem exists to convey:

The Theory of Poetry

consequently it cannot be opposed to the art of the poem. On the contrary, what was said of the other kind of inspiration must be repeated here: the greater the poet's inspiration, the more art he requires. For this is simply to say, that the more the poet has in him to reveal, the more he requires means to reveal it.

The second thing is this. Inspiration, as we are now using the word, is neither the matter of the poem nor the spirit of it, but the two together inextricably compounded. Let me refer you again to that sonnet of Milton's, "On the late Massacher in Piemont." Speaking conveniently, we say that Milton was inspired to write his sonnet by the massacre; but of course that is only half the truth. The massacre would not have inspired the poem unless it meant something remarkable to the poet; and what it did mean we know from the spirit of the poem—that spirit of prophetic indignation which found in this matter the very type of insolent iniquity. We can always see these two aspects of a poem's inspiration—the matter and the spirit; and it need hardly be said that they are no more than *aspects:* they are not separable ingredients. Some occurrence goes home to the poet's mind: that is the matter. In the act of going home, and during its residence there, it becomes charged with what it rouses there: moods, interpretations, sense of import, associations, and whatever else there may be. That is the spirit. The two together compound into an inspiration which, if caught in language, becomes a poem. It follows that the inspiration of poetry is never general,

36

N.B.

Book I "Ring and Book" gives this in poetic form

Introductory

always unique. A poet is never inspired to write poetry at large, but some particular poem. No two poems can possibly have the same inspiration. Even if the matter were the same, the peculiar importance given to it can never be the same. That comes from the mind into which the matter strikes; and no two minds are alike, nor has a man the same mind at any two moments.

What this idea of inspiration involves, as far as poetic art is concerned, we must now go on to inquire.

II

INSPIRATION AND FORM

B Y the poet's inspiration, we are to understand that unique and definite motive which drives him to express himself, and which compels the resulting poem to be just that particular poem and no other, distinct from every other poem in the world. There are always two aspects of an inspiration: there is what we call the matter of the poem; and there is the peculiar value which the matter assumes in the poet's mind and must reveal as white-hot metal reveals the heat it assumes in a furnace: what we often call the spirit of a poem.

Can we make any general statement as to the sort of matter or the sort of valuation which poetry requires? This has often been attempted; but the futility of it is, I should say, getting rather evident. It comes to little more than asserting, as natural necessity, what some of us like to find. Many people, for instance, believing that poets are easily moved by the beauty of things, take it for granted that poetry must begin in some perception of beauty. To which it should be enough to answer,

> O Thou! whatever title suit thee,
> Auld Hornie, Satan, Nick, or Clootie,
> Wha in yon cavern grim an' sootie,

Inspiration and Form

Closed under hatches,
Spairges about the brunstane cootie
To scaud poor wretches!

Hear me, auld Hangie, for a wee,
An' let poor damned bodies be;
I'm sure sma' pleasure it can gi'e
E'en to a de'il
To skelp an' scaud poor dogs like me,
An' hear us squeel.

Was it the devil's beauty that inspired Burns? And did the beauty of things move Dryden to write *Mac-Flecknoe* or *Absalom and Achitophel*, Ben Jonson to write *The Alchemist*, Browning to write *The Spanish Cloister*? All these are poems acknowledged to be conspicuously good. Or think of *The Jolly Beggars*; obviously no theory could live which was contradicted by that superb production. And what inspires it? The *matter* is an orgy of a pack of ruffians in a public house, and the *spirit* is Burns' own heartfelt enjoyment of what is called *low life*. You may say the poet's mind will see beauty where others can only see ugliness. It is possible; but in the poems just mentioned, remarkable care must have been taken to conceal this faculty. To all appearance, at least, these poets seem to have been unashamedly relishing the ugliness of things. And it seems just as clear that poetry may have motives which it would be ludicrous to refer either to beauty or ugliness. Has a poet no right to be moved by common sense—a very stimulating thing, sometimes? Or may he not sum up his experience of men

39

and affairs as placidly as an old Chinese poet did, when
he heard of the birth of his son?

> Families, when a child is born,
> Want it to be intelligent.
> I, through intelligence
> Having wrecked my whole life,
> Only hope the baby will prove
> Ignorant and stupid.
> Then he will crown a tranquil life
> By becoming a Cabinet Minister.[1]

Beauty had little to do with the inspiration there.

More will have to be said about this troublesome
question of poetic beauty. At present, this must suffice. When a poet chooses his subject—or I had better
say, when a subject chooses a poet—there is no necessity for beauty to have any say in the business: but
there is absolute necessity for every subject which
poetry successfully communicates to us, to have thereby
become invested with beauty. That need not have
been the poet's intention; it merely and unavoidably
happens that, when anything is successfully said in
poetry, beauty arrives.

I will briefly mention two other common suggestions
as to the essential nature of poetic matter. Emotion
is sometimes said to be the characteristic thing which
poetry gives us. It is true that poetry has special
means of conveying emotion; but it has special means

[1] From Arthur Waley's *A Hundred and Seventy Chinese Poems*.
Recent English verse can show little to compare with the delicately
assured technique of these versions; and the fascination of their
matter is irresistible.

Inspiration and Form

of conveying many other things as well. To be sure there must be emotion in poetry; for there is emotion everywhere in life. You cannot say anything without bringing in some sort of emotion; and if this is conspicuous in poetry, it is only because poetry is a remarkably complete and many-sided way of saying things. On the other hand, emotion simply as such does not exist. It can be expressed as such, by groaning or screaming. We feel this to be inconclusive, precisely because we know that something more than mere emotion must be happening; and we hasten to require the reason of the groans or screams. What is characteristic of poetry is the fact that it does not leave us asking for reasons. Emotion is there as a necessary part of a satisfactory whole, no more characteristic than any other element in it.

We are swung to the opposite extreme when we are told that poetry has lessons for us. This need not hold us long. Poetry may, among a thousand other things, do some occasional teaching: but if it does, it is not by virtue of its instruction that it is poetry, and the instruction would probably fare better elsewhere. The fallacy—an easy-going misunderstanding of poetry's idealism—is venerable and perhaps immortal, and has kept very distinguished company. The most interesting thing about it is that it should have taken in the two most profoundly artistic peoples in history, the Greeks and the Chinese: and yet the literatures of both could always have supplied refutation as perfect as "Phillada flouts me" is in ours:

41

The Theory of Poetry

Oh what a pain is love,
She will inconstant prove,
She so torments my mind
And wavers with the wind
Please her the best I may,
Alack and well-a-day,

How shall I bear it?
I greatly fear it.
That my strength faileth,
As a ship saileth.
She looks another way,
Phillada flouts me.

Fair maid, be not so coy,
I am my mother's joy:
She'll give me when she dies,
Her poultry and her bees
A pair of mattress beds
And yet for all these geds,

Do not disdain me;
Sweet, entertain me.
All that is fitting—
And her geese sitting;
And a bag full of shreds;
Phillada flouts me.

Matthew Arnold's doctrine, that poetry is a criticism of life, apparently puts the didactic fallacy in a more tactful form, but really sharpens its radical misconception of the poetic activity. What is this activity? So far I have evaded that question, and propose to go on doing so as long as I can. But not because the poetic is difficult to recognise.

Tyger, tyger, burning bright
In the forests of the night,
What immortal hand or eye
Could frame thy fearful symmetry?

If we are looking for poetry, who would think of questioning that? And what does it effect? Is not *criticism* at any rate the very last word one would use to describe it? Language like that simply and purely creates: it makes our minds become a moment of imaginative splendour. What do we care about criticising life while we are living in that style?

42

Inspiration and Form

It is true, nevertheless, that on reflection we may feel some implied criticism of life, when we contrast with the obscure and blundering hurly-burly of every day the clear significant order of things in poetry. Even so, unless a poem were composed in order to draw our special attention to this contrast (which would be very unlikely), we could not call it inspired by the criticism of life. Of course, if you abstract single lines, and wrest them from their purpose in the poem where they occur—that is, if you misrepresent their meaning—you can argue very speciously for the criticism of life in poetry. What a voluminous and various critic has been made out in Shakespeare! For example:

> Rightly to be great
> Is not to stir without great argument,
> But greatly to find quarrel in a straw
> When honour's at the stake.

He can give the rule for all human aspirations in a single phrase:

> Ripeness is all;

or he can be with equal felicity and finality the ironical realist:

> For 'tis the sport to have the enginer
> Hoist with his own petar.

Indeed, so various is his criticism that it is capable of quite irreconcilable extremes, for at one moment

> There's a divinity that shapes our ends,
> Rough-hew them how we will,

43

The Theory of Poetry

and at another

> As flies to wanton boys are we to the gods:
> They kill us for their sport.

The truth is, of course, that to divorce these lines from their context and make morality of them is merely to destroy the art which invented them. That art, the equal of which has never been known, is the art of irresistibly impressing on our minds a sense of character, of particular kinds of human existence: and not only that, but also, as in the quotations I have just given you, an exact sense of the way these particular characters react at a given moment to a given set of circumstances. It is, in fact, like "Tyger, tyger," a use of language which is simply and purely creative: it makes our minds become the imagination of the poet.

If we are confirmed, by rejecting this heresy, in the common-sense and traditional view that the poet is a *maker*, and not a critic or philosopher, we should by now be confirmed also against all those heresies which propose to limit the poet's creativeness to some particular kind of subject. There is no such thing as a poetical subject: or if you like, all subjects can be poetical; but the poetical thing about them will always be, not *what* they are, but the way they come to us. We must leave it to the poets to choose their own themes. It does not follow that we are bound to approve of their choice. It is obviously legitimate to detest a poet's inspiration even when we admire his art; indeed, the vehemence of our detestation may be a tribute to the

44

Inspiration and Form

efficacy of his art. But this is where temperament comes in; and the vagaries of temperament can have no place in the theory of poetry. If any one thinks *The Jolly Beggars* a deplorable affair, there is no contradicting him; many people do think that low life in public houses is deplorable: on the whole, they are people to avoid; but they exist, and that is their temperament. We cannot blame them for it; but we can and ought to blame them, if they allow moral prejudices to obscure in their minds the fiery vividness and subtlety and the keen humanity of Burns' art.

Theory, I said, can make nothing of temperament. But how does this square with the ideal world of poetry, in which, as I said in the last lecture, even evil becomes somehow satisfactory, a necessary contribution to the harmony of complete significance? I was thinking, however, of the *great poems*, in which something like the whole possibility of human experience is represented. There are passages in the *Inferno* which, in spite of their astonishing art, or rather by reason of it, are so abominable that they could never be endured if they existed as separate poems in their own right. But when they are allowed to become in our minds what they were in Dante's—parts of a unified complex whole of experience—then we see that the peculiar satisfactoriness of the complete poem and the exaltation of its final impression actually require these dreadful incidents. In such a work as the *Divine Comedy*, or in the *Iliad, Paradise Lost, Hamlet,* or *Faust,* the prejudices of temperament become mere impertinence;

45

we neither like nor dislike, we accept. But the poet who confines himself to one uncompensated aspect of life—as Burns does in *The Jolly Beggars*—is apt to stir some prejudices against the matter of his work which will sometimes prevent the art of it from making its just effect.

Now by the *art*, I do not mean simply the clothing of the matter in language; I mean as well something that happened to the matter before that process could begin: something that makes it possible for language to convey whatever is entrusted to it in such a way that any aspect of life, high or low, dark or bright, villain or hero, may become exhilarating and satisfying: provided, that is to say, prejudices attached to the matter do not hinder our sense of that peculiar condition of things which is the life of poetry, and which we must now investigate. It is, of course, best not to have any prejudices.

We must first ask ourselves how far it is right to distinguish between the art of a poem and that on which the art is exercised. This is a very old problem. If we are talking of the *subject* or *matter* of a poem, the answer is not very difficult: for what we call subject or matter is nothing but a rough and quite notional synopsis of the poem which we make frankly as a convenience to discussion. There may be some slight difference in the scope of the synopsis implied by the two words. We might give as the *matter* of *Othello* a bare outline of the plot; the *subject* of it would be this informed with some sense of the impression it

Inspiration and Form

makes on us—innocence wronged by villainy working on high-minded simplicity, perhaps. In any case we should recognise that, for precise purposes, any such summary would not be very serviceable. It is not innocence that suffers, but Desdemona; it is not villainy and high-minded simplicity that destroy her, but Iago and Othello. For what the play actually is—for the single complex impression made by the actions and passions of this group of vividly individual persons—for *that* we can only go to the play itself: the art itself is the only thing that can really put to us what exercises the art. The distinction between matter and art is the distinction between the plan of a house and the experience of living in the house: and even the subject would only take us as far as a washed-in perspective.

But the matter of a poem does correspond with something: just as the plan of a house corresponds with something. There was something that came into the poet's personal life from the world outside it, and set the process going which results in a poem: he happened to read a story, he happened to see something or hear of something, something happened to emerge from the impersonal depths of his being. The troublesome thing is, that we can never be sure just what it was; for whatever happened, happened in the poet's mind and under the conditions of his nature. When we hear about it, it has become a poem, and may be a factor there of quite secondary importance. In any case, we are not really concerned with it, except to note, as we already have done, that there is no special quality to be prescribed for it. We may assume it as the thing that set the poetic process going: but until it has been caught up by and dissolved into that process, we must leave it alone. The first thing we can clearly recognise in the poetic process is the stage in which the matter—whatever casual incident of the poet's life may have caught his attention and entered his imagination—has been transformed into an *inspiration:* poetic composition has already begun when an inspiration has come into being.

To determine the relation between the completed art of a poem and its inspiration is a little more difficult; and we should have something tangible to work on. Let us see what an experiment may do for us.

> Like as the waves make towards the pebbled shore,
> So do our minutes hasten to their end,
> Each changing place with that which goes before,
> In sequent toil all forwards do contend.
> Nativity once in the main of light,
> Crawls to maturity, wherewith being crown'd,
> Crooked eclipses 'gainst his glory fight,
> And time that gave, doth now his gift confound.
> Time doth transfix the florish set on youth,
> And delves the parallels in beauty's brow,
> Feeds on the rarities of nature's truth,
> And nothing stands but for his scythe to mow.
> And yet to times in hope, my verse shall stand
> Praising thy worth, despite his cruel hand.

A celebrated critic once regretted that Shakespeare's sonnets had ever been written. He did not like their subject: and was of course quite at liberty to exhibit his eccentricity by saying so. But he went on to imply that their art was bad; and thereby gave us the measure of his critical capacity. Most of us, I fancy, if we have any prejudices relevant here, can sufficiently quieten them to allow Shakespeare's art to effect its magical business. Let us suppose the subject of this particular sonnet may be given as the sense of beauty's perishing. Clearly that is one thing, and the art of the poem quite another. And we should not have to examine very closely in order to realise that, if we want to write down exactly what the poem says to us, there is no way of doing so except by writing down the poem itself. We need not labour the point. What the poem has to say is precisely the same as the way the poem says it: obviously, for our knowledge of what the poem says is neither more nor less than what the language has, directly and indirectly, conveyed to us.

But we can get a little farther than this. What *has* the language conveyed to us? Something more than the series of its images and phrases. They are not like beads on a string. The identity of what the poem says with the way the poem says it, does not mean that the poem itself is to be accounted for by the details of its verbal art; on the contrary, it means that these details exist in the interest of one final presiding purpose. We must use Shakespeare's language in order to have Shakespeare's thought: but it is for the sake of the thought that the language is there. The impression of each phrase is not simply followed by the impression of the next: it enters into, amalgamates with, helps to characterise, the impression that follows. Until at last, in the final summed-up inclusive impression of the complete poem, phrases have combined into lines, lines into quatrains, the quatrains have accumulated their imagery into one richly organised sense of beauty's fatal change, to which the couplet has brought its sudden and plangent modulation of the whole harmony: and with the last word of the poem a unique moment of imaginative experience has completely elaborated and exquisitely defined itself. It was in order to effect this unique moment in our minds that the whole verbal art of the poem was designed; this was throughout the motive of the art, this was its presiding purpose, this was the urgency which called the art into existence and compelled it to be just this art and no other. This was, in fact, the inspiration of the poem. This moment of imaginative experience which possesses our minds the instant the poem is finished, possessed the poet's mind the instant the poem began. For as soon as there flashed into complete single existence in his mind this many-coloured experience with all its complex passion, the poem which we know was *conceived*, as an inspiration. Whatever event in the poet's life generated it, this is the first thing we can take hold of in the composition of the poem; and it existed before the verbal art of the poem was commenced, just as it exists in us after the verbal art has finished. For though it could not have come to us except in these very words, and, in this consideration, may be identified with the verbal art, since we can only have what the language

Inspiration and Form

can give us; yet, once it has come into its complete and vivid existence, it can be attended to and remembered apart from the words. So that it is also possible to consider the inspiration of a poem as distinguishable from the verbal art of it: namely, as that which the verbal art exists to convey and which can be distinctly known as such, however impossible it may be to describe it or express it at all in any other words than those of the poet.

And this distinction must be made, if we are to understand the art of poetry; we must, that is to say, see two clearly marked stages in the composition of a poem. Let me extend our experiment. Here are four short poems, each of which has, like that sonnet of Shakespeare's, some sense of mortality for its subject. I need not ask you to notice, for it is sufficiently obvious, how completely individual this common subject has become in the imaginations of the four poets. That is, indeed, relevant to our argument; but it is not the main thing just now.

This is from Drummond of Hawthornden:

> This world a hunting is,
> The prey, poor man; the Nimrod fierce is death.
> His speedy greyhounds are
> Lust, sickness, envy, care,
> Strife that ne'er falls amiss,
> With all those ills which haunt us while we breathe.
> Now if by chance we fly
> Of these the eager chase,
> Old Age with stealing pace
> Casts up his nets, and there we panting die.

51

2 4 0 4 6

The Theory of Poetry

And now Herrick:

> Sweet, be not proud of those two eyes
> Which starlike sparkle in their skies;
> Nor be you proud that you can see
> All hearts your captives, yours yet free;
> Be you not proud of that rich hair
> Which wantons with the lovesick air;
> Whenas that ruby which you wear
> Sunk from the tip of your soft ear,
> Will last to be a precious stone
> When all your world of beauty's gone.

But now hear Wordsworth:

> A slumber did my spirit seal;
>   I had no human fears;
> She seemed a thing that could not feel
>   The touch of earthly years.
>
> No motion has she now, no force;
>   She neither hears nor sees;
> Rolled round in earth's diurnal course
>   With rocks and stones and trees.

No ordinary sense of mortality there, certainly: as individual in its profound simplicity as the art which conveys it is in its certainty and severity. I cannot help interpolating the technical comment here, that a poem which gives us with unerring precision an experience so remote from all our common habits of thought and feeling, should contrive to do so in words that are nothing out of the common; with one exception—the word "diurnal": and how marvellously, coming just where it does, the mere sound of that word,

Inspiration and Form

let alone the exact rightness of its sense, enforces on
our minds the feeling of brute monotonous motion.

And here is another great spirit, Whitman; here
again a deeper music than those wistful exquisites,
Drummond and Herrick, can give us, though certainly
not more masterly in composition. Yet nothing could
be less like Wordsworth:

A noiseless patient spider,
I marked where on a little promontory it stood isolated,
Marked how to explore the vacant vast surrounding
It launched forth filament, filament, filament, out of itself,
Ever unreeling them, ever tirelessly speeding them.

And you O my Soul where you stand,
Surrounded, detached, in measureless oceans of space,
Ceaselessly musing, venturing, throwing, seeking the spheres to
    connect them,
Till the bridge you will need be form'd, till the ductile anchor
    hold,
Till the gossamer thread you fling catch somewhere, O my Soul.

Evidently, each of these four poems achieves its
purpose by exactly the process I described for that
sonnet of Shakespeare's. As soon as the language has
finished, we are in possession of that individual moment of imagination which inspired the poet to exercise his art in language. I have given you four
characteristic instances of the process in order that you
may plainly recognise, through these remarkable di-
vergences of substance and quality, that which is common to the inspiration of these four poems. And if
I put it in its barest simplicity, you will recognise that

it is common to all poems. In the first place, each inspiration is something self-contained and self-sufficient, a complete and entire whole; and in the second place, each inspiration is something which did not, and could not, originally exist as words.

The whole theory of the poetic art hangs on these two assertions; obvious as they may seem, they deserve all the emphasis we can put on them. The unity of inspiration would, in a strictly logical deduction, be the first thing to establish; but it can be most easily made out as following on the second proposition.

But does this need any expansion? When Drummond saw this mortal world as a hunt—death the giant huntsman and man the fugitive quarry—did he see it in words? The pride of perishable young loveliness flasht its vanity into Herrick's mind when he noted against it the senseless beauty of the unaltering jewel; the lightning of that experience assuredly did not come to him in words. Nor was it in words that the mind of Wordsworth had that entranced experience of becoming one with the unconscious speed of the spinning earth. And when Whitman watched the spider's marvellous instinct exploring space, and suddenly found himself watching his own inexplicable soul, it was not in words that his watch maintained itself.

All this is clear enough; and it holds good for the origin of every poem. Verbal thought has nothing to do with it. It is as experience—imaginative experience—that poetry begins. And by "imagination," I do not mean that it belongs necessarily to the unsubstantial day-dreams of pure fantasy; I mean an experience which, long after its first occurrence, has been continued in the poet's mind by imagination—by the power, namely, of holding something constantly before the mind in keen and vivid definition. I mean also, when I call this experience imaginative, to imply very emphatically that it has not been prolonged as a train of reasoning or reflection, not as an intellectual topic, but simply as experience immediately enjoyable or exciting in itself. It is not the rational or practical or moral value of things that supplies the inspiration of poetry with its energy; but the primitive unquestioned instant value any experience has on the face of it, as a moment when *that which knows* delights to exert itself.

The truth of this is only apparently contradicted by those poems which seem to have some philosophic purpose; by, for example, Lucretius' poem *On the Nature of Things*. This is so obviously not only poetry, but poetry of the noblest and grandest kind, that it would by itself suffice to discredit any theory which could not contain it. But what is the inspiration of Lucretius' poem? It professes to versify the philosophy of Epicurus; and what else is philosophy but verbal thought, to which I have denied the power of poetic inspiration? But never mind what the poem professes to do; what does it actually do? Nobody cares a rap now for Epicurus and his flimsy philosophy.

His sovran method was, not to think too hard about anything—a principle too common to be exhilarating. But Lucretius, with his Roman astonishment at the mere idea of speculation, saw in Epicurus the very type of man understanding his destiny. What inspires his poem is not a particular way of thinking, but a sense of the power of thinking, a flaming exultation in the undaunted courage of man's mind, facing its inscrutable fate and determined not to be overborne. And that, under the colour of expounding Epicurus, is what Lucretius is continually conveying to us in his magnificent verse: the single and central imaginative experience, transcending any verbal thought, of man knowing himself the equal of his fate.

But may not poetry be inspired by a story? And how can a story exist except in words? This, with Homer and Shakespeare for witnesses, may seem the heaviest objection of any. But are they really witnesses against the contention that poetry must be inspired by experience? What would the *Iliad* have been, what would *Romeo and Juliet*, or *Othello*, or *Macbeth* have been, if the original story had not come out of its words, and become alive and real—a reality of personal excitement and suffering—in the poet's mind? A story, as a cause of poetry, is exactly comparable with any other kind of event which may happen to a poet: reading or hearing it may set the process going, but the important and decisive thing in that process is not the story itself, but what the story means

Inspiration and Form

to the poet. Swinburne was moved to tell once more the story of Tristram and Iseult. Why? Was it simply because he wished to repeat the story in more ornamental language? That would have given us something; but assuredly not a poem. The urgency, which insisted on the creation, out of familiar tradition common to every one, of this most individual poem, took hold of Swinburne's mind when the subject of *Tristram of Lyonesse* ceased to be a story told to him, and became a piece of himself, a mode of being alive, an experience of white-hot reality; for it was his own spirit living the lives of Tristram and Iseult—he himself was exulting in their love, and anguishing in their disaster. And because of this (here is the heart of the matter) the whole series of events and passions fuses into one fiery sense of its significance to him. The poet himself tells us what this is in the great *Prelude*, one of the major splendours of English poetry:

> Love, that is first and last of all things made,
> The light that has the living world for shade,
> The spirit that for temporal veil has on
> The souls of all men woven in unison,
> One fiery raiment with all lives inwrought
> And lights of sunny and starry deeds and thought,
> And alway through new act and passion new
> Shines the divine same body and beauty through;
>
> .   .   .   .   .   .
>
> Love, that for very life shall not be sold,
> Nor bought nor bound with iron nor with gold;
> So strong that heaven, could love bid heaven farewell,
> Would turn to fruitless and unflowering hell;

So sweet that hell, to hell could love be given,
Would turn to splendid and sonorous heaven;
Love that is fire within thee and light above,
And lives by grace of nothing but of love;
Through many and lovely thoughts and much **desire**
Led these twain to the life of tears and fire;
Through many and lovely days and much delight
Led these twain to the lifeless life of night.

That is what the story of Tristram and Iseult meant to Swinburne. Not a mere abstract notion of the immortal power of love, but a vivid and actual experience of it in the fortunes and persons of these vivid and actual lovers, who are but forms of Swinburne's own essential spirit. And this single presiding sense of the story's meaning for him dominates the whole of Swinburne's version of it: *inspires* it, in fact; every detail of the version is there because it contributes to and corroborates the complete establishment of the story as a final unity, focussing all its glowing variety into a single incandescence:

Love, that is first and last of all things made,
The light that has the living world for shade.

Fortunately, we can go to poetry itself for an account of this process. The first book of *The Ring and the Book*, which must be reckoned a document of capital importance for these studies, describes with brilliant expatiating energy and clear insight the development of a story into an inspiration. Browning tells us how the story at first attracted him; and at once his attention began to assimilate it to his personality. He poured into it his own sympathies and valuations; the persons of it became characters of his world, they became projections of his spirit, forms of experience and feeling assumed by his own vitality. Every event in the story became impregnated with Browning's sense of the story as a whole; and exactly as he kindled it into a living complex reality of his own, so he fused it all into the unity peculiar to his own unique and characteristic sense of the story's significance. It had no decisive unity before this: it had a certain form of its own, the form which marks any notable occurrence in history. But it was embedded in nature; it had no clear beginning and no clear end. Browning, by taking personal possession of it, lifted it out of nature. It became one complete instance of his characteristic sense of things; from being a series of occurrences, it became one single action, like the single harmonious action of several parts or limbs, moved by one will to one purpose: the central life coordinating the whole complex event being the poet's personal sense of the story's significance, to which his imagination has accommodated every detail. And having been known and felt as this one thing, the story inspires to one whole and final result every nice elaboration of its verbal expression.

Now this is typical of all poetry, narrative or not. Something seizes on the poet's attention. It has importance for him; it means something to him; it delights and kindles his mind with the sense of its significance, of its wide relationship with other experiences. He holds it before him in imagination and recurs to it again and again: not to think about it, but simply to enjoy it in his immediate sense of it. It may be anything you please: the one thing necessary is the mode of its acceptance; and this is poetic in so far as it is acceptance for face-value, for the value of experience as such, and not for any ulterior values that may be reasoned or moralised out of it. Whatever has been thus accepted, brings with it a certain joy and excitement, to which is due the urgency it takes on in the poet's mind, driving him to express it in some appropriate form. But as he attends to it, it reverberates through his nature: it collects feelings and associations round it; other experiences, remembered or imagined, come crowding in with their comment or illumination. So that, when his mind would recur to the original matter which he singled out of the flux of things and held up as an image before him, he finds that the image has become enriched and complicated, and may still have further suggestions and possibilities of relationship to offer: its significance, the impression made by the whole mass on his mind, has widened and deepened and become more peculiarly its own, through the number of elements brought into this special connexion. But imagination will never be satisfied until it has brought out all possible and appropriate enrichment (the degree of which will, of course, vary infinitely); and, what is even more important, will never be satisfied until it can hold the whole complexity clearly before it in one single act of attention, organised into one inclusive experience, isolated into self-sufficing unity by its triumphant internal harmony of unique and presiding significance. Then, when that supremely satisfactory moment arrives, the inspiration has been established; and poetic composition has completed its first stage.

This is what is called the unity of inspiration. Now what right have we to talk about the unity of something that belongs to the inner life of a person unknown to us? Obviously none, unless poetic composition has also completed its second stage. For when the art of poetry is entire, what belonged to the poet's life may now belong to ours as well. Since the verbal art of a poem is urged into existence not only by the vividness of a rich imaginative experience, but also by its power of being impressive as a single whole, the final result of the poem, if it is successful, will be the unification of all its detail into one inclusive and harmonious effect. In one word, therefore, whatever else may follow from a poem being the utterance of an inspiration, this must certainly follow: that the poem will have *Form*. It will, that is to say, however brilliant and varied and elaborated in its parts, be capable of existing as a whole: our minds can accept it as one shapely thing. The analogy of the *shape* of things seen with the understood *form* of a poem is, indeed, unavoidable: just as a building or a machine, however intricate an assemblage of parts, can be taken in and attended to as one thing, because the assemblage has a shape for our eyes—so a poem can be attended to as one thing, producing one complex effect, because it has form for our minds. And this is required not because form in poetry is conventional, or expected by a sort of etiquette; but because the form of a poem is its way of communicating to us something essential in the poet's inspiration. The form of a poem is a necessary contribution to its meaning, for it conveys the peculiar unity of significance which the matter had assumed in the poet's mind; and without this unity of significance, the expression of the matter would have been incomplete and crippled.

Every inspiration has its own unity, and every poem should have its own form, since the form must be the efficient equivalent of the unity. There will therefore be an endless range of what form in poetry has to say to us. "Soul is form"; and if the soul of an inspiration be one intense masterful emotion in which the whole substance is transparently dissolved, the poetic form resulting from it will be lucid, close, and rigorous, clearly dominating all the detail of its matter:

> Ah, what avails the sceptred race,
>   Ah, what the form divine!
> What every virtue, every grace!
>   Rose Aylmer, all were thine.
>
> Rose Aylmer, whom these wakeful eyes
>   May weep, but never see,
> A night of memories and of sighs
>   I consecrate to thee.

But the form of poetry may also be flowing and elastic: when there is quite another kind of unity to be conveyed. Yet it may be quite as decisive. Read Browning's *A Light Woman*, for example. As the poem proceeds, you cannot help translating its verbal art—the conversational tone of the words, their fine shades of meaning, their metaphors and swift allusions to related feelings and ideas, their subtly modulated rhythms—you cannot help translating the words into the very life of the characters and emotions they mention. But as soon as the poem has finished its verbal art, not only the vivid evocative power of the words, line by line and stanza by stanza, has affected us, but the whole proportion and connexion of the parts; and we feel that tense unresolved situation as a single thing, as a single moment of rich imaginative experience: there it is, complete and self-contained, a complex dramatic moment perfectly crystallised. In that single and final impression of the completed poem, we feel, as far as we are capable of it—we at any rate have the opportunity of feeling—what the experience meant to Browning: its significance as an emblem of life itself, a significance which, though it came to us through words, nevertheless goes far beyond them; for it is nowhere the actual meaning of the words, and it is more than the total of their meaning. It is the meaning of the *form* of this total, the meaning of the peculiar disposition and internal adjustment of all that the language says, together with the effect of the language as an accumulation of rhythmical sound. It is a whole much greater than the sum of its parts. When we can hold everything that the poem can give

The Theory of Poetry

us in one harmonious act of attention, it becomes to us what it originally was to Browning: a single experience, with its own immediate value and significance—the peculiar significance given, without ulterior valuation, by just such elements being fused into just such a relationship. Now this is no more than to say that the poem was prompted by an inspiration, and that the inspiration has revealed itself as the form of a poem. And that would be true of anything we can call a poem. If every poem, to be worth anything, must have been inspired by an imaginative experience, it follows that every poem must have Form—its own Form.

III

TECHNIQUE

I N the composition of a poem, as I have already said, we are to distinguish two stages. It does not matter much what we call them; but unless we can see pretty clearly the remarkable difference between what is usually called the *Conception* of a poem and what is called its *Technique*, we are not likely to understand the peculiar nature of poetic art.

As to the *Conception* of a poem, not much more ✓ *Summary.* needs to be said. This is the stage in which the in- *N.B. §* spiration of some imaginative experience completely establishes itself in the poet's mind, as an affair of clear imagery, vivid importance, and delightful excitement: also as a focus of varied and perhaps only just suggested associations and allusions; but above all as a single inclusive harmony, however complex, of all that it contains. Verbal art has no place in it. It may complete itself in an instant and without conscious effort; or it may be a gradual development and, in ✓ part at least, have been deliberately thought out. It certainly will have been this latter, if it is the conception of a dramatic or narrative poem, requiring a considerable organisation of parts; and in that case, no doubt, verbal thought will have helped the process of conception. But only for the purpose of clarifying

65

or developing the poet's own sense of what he wants to say, not for the purpose of saying it: only for the purpose of elaborating his imagination, not for the purpose of communicating it.

The art of poetry, however, does not exist until both stages have been accomplished. A man is not to be accounted a poet simply for being sensitive or excitable. A sunset may mean wonders to him; an old story may have fired his fancy into a rapture. But he is not a poet unless his wonders and raptures have ceased to be private to himself, and have become available to every one. A poet, that is to say, is not only a man of remarkable imaginative life, but a man who can express this.

Now expression is a somewhat ambiguous word. It means two quite different things in the two stages of poetic composition. This is what I want to stress in this lecture; for otherwise the peculiar manners of poetic technique might seem a mere affair of traditional etiquette. In the stage of conception, an inspiration *expresses* itself by the mere fact of being unmistakably and vividly *known*. As soon as the poet is perfectly aware of his own experience—of all that can be seen and felt in it—of all that it is and all that it means to him—then, as far as he is concerned, expression is complete: the event, whatever it was, has expressed itself to him, and he has expressed himself, in his experience of it. But if a poem is to come of this, what happened in the poet's mind must somehow be made to happen in other minds: the image and its

The Maker
ποιητη

66

Technique

meaning must be conveyed to us. That is to say, some vehicle must be contrived to carry it; for it cannot carry itself: by no possibility can an experience in one man's mind be transferred bodily and directly out of his mind into ours. So now begins the stage of technique: the stage in which something which does not exist as language—namely, an event in the poet's life —has to translate itself into an existence alien to its first nature: into the existence which is given by language. For not otherwise could it escape from the privacy of the poet's own mind; and it is, once more, the essential thing in poetry, that imagination should thereby escape from the self-consciousness of the poet and become the property of the whole world.

When, therefore, we say that a poet's *technique* is expressing his imagination, we mean something vastly different from the automatic and immediate expression that comes about when, in the privacy of his own consciousness, the poet *conceived* his work. We mean that his inspiration is urging something other than itself to act as its interpreter; we mean that his vivid and compelling experience is organising all the resources of language to combine into an unmistakable *symbol* of itself. One remarkable aspect of this process has already been noticed: the language which expresses a poetic imagination must show a certain *form*, in order to symbolise the original unity of its inspiration. Now this poetic form, as we have seen, results gradually from the organic connexion and proportion of the parts, whereby a sort of shapeliness finally presides over their combination, enabling them noticeably to make one single complex impression. But what does this mean? It means that technique must *first* express the substance of its inspiration, and *then* the peculiar harmony in which the substance was disposed. Poetic technique, that is to say, will always have two aspects. We may regard it as giving some equivalent to the *harmony* of its inspiration, in which case we call it poetic *form;* or we may regard it as equivalent to the *substance* of the inspiration, in which case we call it poetic *diction.* We shall see presently how closely and inevitably these two aspects are related; and that I mean by these terms no more than two aspects of one continuous process need hardly, indeed, be said. There are those who will deny any distinction between substance and form in poetry; but surely, if it is allowable to say that a billiard ball and a tennis ball have the same form but different substance, we may permit ourselves a similar discrimination in poetry.

And this brings me to an important consequence of the symbolic nature of technique in poetry: namely, that it is never exact. How could it be? Look only at the fact we have just noted, that technique has these two distinguishable aspects of diction and form. The poet, in order to express himself in language, has to build up, phrase by phrase and moment by moment, the substance of his experience: instead of attending to it as a whole, he has to attend to it bit by bit, breaking it up into its elements and concentrating on their piecemeal translation into language. But all the time

Technique

he has to be providing for the final moment, when the series of these moments is to make one harmonious and inclusive impression, similar to the impression originally made on himself by his inspiration. It could hardly be expected that the result of this gradual and complicated process would be an exact equivalent to his imagination, which presented itself to his mind in the instantaneous harmony of its substance. It must be remembered that the effort has been not so much to embody an inspiration as to symbolise it; and symbolic expression must anyhow be indirect, since it means the expression of one thing by exhibiting its influence on another. But something else must also be remembered. The thing which has to be expressed—imaginative experience—is infinitely variable; but the thing which has to become its symbolic expression is not. Language is a finite medium; it can only respond to the urgency of imagination in a limited number of ways. It is true that a skilled artist in language can get an enormous range of modulation out of its resources; but nevertheless he has to canalise, as it were, his inspiration into the special kinds of symbolism which are possible in language. The tradition of poetry, in fact, is nothing but the accumulation, from countless ages of experiment, of the knowledge how to make language approximate most closely to the infinite variety of imagination. In any case, it can only be an approximation; and if I speak in the sequel of poetic expression being "precise" or "perfect" or "just," I must be understood to mean, within the limits set by the nature of language.

The Theory of Poetry

A good illustration of the way poetic technique may be content (and I should add, safely content) with approximate symbolism, may be found in certain kinds of poetic form. I said that every poem must have its own form, and that the form of every poem has in itself unique meaning; since it is this final shapeliness of the whole impression which answers to the unique harmony of imaginative substance in the poet's inspiration. And the form of a poem must include not only the disposition and proportion of the thought, which we shall call its intellectual form; but also the arrangement of its rhythms and rimes, which we shall call its instrumental form. Both kinds combine and reinforce one another in enabling us to take in the poem as a single and orderly whole. Now it is clear that every poem must have its own intellectual form; but instrumental form, which should be just as individual, is often common to a very large number of poems, and can be described apart from any particular poem as an abstract and rigid pattern. Here, for example, is a well-known triolet by a brilliant poetess of to-day:

To a Fat Lady seen from the Train.

Why do you walk through the fields in gloves,
Missing so much and so much?
O fat white woman whom nobody loves,
Why do you walk through the fields in gloves
When the grass is soft as the breast of doves
And shivering sweet to touch?
O why do you walk through the fields in gloves,
Missing so much and so much?

Technique

How admirably does this intricate little pattern of rhythm and rime fit the tone and mood of the poem! There is artifice in it, no doubt. One sees why nobody *loves* the woman: it is because she wears *gloves*. Quite another relationship with society would have been recorded, if the authoress had happened to be an enthusiast for walking the fields barefoot; the poem would have had to go

> Why do you walk through the fields in boots,
> Missing so much and so much?
> O fat white woman whom nobody shoots,
> Why do you walk through the fields in boots
> When the grass is tickling soft at the roots
> And shivering sweet to touch?
> O why do you walk through the fields in boots,
> Missing so much and so much?

You notice how a slight verbal change, which leaves the external form practically unaltered, has given us quite another poem; and yet the form seems just as valid as before.

Now this was a case of ready-made or *prescribed form*. A certain arrangement of lines is ordained and may not be departed from. The form precedes the poem, as an abstract pattern which the poet has to fill in with his matter. It seems, then, that instead of being a necessary expression of inspiration, form may be arbitrarily imposed on it; and yet may be entirely satisfactory.

I do not think anything like *prescribed form* is to be found earlier than the troubadours: the discovery

71

of its possibility is perhaps the most conspicuous relic of the exquisite civilisation of Provence. The Greeks had, of course, a passion for strict and noble form; but Greek form was always appropriate to and varying with the poetic occasion. Pindar and Simonides would, I fancy, have scorned an invitation to write a sonnet—to make up so many lines in such and such an arrangement, irrespective of the theme. They would have found nothing offensive in being asked to write an ode to a team of mules; they would, for pay, have done it pompously and superbly, addressing the mules as "daughters of whirlwind-footed horses," or something in that style. But sonnets, I think, would have been too much for their artistic consciences. Yet not only sonnets, but ballads, triolets, rondeaus, sestinas, villanelles, and the rest of the Provençal and Early French prescribed forms of poetry have established themselves in the European poetic tradition. We need think only of Dante's sonnets, and that grand impassioned sestina of his; of Villon's ballades; of the many glories of our English sonnets—the sonnets of Spenser, Shakespeare, Milton, Wordsworth and Keats. "Scorn not the Sonnet," says Wordsworth: and the poem is formidable evidence not merely for its array of convincing instances, but also because these instances are enabled to assert themselves so splendidly, for the precise reason that they are themselves given in the form of a sonnet.

The sonnet, indeed, has made itself so generally useful, that it is difficult to imagine how modern poetry could do without it. The other prescribed forms are

Technique

too curious in their repetitions and riming to be successful except in a very limited scope. But the sonnet, though doubtless it began in love poetry, has triumphed in every kind of mood. What, then, becomes of our doctrine that form in poetry is produced as the symbol of harmony in inspiration? We know quite well how sonnet-form is produced; one simply has to follow the prescription: fourteen lines of a certain length and rhythm, with rimes falling in certain places. Into this one fits any theme that will go into it; and there is the sonnet. How can we pretend that a form thus arrived at can have any symbolic responsibility at all?

But it has, of course; that is precisely the problem. Look at Wordsworth's sonnet on Toussaint l'Ouverture, and ask yourself if anywhere in poetry instrumental form chimes into a harmony more exquisitely appropriate to its matter; if correspondence between the movement of the rhythm and the procedure of the thought could combine more beautifully or securely into the right finality of a single complex impression. The form, in fact, is signally expressive, in spite of being ready-made and exactly prescribed. And when we think of similar successes achieved by Dante, Petrarca, Ronsard, Milton, we are tempted to think, perhaps, that no more is required for success than to follow the rules.

But we forget the failures. I do not know what the percentage of successful sonnets may be in the vast welter of sonnets attempted with every regard to the rules; but I am sure it would work out to a decimal beginning with many noughts. The sonnet has been compared to the bed of Procrustes. We are not told how many of Procrustes' guests exactly fitted his bed; but if he went on long enough having people to stay with him, he must have found some. In the case of the sonnet, we do know of many guests who exactly fitted the bed; but we also know of a prodigious number who had to be lopped or stretched. Even in such an accomplished sonneteer as Rossetti, there are very few sonnets in which the inspiration does not, under its handsome coverlet, audibly stifle some groan of discomfort.

Still, there are those notable successes; we must account for them. They vary enormously in the nature of their themes; and yet the same conventionally prescribed form does equally well for all of them. It cannot be mere accident; it cannot *just happen* that the same form will be equally right as a part of expression for such an immense range of moods. But the solution is obvious. Language is not capable of exactly symbolising every possibility of imagination. But it can approximate so closely to its original that the defect will be unnoticeable, and our delight in the vigour of its sufficient accuracy will leave no room for dissatisfaction. And yet, since it is only an approximation, a species of symbolism may be equally adequate for things which are not indeed the same, but sufficiently similar to be classed as one kind of things. So in the case of sonnets: experiences very different in the elements of their imagination may yet all exhibit the same sort of in-

clusive harmony; and it is the harmony, not the substance, which form has to symbolise. The unity of
several inspirations can never be quite the same; but
it may be so similar that one approximate form will
serve for many cases. Hence the validity of sonnet-
form. The author of a successful sonnet does not set
out to substantiate a certain prescribed form. He has
his inspiration; and it impresses him with the peculiar
harmony of its elements. His knowledge of his craft
tells him, that for this peculiar harmony, the nearest
symbol in poetic form will be a sonnet. The sufficiently
appropriate form was there, ready to be used.

It very often happens, of course, that widely divergent themes, working themselves out into their natural
forms without any prescription, will nevertheless, in
lyrics and epigrams, arrive at the same instrumental
form. This means, that it was as near as the poet's
expression could get, in the finite medium it was using.
It was the singular achievement of Provence, first, to
recognise the constant recurrence of similar unities in
varying substances; secondly, to devise and perfect the
poetic forms which would, as far as language can, most
closely symbolise these recurring kinds of harmony.
For anything like the subtlety and insight of this discovery we look in vain through the civilisations which
followed the murder of Provence in the most bestial
of all crusades.

I have discussed at some length this special question
of approximate form in poetry, in order to emphasise

the inevitable limitations in the symbolism of which language is capable. The poet's imagination, in all its rich complexity as a moment of intense and real experience, must use, in order to make itself communicable, a medium which will only respond to it in certain well-defined directions. How poetry contrives to make language respond in these directions so subtly and vividly and expansively that, for all its limited scope, it can convey to us the authentic life of the poet's mind—that is what we must now go on to study. But first we must see more exactly what poetic symbolism in language means.

It is often unmistakable enough: and chiefly when words are made to impress our imagination without any precise logical coherence. Here, for example, is the dirge from *The Two Noble Kinsmen:*

Symbolism in language //

> Urns and odours bring away,
> Vapours, sighs, darken the day.
> Our dole more deadly looks than dying;
> Balms and gums and heavy cheers,
> Sacred vials fill'd with tears,
> And clamors through the wild air flying.

The logic of that is not very apparent; but as a verbal symbol of lamentation it is the very thing. The suggestion of its images, the sound of its syllables (*urns and odours*), the expansion of its feeling (*vapours, sighs, darken the day—clamors through the wild air flying*) produce an emotional coherence which we do not have to understand: it comes home to us directly,

Technique

instinct with meaning we need not analyse. This, we are tempted to say, is pure symbolism.

The same sort of thing is often found in *refrains*, in which images are joined not for any logical meaning, but for the indefinable yet unmistakable force of their combined associations. The romantics, always ready to escape from rational values, were fond of this; and certainly discovered some pleasantly irrational effects. *Two red roses across the moon*, for example. Reason may protest as it likes that the phrase says nothing. It says nothing reasonable, indeed; but as a mere symbol made of colours and associations, surely it works like magic. Parlour magic, perhaps; but nevertheless delightful:

> There was a lady lived in a hall,
> Large of her eyes, and slim and tall;
> And ever she sung from noon to noon,
> *Two red roses across the moon.*
>
> There was a knight came riding by
> In early spring, when the roads were dry;
> And he heard that lady sing at the noon,
> *Two red roses across the moon.*

And so on! Many find this sort of thing puerile; Calverley thought the lady might just as well have sung "Butter and eggs and a pound of cheese." Why roses, and why two of them? And why across the moon? There is no why: except that, by merely bringing these images together, Morris created the perfect symbol for that enchanted mood of his youth. A red rose does

77

not simply mean a flower in a garden, though that is a great deal of meaning; the moon does not simply mean a silver brightness at night, though that too is a great deal of meaning. Who can say how much *suggestion* these images draw along with them? It was mainly on this that Morris, with the guileless cunning of his youthful technique, relied for the efficacy of a symbolism as innocent and thoughtless as a child's.

It is indeed obvious that words, if luck helps the choosing of them (and luck, when reason retires, must always be a chief partner in the affair), can be made so convincingly suggestive apart from syntax or logic, that poetry will often rely on this alone. The suggestion can come as much from the sound of the words as from their meaning. It is common with the Elizabethans. Thus Peele gives to Paris and Œnone a lyrical dialogue in this style:

Œnone. Fair and fair and twice so fair,
  As fair as any may be:
  The fairest shepherd on our green,
  A love for any lady.

Paris. Fair and fair and twice so fair,
  As fair as any may be:
  Thy love is fair for thee alone
  And for no other lady.

It would be difficult to dilute the logical meaning of language further than that. But what then? The mere music of the words, however little sense they

Technique

have, is a sufficient symbol of the delicious fresh gaiety which Peele had in his mind.

But neither the Elizabethans nor the romantics thought that this purely illogical symbolism, whether of meaning or of sound, would supply by itself a sufficient technique for poetry. Such a belief has, however, been not only asserted, but practised. It is a signal instance of the danger of theories which declare what poetry ought to be. This theory alleges, that since poetry in its use of language must anyhow be symbolic, the more obvious and ostentatious its symbolism, the better it must be as poetry. Accordingly, the symbolist poets of France—led by a man of genius, Mallarmé, and aped by a horde of camp-followers, the Futurists and Imagists—sought to empty the technique of poetry of all logical meaning and rational coherence; everything but the bare symbolism of words. This absurd and arbitrary restriction not only limits our imaginations to the region of clouds, and makes us, even amid the exquisite clouds of Mallarmé's vague but many-coloured mind, yearn for clear light and clean outline; it actually restricts the suggestive power of words themselves, the power which the symbolists chiefly rely on commanding.

For the instrument of poetry is not so much *words* as *language;* not so much the separable meaning, however expansive, which can be assigned to this word or that, nor even to this phrase or that, but the continued organisation of this into language, into the process of *verbal thought,* in the broadest sense. We do not, as some have supposed, get away from symbolism by this extension; we merely get away from the crude and elementary limitation of it practised by the so-called symbolist poets. Language as the vehicle of connected and coherent thought must still be only a symbol in poetry; for it is not thought which urges poetry into existence. A poet's motive will always be the immediate delight of experience; and if he has to reduce this to thought, it is not because we require him to think *about* experience, but (so far as is possible) to think experience itself: that is, to think in language a symbolic equivalent to it, simply because then he will have in his mind something he can communicate.

And the poetic instrument must be the continuous organism of language, and not merely the separable force of particular words and phrases, for two main reasons: First, because it is only when language assumes the nature of connected and orderly *thought*, that it is capable of that firm and delicate *structure* by which alone the power of words can assume the harmony and distinct shapeliness of meaning required for a work of art—to enable it to exist in its own single, complete, and self-contained nature. Poetic language must, in fact, first be *syntax;* or it will never achieve the unity of *form.*

vg: cubist verse.

But the second reason is, that it is only when words are made into a continuous texture—only when each word is chosen to contribute to the sense of many— that their individual genius can have its full effect. There are no creatures in the world so sociable as words; and until we see them taking their part in the society of other words we cannot know what they are capable of effecting. As the next lecture will indicate, the concealed energies and delicate suggestions of words are of vital importance to the texture of poetry. But not only can they never be fully revealed, they can never (a much more serious requirement) be definitely and precisely directed, except when they are fitted into the massive coherence of syntax. In poetry, as in any other intelligible use of language, words are the servants, but the master is grammar.

This, however, is only one side of language. We hear it as well as understand it. But here again language must be continuous and organised, rather than an affair of separable qualities, in order to be adequate as a symbol of imagination. For the continuous sound of language is its rhythm; and the rhythm of language can symbolise as nothing else can the emotional comment with which mind accompanies its experience. Moreover, rhythm, like syntax, is capable of organising its sequence of momentary effects into one inclusive major effect; and is, therefore, the means whereby a poem may be heard, as well as understood, as a unity. Rhythm, that is to say, as the audible counterpart of syntax, is the means of the instrumental form which corresponds to the intellectual form of the meaning. Both are required in poetry; because its technique can only be adequate to the whole force of imagination by taking the fullest advantage of everything language is capable of doing. And just as the suggestion of in-

81

dividual words is brought out and directed by their function in syntax, so the scarcely less important expression due to *syllabic sound*—the quality of vowels and consonants in combination—becomes evident by its place in the continuity of rhythm.

These are the four channels in the medium of language along which the infinite complexity of poetic inspiration must flow, in order to express itself. Words have their straightforward meaning, which can organise itself into a wholeness of significance greater than the sum of their separable effects; and yet each word has an individual genius of its own, capable of suggesting more than it seems to say. But the contexture of the words must also be heard as a continually growing rhythm, whereby the force of the individual sounds not only enlarges the expressive power of the words but adds to the structure of the thought the structure of an evident pattern of sound. And within that pattern, sequences of vowels and juncture of consonants will contribute their elusive but invaluable persuasions.

Now the purpose of all this is *symbolic*. That is to say, language succeeds as poetry by handing on whatever has been entrusted to it; and a great deal more has been entrusted to it than analysis will ever discover. Language is not the vehicle of inspiration in the sense of being a receptacle into which the poet pours his mind for purposes of transmission, and out of which the reader then extracts what it contained. Language in poetry is a transmission of energy rather than of substance. It sets the reader's mind working and di-

rects the tendency of the work. It urges us to live
for a time in a particular style of imagination—the style
of the poet's imagination: but it is our own imagination
that really does the business of poetry. In other words,
the symbolic nature of language in poetry means just
this: that it is a *stimulus* for our minds, though a stimulus of a very determining character. The whole purpose of a poet's technique is to make a moment of his
experience come to life in other minds than his. He
assumes that we have an imaginative life similar to his,
and provides himself with means to rouse it and take
charge of it; but his language can do no more than that.
For a poem must end as it began—in a private act of
imagination. This, secluded in the reader's individual
mind, can never be quite the same as it was in the
privacy of the poet's mind; not only because no two
minds can be the same, but also because the poet has
had to rely for his communication on a limited and
therefore imperfect medium. But since this medium
works symbolically—that is, as a stimulus—its limitation is less serious than might be supposed. For imagination is not to be roused in separate bits. Rouse it at
one point, and the response goes thrilling and reverber-
ating through the mind with messages summoning all
sorts of sensuous and emotional associations to come
and join in the answer. The skill of the poet consists
in rousing just that tract of imagination, and rousing it
in just that way, which will produce a train of associations similar to the complex of feeling, image and idea
he vividly possessed in his own experience. He cannot

[handwritten margin note: Someone has said there is no poem until it has been read. A half-truth, but it is merely a stimulating truth.]

[handwritten margin note: A poem is a compliment.]

[handwritten margin note: We get out largely what we bring to our reading.]

directly *say* all this; and that is why poetic language requires such refinement and intricate subtlety of texture: it has to expand into much more than it apparently says. Clearly, this is due to the power of language not as an informative medium, but as a stimulus: it is the reader's imagination which has to expand, however this may be due to the influence of the language.

This, then, is what the symbolism of language in poetry really means; this is how it hands on what has been entrusted to it. The poet's communication will always take place in private; and it will always take the character of the mind which receives it. But it is nevertheless a true *publication* of the poet's experience; first because it is available to all minds, and secondly, because, however qualified it must be by the reader's individual nature, it is possible to use language with such precision and yet with such expansive power of suggestion, that the common humanity of all minds will similarly respond to it. The radiant persuasions of sense and sound in a poet's phrases, marshalled by the structure of his thought into an inclusive harmony, will effect an experience in the reader's mind which may be, so far as it is possible, the *imitation* of the poet's experience. And this is the true sense of that ancient, much debated, and much misunderstood doctrine, that poetry is a kind of imitation: the sense, namely, that the purpose of poetry is to effect in the reader's mind an imitation of what happened in the poet's mind. It does this by the expansive symbolism of which language is capable; and the term may be legitimately

Technique

and conveniently transferred from the result to the instrument. We may say that poetic language is language which imitates the inspiration of the poet; and that will mean, language which employs simultaneously every available means to symbolise it.

But if we are asked how poetic language differs from other language, our answer must be, that it differs simply in the degree of its imitation. For all language is, or was originally, symbolic. It is no longer this in the technique of rational thought: language has become the embodiment which realises its nature—though even here we may remember Abelard's profound paradox, that though the language exists for the sake of the thought, the thought exists by means of the language. But fortunately we are not as a rule engaged in purely rational thought; everywhere else we shall certainly be making some symbolic use of language. If we are engaged in conversation we are no doubt using tone of utterance to imply much of what cannot be directly said. Think how many kinds of affirmation you can *speak* with the one word *Yes*, by using falling, rising, or mixed tones: *Yès*—provisional agreement, but you are a little dubious; *Yés*—you agree so far, but you would like to hear more; *Yês*—you agree heartily and are surprised to be so convinced; *Yěs*—you do not agree at all, but think it polite to say you do. Of course, these tones, and their implication, allow of innumerable modulations. But this sort of thing is evidently not to be relied on if, as it has been for thousands of years, the chief medium of literature is the written word. For though the written word must be mentally translated into the spoken word in order to be effective as art, it is not the artist who does this, but the recipient. The poet's language must supply the lack of that most expressive thing, tone of voice, by the nicety of the other devices he employs. But all these devices enter, in some degree, into any use of language, unless it be pure argument like Euclid's *Elements* or Spinoza's *Ethics:* except in such rarefactions of thought, we must always rely, speaking or writing, on something more than the analysable meaning of language: we must rely on some degree of expansive response to the stimulus of language as well as on the sense it actually carries. And all the poetic methods of symbolism which I have mentioned may be used more or less effectively even in easy-going conversation.

How then do we distinguish poetic language? The fact is, I think, that there is no hard and fast distinction. It has often been asserted that by poetic language we mean the presence of metre. Now, as we shall see, metre is, beyond doubt, the kind of rhythm most suitable as a rule for the purposes of poetry. But metre is simply one of the devices available to poetic expression; and if it happens that some other kind of rhythm will do just as well or better, and if everything else we require is there, it seems merely arbitrary to withhold the title of poetry. A definition of poetry would surely look very foolish, if it would exclude the English versions of *Job* or *The Song of Songs*.

Technique

I would put it in this way: the passage from prosaic to poetic language is the passage from language which *describes* what is happening in the author's mind, to language which *imitates* this. There must be an infinite number of stages between merely descriptive language (probably for some ulterior purpose, such as giving information or stating a case) and language completely imitative (for no other purpose than to be just that). But if you could make a scale of literary art, passing by degrees from the extremely prosaic to the extremely poetic, you would find that your scale really represented the passage from the language which simply tells you about the author's mind, to the language which can make the author's mind come vividly to life again in yours. And you would find that the nearer you got in your scale to perfect imitation, the greater addition was being made to the grammatical sense of language: the greater use, more intricate, more subtle, more precise, was being made of all its powers of stimulation, whether through meaning or through sound; until at last you arrived at the stage where grammar fuses the symbolism of meaning and sound into a moment which imitates beyond any analysis the poet's rapture of complex experience—sense, feeling and idea—as authentically as this:

> When the hounds of spring are on winter's traces,
>   The mother of months in meadow or plain
> Fills the shadows and windy places
>   With the lisp of leaves and ripple of rain;
> And the brown bright nightingale amorous

Is half assuaged for Itylus,
For the Thracian ships and the foreign faces,
The tongueless vigil, and all the pain.

Thus to account for poetic language, simply by the degree of its power to *imitate* rather than to *describe* imagination, or, if you like, by the degree of its simultaneous complexity of symbolic devices, takes us round several difficulties which beset more rigid definitions. For instance, language is often poetic to some and not to others; but our account obviously allows for variations in individual response to language. Some minds may not be capable of mustering the required associations round a particular kind of appeal; and in that case the language clearly can produce no experience in their minds imitative of the poet's.

Again, the spirit of poetry may only occasionally visit a writer's style. In the midst of the unquestionably prosaic, a paragraph, a sentence, a single phrase even, may strike us as being just as unquestionably poetic. And, since we are not relying on any one quality, such as metre, for our criterion, but on the intricacy of all the appropriate qualities, whatever they may be, it should be no more difficult to account for poetic prose than for prosaic versification. A paragraph of De Quincey suddenly becomes poetry when, instead of discoursing about things, he allows his imagination to take hold of his language and to elaborate it so completely that every shade of meaning and turn of rhythm will help to excite in us the actual emotions and visions which he had enjoyed. But if, on the other hand, the

Technique

texture of a writer's words has not the manifold subtlety and nicety of stimulus which alone can give to us the sense of experiencing something (even though that something be an intellectual experience)—if he is merely telling us *about* something—then it will not come any nearer to the condition of poetry for being versified.

But poetry in this sense is simply *diction:* it is that language which imitates as perfectly as may be, moment by moment, the very life and vigour of imagination with all its unaccountable swift suggestions and illusions. But technique must be capable of achieving something more than diction; the art of poetry does not perfect itself unless it gives us not only *poetry,* but *poems.* In a poem, imagination is self-sufficient and self-contained; it exists entirely within its own right and for its own sake. It must, that is to say, exist as a unity of its own; otherwise, its existence is imperfect. Here we resume, from the technical point of view, that prime poetic requirement with which the last lecture concluded. Now it may be that a writer's imagination has never perfectly come into existence: it has never isolated itself from the rest of his thought and made itself distinctly known, complete in its own significance. Or it may have done that, and yet the writer has not been able to manage his art firmly enough to express it as a single coherence of elements. For, in order to let language take charge of it, it was necessary to disintegrate it and express it piecemeal. If, however, the author has during all the effort of

89

composition held the original unity of conception steadily before his mind, and has expressed every part of it in its exact proportion and right relation to the whole, then the sense of his words will build up an intellectual harmony, and the sound of them will build up an instrumental harmony: both sense and sound being, in poetry, equally required for expression. Diction, that is to say, will have become form: poetry will have become a poem. When the art of poetry is perfect, we have not only such texture of language as can perfectly imitate momentary imagination, but language which can draw imagination into wholeness of self-sufficing harmony: and that not by any imposition, but simply by the natural accumulation of the precisely right expressions, moment by moment. Poetic form means simply this: that by provision made for the whole through every part of the texture of a poem, what had to be disintegrated into language cannot but finally re-integrate itself into a single imaginative experience. For, once more, an imaginative experience which has been so distinctly known that it has urged the poet to express it, has not properly been expressed at all if it has not been expressed as a unity.

IV

DICTION: THE MEANING OF WORDS

A GOOD deal of the theory of poetry has now been broadly outlined; and after noticing one or two fallacies which it exposes, I had better summarise its main results, in order to show how the outlines must now be filled in. The art of poetry consists both of having something to say and of saying it. *Speechless poets—mute inglorious Miltons* and so on—do not concern us: indeed, they are not usually invoked as creatures at all, but rather as harmless tropes, like *wise fools* and men who *achieve the impossible.* But sometimes the *dumb poet* is offered more seriously to our notice. He signifies now not pathetic *failure to be a poet,* but on the contrary a triumphant soaring beyond the reach of language. There may be these spiritual triumphs; but so long as we are merely told about them, we have to take them on trust; they have nothing, at any rate, to do with poetry, unless they at least try to make themselves communicable. And when we remember what Dante and Shakespeare did manage to communicate, we may suspect that these unspeakable exaltations are only, after all, another kind of poetic failure: the *art* was lacking. So, when Samuel Butler says, "The greatest poets never write poetry—for the highest poetry is ineffable," we recognise it as a case of what Hobbes calls "the frequency of insignificant speech." This ineffable poetry is as good as a square circle. It has no function but to enable Butler to seem profound when he is only talking sentimental nonsense —which is usually what he does talk when art is the topic.

Let me, for a moment, touch on two other popular figments: the poet whose work has more matter than art, and his companion in misfortune, who has more art than matter. How can poetry have more matter than art? As far as we are concerned, the poet has just as much matter as he has art to convey it; if there is matter in him for which he has no art, how do we know anything about it? We may sometimes feel that a poet is trying to say something and is not succeeding; but in that case we do not know what he wants to say, we only hope there is some reason for his exasperated fumbling. This is to give us neither matter nor art; for if the matter does not arrive, there is no art. When we do gather what he wants to say, then obviously, somehow or other he has said it. He may not have said it well; he may be deficient in art. But the result of that will be not too much matter, but too little. Whether that was due to poverty of inspiration or of art, we cannot tell; for we can only know his inspiration by his art. Browning was both blamed and praised for loading his poetry with matter while disdaining art. This was simply a formula for avoiding criticism; it repressed inquiry into the unusual character of his art, and into the fact that its oddity sometimes succeeds, sometimes fails. But it fails precisely when it conveys to us only dead matter—intellectual stuff that will not come to life: it fails, that is, because its matter, far from being excessive, is deficient—there are only the bones of it, not the breathing flesh.

Swinburne, on the other hand, is still quoted as the type of poet who exhibits art without matter. Again, a phrase takes the place of criticism. Why is Swinburne's work sometimes so thrilling, sometimes so dull? He had found out certain devices which in his earlier work had done such wonders that he went on using them whether they were appropriate or not. Was this excessive art? It was a woeful lack of art. Art without matter can only be, in poetry, language without meaning: which is as much as to say, language that is not language. Swinburne may have come near to that; but the nearer he came, the less art he showed, for the art of poetry is simply the art of electrifying language with extraordinary meaning. Art without matter is not art at all.

When therefore we come across language which is instinct with an exceptional degree of meaning; when it not only conveys ideas or the way things happened, but can make those ideas enact themselves in our imagination as sensuous and emotional experiences, or can turn the way things happened into the very sense of their happening: when language does this, we recognise that we have poetry before us. The detailed theory of poetry must therefore proceed to examine into the means available for this; and these, as we have seen, will resolve themselves into special uses of the dual nature of language—its nature as *sound* which is also *meaning*. Sound of words will have a meaning of its own in poetry, not to be given in any other way; and the meaning that is ordinarily conveyed in the sound of words will prove capable of a subtle expansive reverberation, which seems to detach itself from the sound and go summoning images and feelings from remote regions of the mind to come and share its life. These are the two aspects of language which the learned call phonetic and semantic; they are not properly separable, but their effects can be discriminated.

By noting these effects (which we shall now do more minutely in this and the following lecture), we may collect some notion of what it is that poetry peculiarly has to say. But this, whatever it is, we cannot help but note also, does not come to finality of expression unless the poetry has also become a poem: unless, that is, it has achieved a certain self-sufficient and complete coherence of independent existence. And this independence is due to the fact that there is a further meaning to be got out of the sense and sound of language: the meaning we indicate by the word *form*. This is the final and resultant success of all those serial qualities we shall have considered as *diction*, and is not therefore to be discussed as though it were a separable imposition; but when we come to it, we shall also have come to considering what it is that poetry finally exists to say to us. We may therefore content ourselves, in

The Meaning of Words

the last lecture, with discussing *poetic form* in general under the guise of *poetic significance*.

There is always more in our minds than we can put into words. The peculiarity of poetic language is merely one of degree: it manages to mean more than other language. But language can say things directly or indirectly: along with its explicit meaning, a great many things may be, with tolerable certainty, implied. And what our words imply, even in everyday affairs, is often very important. Who does not know that a sentence grammatically innocent may imply something very injurious? But the indirect (yet unmistakable) implications of language are of crucial importance in poetry. For language as a means of explicit statement —as a merely grammatical instrument—is pretty much the same everywhere; so that if we are to have an unusual degree of meaning in poetic language, it must be by means of its indirect or, as we say, its suggestive powers. Moreover, what language explicitly says is *thought;* and thought in poetry is only the symbol of experience. How verbal thought—the syntax of language—is to work symbolically in our minds and be *experienced* there, is largely determined by the mood and the associations which accompany it; that is, by what the texture of it is made to imply.

Thus, when we are discussing either the meaning of words in poetry, or their sound, we naturally take first the momentary effect of individual words and phrases; but we shall go fatally wrong if we ignore the continuous organisation of words into syntax and rhythm.

95

The Theory of Poetry

Their vague and changeable suggestion can only become reliable and distinct when it is governed by the presiding force of verbal *construction;* and it is only by syntax that meaning, only by rhythm that sound, can become form.

The imperfections of language make themselves uncomfortably obvious when we are trying to be clear about language itself. We talk of poetic meaning and poetic sound: but how can sound be poetic unless it also has some sort of meaning? True, it is not a definable meaning; not indeed a meaning language can convey by any other means than the mere sound of its words. For if there were another way of expressing what rhythm, assonance, and so on, can so forcibly charge our minds with, the technique of poetry would not need to be managed with such a strict regard for them.

We can avoid some of this confusion by adopting terms already mentioned: "semantic" for *the meaning of the sound* and "phonetic" for *the sound of the meaning.* But we are still liable to confusion when we go on to dissect, as we must now do, the semantics of language in poetry. For what is the meaning of a word? In the usual sense, it is that for which we consult our dictionaries; it is what the word contributes to the syntax of a sentence, to the structure of the thought; it is a word's definable or logical character. But, though there must be this sort of meaning in poetry, as everywhere else in language, there must be much more than this. If a writer cannot invest his syntax with something of what we call the magic of words, we deny

The Meaning of Words

his right to the title of poet; but if he can make his individual words live in a special and unusual way in his verses, he may have scarcely any other power, but we allow him to be a poet. This "magic of words," however, is clearly only a species of meaning; but it is so noticeable in poetry and so characteristic that we should be able to refer to it distinctly. For this purpose it will be enough if we agree that a writer, for his work to be accounted poetry, must be peculiarly intent on the *values* of his words in addition to their straightforward and explicit meaning.

What the value of a word is in poetry can be easily illustrated:

> She lived unknown, and few could know
>   When Lucy ceased to be:
> But she is in her *grave*, and, Oh,
>   The difference to me.

The extraordinary value of the word *grave* there is plainly not to be discovered by looking it up in a dictionary; and it is a very special and distinct value, due not simply to the word itself, but to the position of the word. It would not have quite this value anywhere else; the value is elicited by the fact that the word comes just where it does in the structure not only of the verse but of the whole poem. No doubt the sound of the word has much to do with its remarkable value, but just now I am attending to the semantic value of it.

And exceptional semantic value of words is so conspicuous in poetry that we naturally take it as the first sign that language is succeeding as poetry.—Life is like a man play-acting: that might do for prose. The language is a mere abstract of the idea that prompts it—an idea that, as we reflect on it, may perhaps come to life in our minds; but if it does, there is nothing in those bare words to determine what sort of life that shall be. But when life is

> a poor player
> That struts and frets his hour upon the stage,

there is no question of the idea *coming* to life: these words infect us not more instantly with the idea itself, than with the unique and rich reality of life it assumed in Shakespeare's mind. This—this compound of vivid mood and imagery—must now be its life in our minds: for it has come to us in the language of poetry, the language which can charge the syntax of its words with such vigorous and nicely appointed *values* as those of "struts" and "frets," liberating and adjusting the energy of their suggestion so that we must respond by seeing and feeling as well as by understanding.

We can, of course, only appreciate the full value of these words by taking them in their context; the whole marvellous speech in which they occur characterises their force. This contempt for the self-important fuss of life follows hard on contempt for its pallid imbecility—"life's but *a walking shadow*"; and life as a player that "*struts and frets*" has ten times the value for imagination when, immediately before, life was a "*walking shadow.*" And see what a special and unmis-

takable value the common word *walking* has here, over
and above its plain lexical meaning, by the mere fact
of being combined, in just this context, with the word
shadow. Context is always the decisive thing for the
value of a word in poetry; and a mere snatch of the
context may indicate how greatly the *value* may alter
while what we call the *meaning* remains the same:

> Life's but a *walking* shadow . . .
> Through the dear might of him that *walkt* the waves . . .
> She *walks* in beauty like the night . . .
> Swiftly *walk* over the western wave, Spirit of night. . . .

Each of these phrases turns on the same word; in each
it has the same meaning; and in each it has a markedly
different value. But in fact what we call the meaning
of a word—its explicit, permanent, lexical meaning—
is no more than the sense which is common to, and will
plainly persist through, all possible variations of its
value: I am thinking, of course, of the words which
have something more than a purely grammatical function. What the dictionaries give us for verbs, nouns,
adverbs, and so on, is merely a handy and ready sort
of general formula for each word's potential value:
a formula more or less comprehensive according to
the price of the dictionary.

Certainly, the more poetic language is, the more it
relies on those suggestions which perhaps can only be
revealed—which at any rate only become unmistakable
—by an exquisite skill in the combining of words. The
dilating splendour of such a phrase as this:

The Theory of Poetry

> The baby figure of the giant mass
> Of things to come at large,

is wholly due to the fine interaction of secondary meanings, qualifying each other and expanding round the central idea of the words. Or, for a final instance, take this stanza from Milton's Nativity Ode:

> For if such holy song
> Enwrap our fancy long
>   Time will run back, and fetch the age of gold,
> And speckl'd vanity
> Will sicken soon and die,
>   And leprous sin will melt from earthly mould,
> And Hell itself will pass away,
> And leave her dolorous mansions to the peering day.

One could discourse for long enough on the values of the words there. There is not one of the significant words in that stanza, which has not been compelled, by its combination with the other words, to reveal some special force in its meaning, or at least to make its meaning unusually vigorous: in either case, to insist on our minds responding to it not merely by understanding the thought, but by sharing a concrete and manifold experience of imagination. Look only at the astonishing value here of that common word "fetch" for example: "Time will run back, and *fetch* the age of gold": why, you can see Time doing it. And "the peering day"! It is the accuracy with which the precisely right values are fixed in the language that should move our wonder, as well as the penetrating vigour of the words. Milton's visionary exultation over the final

The Meaning of Words

destruction of evil reached its height when he saw, and in seeing *became*, the mildly inquisitive day at last examining with its immortal equanimity the broken deserted hiding-place of its enemy; and into that actuality of sympathetic experience our minds are quickened when we reach those magical words,—"the *peering* day." It is a magic which is due not simply to the releasing, but also to the exactly right adjustment, of unsuspected force; as we may see when we think of the vastly different magic the same word may exercise in other contexts:

> When daffodils begin to *peer* . . .

> Tell me, if this wrinkling brow
> . . . *Peers* like the front of Saturn.

We must not, in fact, think of the values of words in poetry as of something which the poet *adds* to their meaning, however noticeable it may be that a poet's words do mean more than is usual to them, and however convenient it may be to emphasise this extra meaning in the discussion of his art. The poetic value of words is nothing but an exceptional qualification of meaning, due to the suggestion of exceptional richness in particular associations, brought out by the context. But we must try to understand just what these values are and how they are possible, if we are to understand what poetry makes of them. In the first place then, they are inherent in the words: a poet cannot get more out of a word than the general use of it will allow. All he can do is to elicit, out of the word's accepted whole possibility of meaning, just that precise part of it which will exactly serve his turn. That words have naturally a certain indiscriminate magic in them on which the artist in language can but draw, is pleasantly exemplified in the profane version of that mysterious etymological parable, the Naming of the Beasts. Adam, it appears, made some difficulty about the business—a purely logical difficulty. But Eve was ready for him. If Adam would drive the beasts in front of her, she would name them as they went by. So, as the first beast ran past her, Eve calls out: "Well, that, of course, is a bear." "Now whatever makes you call it a bear?" says Adam. "Why," says Eve, "it looks like a bear."

And so it does. It at any rate looks vastly more like a *bear* than any *meaning* of that word which a dictionary will give you. Here, from an unimpeachable source, is the dictionary meaning of the word: "Heavy, partly carnivorous, thick-furred, plantigrade quadruped." Out of that we may, indeed, collect something like the look of a bear; but nothing that can compare with the indisputable instantaneous vigour of the word itself. And yet what is the look of a bear? It may be a sitting bear or a slouching bear, a dancing bear or an angry bear, a bear in a cage or a bear on a mountain. All these appearances, variable without end, may be evoked by the word *bear;* the infinite possibility of them surrounds like a cloudy halo the nucleus of strict and constant meaning in the word. That meaning, except per-

The Meaning of Words

haps in works of science, can hardly occur in language in its mere simplicity; it can hardly fail to draw along with it something of what Eve found in the word—something of the look of a bear. But what kind of bear, and what kind of bearish attitude, must depend on the context. The word, in fact, will almost always have some special value radiating out of its strict meaning; though it may be so faint as to be negligible. But when the word strikes us as poetic, its suggestive value must have become as considerable as its plain meaning; some one of the infinite possibilities of bear-life will have been vividly and definitely elicited out of the general sense of the word by its context. Elicited out of it: not added to it. The poet has not *improved* the sense of the word by investing it with a value of his own; all he has done is to narrow and intensify the vague possibility of "bear" into some specific and appropriate bearish behaviour. The *value* he gives to the word is simply its noticeable release from the artificial existence of an average *meaning* into the individual vigour of some particular vitality.

But whence is it that words have their infinite possibility of poetic value? How is it that the same meaning can exert itself in such various directions? We have not, so far, formed any exact notion of what word-values are: we have only seen their unexplained presence. We must try to form some notion of the nature of words in civilised speech. A good deal may be learned about them by contrasting them with the words

103

of uncivilised speech. We gather, from evidences collected among savages, that the parable of the Naming
of the Beasts requires some important modification.
That ceremony must, in fact, have been incredibly
gradual. If we could go back to primitive language,
we should find, apparently, that there was no such thing
as our word *bear*. What we should find would be
words, whole and indivisible, and all entirely different,
for *bear-here, bear-there, bear-close-to, bear-far-off,
bear-running-at-me, bear-running-at-you;* and so on. I
do not know that these instances have ever been recorded: but they are in exact conformity with the main
principle of primitive vocabulary, and about the principle there seems to be no doubt. We may think it the
most natural and unavoidable thing in the world, to
use such simple pronouns as "I," "she," "he," and the
rest. But savage speech is a long way from these re-
finements. Instead of them we find words—not what
we call compound words, but single homogeneous
words—for *he-absent, he-present, she-absent, she-
present*. And besides these we find words which combine the idea of presence or absence with some idea of
action: *he-walking-about-over-there, she-sitting-down-
here*. And further we find such forms as *all-of-us,
some-of-us, I-by-myself, I-amongst-others:* and so on.
These are authentic; and they are enough to show the
extraordinary complexity of savage speech, judged by
our notions.

But, like all the other complexities of the savage
mind, this vast and elaborate vocabulary springs from a

profound simplicity; as, on the other hand, our simple forms of speech answer to a very complex habit of mind. All our civilised language betrays the habit of analysis and abstraction; the most concrete words we can think of are abstract compared with savage words. What more concrete to us than the word "*bear*"? But *bear* pure and simple does not occur: it is an abstract from experience of bears doing various things and variously affecting us. And it is these whole experiences which the savage brain labels with words. For the essential thing about the savage brain is that it does not analyse. It would never think of naming such an abstracted ingredient as *bear;* what it would name instead would be large masses of experience in which a bear played its unanalysed part—*bear-running-at-me* or *bear-running-at-you.*

Civilisation, however, does not alter the facts of experience; it still comes to us, as it came to primitive man, in lumps. But our mode of dealing with it has altered. The civilised brain analyses its experience; and language obeys the habit. Out of such remarkably diverse lumps of experience as *bear-running-at-me* and *bear-running-at-you,* civilised language selects some characteristic and constant element and names that: such an element as the abstracted existence of a bear. The result is, that round the one word *bear* cling, as possible suggestions of ulterior significance, all those moods and circumstances contained in the various primitive words which name the various masses of experience concerned with bears: the same word, in civilised speech, may according to its context suggest such completely opposite notions as the appalled horror of *bear-running-at-me* and the not wholly unpleasant exhilaration of *bear-running-at-you*. That is to say, the same word, with what we call the same meaning, may have many utterly different *values*.

Now what is the gain of this to poetic technique? It is scarcely too much to say that the change from synthetic to analytic habits of speech made poetic diction possible—the poetic diction known to Greece or China or Modern Europe. The opposite opinion has been held; it has been thought that savage speech must result automatically in a sort of natural poetry, from the fact that everything it mentions is referred directly to the realities of experience in which it is involved; the speech of a savage is therefore a series of vivid and concrete images. This is true enough; and this is what poetry essentially is. Now all civilised language, in comparison with savage, is analytic; what the savage can give in a single word the civilised person must build up in a phrase of several words, for he has lost the power of directly naming experience in the mass. But he has lost it in order to gain inestimably: he has gained the possibility of easily referring the same thing to an infinite variety of experiences, by using the same word in an infinite variety of contexts. Savage words are inflexible; for the more complex the direct meaning of a word, the fewer the occasions in which it will be exactly appropriate. It can only have the value of its obvious and open meaning; it can only exert itself in

The Meaning of Words

one rigidly definite direction. When a savage, in order to name a thing, names a notable experience in which that thing occurs, he certainly gives his speech a power of evoking living imagery; but he cannot name every experience in which the thing may occur, and the more he complicates it with this or that set of circumstances, the more rigorously he limits the associative power of the words which contain it. But when the analytic habit of civilised speech disentangles things from the experiences which involve them, while yet leaving it open for any such experience to take hold of the thing at need, the associative power of words becomes infinitely variable. Any mood, any circumstance, may be attributed to the thing, if the word for it be combined in the right phrase. It would seem, then, that the more analytic language has become, the greater its possibility of poetic diction; for the larger and the more variable will be the scope of its words in building up suggestions of the full realities of experience, while yet the *phrase* in civilised speech can be just as vivid as the uncivilised *word*.

The contrast of the rigidly concrete words of savage speech with the flexible and infinitely applicable vocabulary of civilised speech shows us, at any rate, the source from which our words derive their *values*. It is experience; the value of a word comes from continual use in connexion with action, with the realities of living. No two actions, no two moments of life, can be quite the same; but the words for them may very well be the same. Action never repeats itself; but language has to be for ever repeating itself. Hence words, by continually being used for slightly different actions—for slightly different moments of life—get charged with infinite possibilities of variation and gradation in significance; and the longer they remain in *living speech,* the more complex the aura or halo of subtle suggestions clinging round them—suggestions of varying action and varying quality of action. Moreover, the same sort of action, given by the same word, may recur enveloped in very different masses of experience; so that round a word may cling not only suggestions of variety in what we call the same action, but of variety also in the whole environment of moods and relations with other experiences. The finest verbal skill, therefore, is that which can securely use this variety of suggestion; which can pick out of it just the one appropriate sector of it and make that unmistakable; so that a word may be able, while it is impressing on us its direct meaning, at once to call up in our minds the right accompaniment of vividly related experience. This is what we mean by richness of language, and this kind of riches is what poetic technique specially aims at; for by its means you get crowding into a single phrase a whole system of significances which, if it is rightly organised, may exactly convey the complex pressure of imagination urging the language to become its equivalent. It follows that the words in common use will be the really poetic words; for constant use in connexion with perpetually varying action keeps them electric, charged with a plenty of secondary meanings.

The Meaning of Words

This is the reason why Saxon and Norman words do better in English poetry than later imported Latinisms and Greekisms. It is not simply that the Saxon and Norman words are older, but that they have been made rich in suggestive power by their use in the common needs of life. Of course, poets will always delight in rare or archaic or even dialect words—in anything which may increase the range of expression and give it some desired peculiarity. But it is the common words that have the finest triumphs in poetry, because they necessarily have the greatest suggestive power behind them. And we can see now how dangerous it is for poetry to develop a language of its own; when, at any rate, the select conventionally poetic vocabulary tends to consist of words withdrawn from the rough and tumble of everyday speech. For it is everyday speech, with its innumerable slight variations in usage, that keeps a word alive with poetic power; whereas a word traditionally reserved for poetry may get a great deal of use, but of use that tends always more and more to repeat itself: and this, far from enriching, will very soon exhaust the word's suggestive influence. There are many words, admirable in themselves, which no scrupulous poet would nowadays venture to use: simply because they have become exclusively poetical. Who now would dare to say a place of trees was *bosky,* or that water was *wan?* Excellent words: but spoilt by long withdrawal from the freedoms of spoken life into the conventual routine and seclusion of literature: their *values* have been exhausted, because, while com-

mon affairs would have nothing to do with them, poetry
kept them all too busy.

The sterility of conventionally poetical words must
not be misunderstood. It is not so much disuse as mis-
use which spoils the elasticity of a word; it is the familiar employment of its meaning in one constant literary direction that makes a word rigid, and takes the
magic out of it. But unfamiliar words may appear
in poetry with all their magic still fresh and active in
them. Indeed, it would be ridiculous to think of limiting poetic diction to contemporary speech. The English language is not an affair of any particular time, and
the whole of it is open to the poet. Even the so-called
archaic and obsolete words may be invaluable to him;
especially as it is never safe to say that a word is obsolete: many words which the dictionaries declared had
gone out of employment are back again now in active
life. But whatever departures the poet makes from the
vocabulary of everyday talk, whatever unfamiliar and
literary words he may use, he can only make such words
successful as poetry on one condition: namely, that he
imagine them into the spoken life which is actually denied them. Only thus can he truly know the words,
and be competent to manage their complex vitality and
adjust the niceties of their behaviour. Otherwise he
might as well be playing with counters. But unfamiliar
words do sometimes obscurely survive in actual speech;
far better than imagining an archaic word back again
into spoken life, is to hear it in natural and careless
use as a dialect-word; and fortunately this may still

happen. Country folk, indeed, have an odd way of bringing out the suggestive power of words. Some time ago I asked two people, who knew the cottage where I was staying, what sort of a flower a certain climbing rose had: I asked a parson and a plowman. The parson said, "Oh, it's an awfully jolly little thing!" The plowman said, "Oh, it's an innocent little blow!" The plowman gave me the better notion of the rose in flower. And, in that careless phrase of his, he proved that the obsolete word "blow" still has magic living in it, and that an old and exquisite value in the word "innocent" still survives for any one who can use it.

But let a poet venture as far as he please in unfamiliar diction—reviving old words, capturing dialect words, or it may be schooling new words; the staple of his art must nevertheless always be the living, infinitely variable speech he hears about him. The magnificences and splendid surprises of diction have their best chance of success when they are immersed in the nameless indefinable electricity of common speech. It is pretty generally agreed that English literature has never known such a display of verbal magic as in the Elizabethan period; the least of the Elizabethans can thrill us with the sheer vitality of his words. It is because the accent and the idiom of Elizabethan poetry was always as close as possible to the accent and idiom of speech. Poetry then found its prime material not in a language broken in by literature, but in the language of people talking, full of the rapid shades and gleams, the expressive irregularities and careless experiments, of conversation. It could not be otherwise; an Elizabethan poet had hardly any other language to draw on except the language of speech; English as printed literature scarcely existed for him. Elizabethan poetry took place in the midst of life; and it eagerly used the language of life, even the slang of life. Subsequently, poetry went into a corner; and it was then that poetry developed a conscience about the use of slang.

It is certain, at any rate, that a poet, in order to make his language the vivid symbol of imagination, must make careful and emphatic use of that potential vitality which lies implicit in the obvious meanings of words; and in order to do that, he must always keep his mind in closest touch with the changeable spoken life of language. And this applies not merely to separate words. The subtle, hardly definable, but very notable vigour given by common speech exists just as keenly in phrases and idioms. The sort of vigour I mean, with its singular nicety of expressive effect, may be illustrated by the various colloquial uses of the word *take*. Thus, a poet may *take in* his public, and the public may in consequence *take to* the poet, and he may then be *taken up* by eminent ladies; but perhaps a critic will *take down* the poet, chiefly by *taking him off*; whereupon the poet will *take on* the critic. Will any one say these are too colloquial for poetry? I cannot see why *take in* = *deceive* should not be as proper a phrase as *come off* = *escape*, which Milton used. It is

The Meaning of Words

not easy to say what it is that is so very much alive in such phrases; but certainly the kind of vigour they illustrate is of inestimable value in poetry. Think of the effect Milton got from the phrase I have just mentioned, an effect every one must have noticed:

> I knew the foul inchanter though disguis'd,
> Enter'd the very lime-twigs of his spells,
> *And yet came off.*

And as there the words shift from pomp to colloquialism, so they at once shift back again from colloquialism to pomp:

> *If you have this about you*
> (As I will give you when we go) you may
> Boldly assault the necromancers hall.

And in the whole splendid compound of significance, is it not due to the masterly use of the keen swift vigour of colloquialisms that the more solid forces of the big words are so telling? The passage is a perfect example of the right admixture of the common and the lordly in poetic diction; but it is to be remarked that Milton, having triumphed through all the lordly splendours of which English is capable, ended by relying chiefly on the words and idioms of common speech.

There can be no doubt that the vocabulary of poetry must be far larger than that of ordinary speech, simply because a poet has both larger and subtler matters to express than arise in the usual business of life; and he must therefore be free to elaborate his diction out of the language of the past as well as of the present. But certainly poetry will always be in danger when poets are afraid of being colloquial in their language. So far as one can make out, this was by no means a fear that afflicted such studious artists as Sophocles and Dante, any more than it troubled Shakespeare or Milton. And colloquialisms are not so perishable as is sometimes supposed. *Let on*, in the sense of *blab* or *boast*, seems the very phrase for poetry, in the forthright strength of its expressiveness. Is it only an evanescent modernism? It seems too good for that; and in fact the very phrase occurs, with wonderful effect, in poetry written centuries ago. A torturer in the Wakefield crucifixion play says of Christ:

Lo, he *lets on* he could no ill;

that is, he boasted he was incapable of evil. Instances just as remarkable could be multiplied.

What holds good of words and phrases, holds good too of syntax. If there is such a thing as poetic syntax, it is the syntax of language spoken. But the argument need hardly be carried further. Think only of the extraordinary expressiveness gained in spoken English from the order of the words in a sentence; here we come on something like the values of words as distinct from their obvious meaning: but now it is the value of a whole sentence of meaning, changeable according as the order of the words may be changed without loss of logical force. No poet who knows his business will neglect so fine a means of conveying shades of significance. But on the whole the structure of thought in language does not offer such scope for exceptional, immediate expressiveness as the diction which builds up that structure; we naturally look for poetic quality in words and idioms rather than in the planning of sentences, the quality of which has no great range of variation. The chief importance of syntax in poetry is of another order. It is not remarkably concerned with the actual symbolising of imaginative experience which we call *poetry;* it is rather concerned with the organisation of this business into *poems.* The intellectual shape of poetical matter—the coherent isolation of it into self-sufficient organism—to effect *that* is the affair of syntax in poetry. Without it, we could never know the real significance of poetic detail; but the detail must first be there in order to give syntax a function at all. Given poetic matter, conveyed in the vigours and delicacies of diction, it is the continuous organisation of syntax which moulds this into that intellectual unity, the achievement of which we call form.

V

DICTION: THE SOUND OF WORDS

I HAVE insisted on the importance to poetic theory of the spoken life of words as regards their semantic qualities. Now, words, of course, are sounds which symbolise ideas: we listen to them for the purpose of understanding them. But it is well known that words, especially combinations of words, very often produce remarkable effects by their sounds over and above the necessary and open conveying of meaning; the mere existence of such terms of linguistic criticism as euphony and cacophony witnesses to this. The art of poetry endeavours to make language not so much the vehicle of thought as the equivalent of experience itself; and it can only do so by deliberately using every quality which language is capable of exhibiting—and by using, as far as possible, all the qualities appropriate to its purpose simultaneously. Accordingly, we find that the phonetic aspect of language is in poetry very conspicuous; so much so, that the meaning of the words cannot impress itself on our minds without the sound of the words distinctly impressing itself also. It is not merely that we become aware, as we seldom do elsewhere, that it is *sound* to which we are attributing meaning; nor is it that the effect of sound over

The Sound of Words

and above its regular symbolism of meaning is simply
an effect of euphony. The whole sound of the words
and the whole of its effect—whether as the necessary
sign of grammatical meaning, or whatever may be re-
dundant to this (e.g., rhythm)—must contribute so decisively to the art of poetry, that its *audible technique*
may well be discussed separately; not indeed because
verbal sound operates on its own account in poetry, but
because it is an addition to the common use of language so notable and so characteristic that its contribution cannot but be distinguished.

When, therefore, we consider the phonetic aspect of
poetry, it is obvious that we assume the spoken existence
of language; so obvious that it might hardly seem
worth mentioning. But we are sometimes apt to forget, even in this connexion, that language has, and has
had for many centuries, a double life, in poetry as elsewhere. Language lives as the spoken word, and it lives
also as the written (or printed) word. The spoken
word cannot be anything else than sound accepted as
the symbol of an idea; and the written word was originally the symbol of this spoken sound: that is to say,
the symbol of the symbol of an idea. But the written
word can be, and has long since in part become, something else than the symbol of a symbol; it can be a
symbol in its own right. For the human mind will
always short-circuit a process when it can. As soon
as the habit of *reading to oneself* was established, the
second-hand symbolism of the written word was short-
circuited; and the written word became itself the symbol

of the idea, without having to pass through the symbolism of sound. Printing has fixed this short-circuit in our civilised mentality so deeply that many of us are scarcely aware of it.

Language, as communicable symbolism of ideas, has two modes of existence: it exists as audible signs and it exists as visible signs. Generally, the only practical relation between the two kinds of signs is that they both refer to the same thing: the English we read has almost given up pretending to have anything to do with the English we hear. As a rule, when we are reading to ourselves, the printed word refers immediately to its idea; the sound of the word very likely comes in, but it is not required, and may be due to association with the idea as much as to taking the letters as phonetic signs. The sound of the word at any rate only comes in as a faint unnecessary accompaniment, to which we only attend as a sort of mild corroboration. But, though it may be proper enough to read our newspapers in that style, it will not do for poetry. Poetry consists absolutely of the word spoken and heard: the printed word must always be frankly the symbol of articulate sound. We must hear what the poet has to say; if we are reading to ourselves, we must hear it mentally. Otherwise we shall miss half his technique; and that means, we shall miss half of what he is trying to express.

But there is still something to be said on this matter; the visible word is not to be dismissed in poetry altogether, in favour of the audible word. There is no doubt, in fact, that the existence of language as printed words has had a profound influence on the art of poetry, though it would take too long to investigate this here exactly. We read poetry to ourselves more often than hear it read aloud; and poets, consciously or not, have taken advantage of this. Poetry will always take advantage of anything that will increase or refine its expressive power. I said, that the printed word in poetry must *always* be taken as a symbol of an articulate sound. I did not say, it could *only* be taken so. When we read poetry to ourselves, it is not, I think, the usual thing to refer the word to the sound and thence, *through* the sound, to the idea; I think rather we refer the printed word immediately to the idea and simultaneously to the sound as well. And this is important; for eye-language is a much subtler and nimbler affair than ear-language. We can get, in printed language, in the appeal through the eye, a more instant and more certain apprehension of fine associations of ideas, of delicate shades of significance, than you can ever get through the ear. One of the chief differences between such an art as Homer's and such an art as Dante's or Milton's is that Homer never thinks of any appeal but through the ear; whereas Dante and Milton both know their verses will meet with eyes as well as ears. Their art is certainly not greater than Homer's, but it has finer modulations of significance. The thing is, that Dante and Milton, like every other printed or written poet, take advantage of the eye-appeal without losing the ear-appeal. However, we are not concerned with this just now; for of course the eye has nothing whatever to do with that part of expression which is specifically due to the sound of language—rhythm and rime, for example; and it must be admitted, that mental hearing is never quite as good as actual hearing: the *sound* of poetry is always more impressive and expressive when it is actually sounding than when it is imaginary. Really to know a poem requires a double experience of it: it requires that it should be read aloud, and that it should be read to oneself.

One or two points should be noted before we proceed to study the function of verbal sound in the art of poetry. We saw that, as regards the semantic aspect of poetry, words are effective both by the meaning which they contribute to the syntax of the sentences, and by the individual value which they have according to their place in the sentence. Just so the sound of words is effective both by contributing to that continuous organisation of sound which we call *rhythm* (corresponding therefore with *syntax*), and by the individual quality of their vowels and consonants which we may call their *syllabic* sound (corresponding with semantic *values*). The effect of syllabic sounds cannot, any more than the effect of semantic values, be reduced to a system; but as for rhythm, since, like syntax, it is in its essence organisation, the rules which govern its effect should be discoverable. There was no need for any special discussion of syntax in poetry, since it must be, to all intents, the same as syntax anywhere else. But rhythm in poetry commonly assumes a very special

The Sound of Words

character, the effect of which is elsewhere regarded as inappropriate, if not unseemly: poetic rhythm therefore must be discussed with some particularity. Since rhythm is some organisation presiding over the continuity of sound in language, its discussion requires us to consider verbal sound in masses; but neither is it possible to consider the poetic effect of *syllabic* sound in isolated words. Just as the value, or suggestive power, of a word does not reveal itself unless the word is brought into combination with others, so the expressive effect of syllabic sound is nothing in words taken singly. It is when one word sounds against another, or falls in with the sound of another; it is in phrases and sentences, with variety or assonance of vowels, with repeated or contrasted consonants, that syllabic sound becomes expressive.

This is a good deal more than euphony. Euphony at bottom is the adaptation of language to convenience of articulation. A sentence hard to pronounce is said to lack euphony; but it does not follow that it will be unpleasant hearing: we sympathise with the trouble of the speaker, or are conscious of our own. We may also include in euphony, however, the avoidance of jingling repetitions of sound that unpleasantly irritate by obtruding on our attention. But, whether the result be pleasant or not, euphony may be deliberately violated in poetry, if something expressive is to be gained. Browning, for instance, often chose to force on us the expressive sound of his syllables by downright cacophony. In *Through the Metidja*, he achieves, at the expense of grammar and perhaps sense—certainly of lucidity—a portentous jingle of continuous rhyming on one not very charming diphthong; the cacophony is certainly deliberate, for the purpose of thrusting on our notice the mood of mesmerised fanaticism in the poem: a mood almost wholly conveyed by the emphatic monotony of the rhyming. The experiment is a doubtful success; but the poem called *Popularity* shows a masterly power of alternating euphony and cacophony exactly as the occasion requires. It is no glib sort of euphony which this stanza gives us, for example, but that rarer euphony which can hold a wealth of sharply contrasted sounds in strong and intricate discipline:

> Who has not heard how Tyrian shells
>   Enclosed the blue, that dye of dyes,
> Whereof one drop worked miracles
>   And coloured like Astarte's eyes
> Raw silk the merchant sells?

But from that rich ceremonious flow of vowels and consonants Browning proceeds to this:

> Yet there's the dye—in that rough mesh
>   The sea has only just o'er-whisper'd!
> Live whelks, the lips'-beard dripping fresh
>   As if they still the water's lisp heard
> Through foam the rock-weeds thresh.

If not quite cacophony, that is certainly not euphony. The tongue has to walk delicately there, for fear of tripping among those jostling consonants and abrupt vowels. But the very absence of euphony compels us to notice how vigorously the sound of the words suggests the washing of sea-water. Instantly, however, the mood changes and expands, and at once an exquisite and most noticeable euphony surprises us with its contrast; now it is the inviting ease with which syllable follows syllable, that opens to us a subtler and less imitative propriety of sound to sense:

> Enough to furnish Solomon
>   Such hangings for his cedar-house,
> That, when gold-robed he took the throne
>   In that abyss of blue, the Spouse
> Might swear his presence shone
>
> Most like the centre-spike of gold
>   Which burns deep in the blue-bell's womb,
> What time, with ardours manifold,
>   The bee goes singing to her groom,
> Drunken and overbold.

And then, after that lordly music, how does the poem end? With a cacophony that many readers still, it appears, find decidedly shocking:

> And there's the extract, flasked and fine,
>   And priced and saleable at last!
> And Hobbs, Nobbs, Stokes and Nokes combine
>   To paint the future from the past,
> Put blue into their line.
>
> Hobbs hints blue,—straight he turtle eats:
>   Nobbs prints blue,—claret crowns his cup:
> Nokes outdares Stokes in azure feats,—
>   Both gorge. Who fished the murex up?
> What porridge had John Keats?

Yes, the sound of those verses is hideous. And just for that reason you cannot help attending to the sound, and perceiving how amazingly expressive it is, simply as sound. What makes the words so remarkably animated here? It is the intensity of ferocious and amused contempt with which they are charged. And where do we find that? Scarcely at all in their meaning, almost entirely in their sound.

But euphony is a mere fringe of the real matter. It is obviously in a poet's own interest not too seriously to offend our mouths and throats without good reason; but, on the other hand, our vocal organs are really very willing creatures; if we leave them to it, they will despatch without much fuss combinations of letters that look on paper formidable enough.

The main question is not of pleasant but of expressive sounds. The most elementary kind of expressive sound in poetry occurs when the words, in the act of mentioning some particular noise, themselves make a noise recognisably like it. This may not be a very astonishing feat, since the words for noise are in a great many cases formed on the imitative principle. The skill is to carry the imitation on to the neighbouring words. Tennyson gives a famous example of it in the close of that beautiful idyll in *The Princess:*

> Sweet is every sound,
> Sweeter thy voice, but every sound is sweet:
> Myriads of rivulets hurrying through the lawn,
> The moan of doves in immemorial elms,
> And murmuring of innumerable bees.

The Sound of Words

We need not discuss a device so noticeable. As a rule, its effect must appear too trite and obvious for serious art. Much more effective is it when the poet discreetly hints at a sound by his vowels and consonants without actually mentioning it, as Matthew Arnold does in the line

> Crossing the stripling Thames at Bablockhithe;

where for a moment, in those S's and L's, you *hear* the little brook among its pebbles. But of infinitely greater importance in the art of poetry is that subtler expressiveness of the mere sound of words, when what is conveyed has nothing to do with sound. This is a purely empiric affair: it has simply been found out that certain combinations of verbal sound may suggest feelings and moods, and even other sensations. Thus when Cowper's great ode starts off with

> Toll for the brave,

we are at once aware of the solemnity of the poet's inspiration. Or, to go back to Tennyson's idyll, which is from beginning to end extraordinarily felicitous in its marriage of sound and sense, when we come to the line

> Or hand in hand with Plenty in the maize—

does not the very sound of the words *mean* ease and gentle happiness? And in the line

> Or red with spirted purple of the vats,

125

that doubling of the vowel sound of *purple* in *spirted*, does it not somehow emphasise the *colour* of the words? And can any one escape the grander significance of the sound here?—

> the firths of ice
> That huddling slant in furrow-cloven falls
> To roll the torrent out of dusky doors.

There is, no doubt, the sense of hurling mountain water in that last line; but the whole sequence of vowels has a much more general suggestion—a suggestion of immense descent, of opening downward into gulfs. It is perhaps more difficult to define what the sound does for us in

> let the wild
> Lean-headed eagles yelp alone;

but it does something very decisive—it has a suggestion somehow of remote fierceness and loneliness.

Such instances, perhaps, are too liable to individual interpretation. I will give you one that cannot but command agreement. In *Paradise Lost* there is a tremendous passage where the devils are punished for interfering in man's world. They are turned for a season into serpents of all kinds:

> Scorpion and Asp, and *Amphisbaena* dire,
> *Cerastes* hornd, *Hydrus*, and *Ellops* drear,
> And *Dipsas* . . .

and afflicted with the sight of trees laden with fruits of glorious rind which they are impelled to taste, only

The Sound of Words

to fill their mouths with loathsome dust. Milton, as he alone could, electrifies the lines that narrate this with a perfect frenzy of infuriated disgust: and a good half of the passion is conveyed by the mere *sound* of his words:

> greedily they pluck'd
> The Frutage fair to sight, like that which grew
> Neer that bituminous Lake where *Sodom* flam'd;
> This more delusive, not the touch, but taste
> Deceav'd; they, fondly thinking to allay
> Their appetite with gust, instead of Fruit
> Chewd bitter Ashes, which th' offended taste
> With spattering noise rejected; oft they assayd,
> Hunger and thirst constraining, drugd as oft,
> With hatefullest disrelish writh'd their jaws
> With soot and cinders fill'd.

It is not often that the texture of syllabic sound conveys anything quite so definite as that. In varying degrees, however, its expressiveness is ubiquitous in poetry: the sound of words is always there much more effective than its necessary symbolising of plainly intelligible meaning. The varieties of interpretation of sound-suggestion should not make us sceptical about it. The poets use it for insinuating what cannot be given as direct grammatical meaning; but when we try to define it, we try thereby to reduce it to grammatical meaning. This cannot be done: we can only edge clumsily towards it. Some will try to take it on one side, some on another; but great differences of interpretation do not necessarily mean any serious difference in the way the suggestion has been *felt*.

Milton, however, has brought us to a point where our discussion may conveniently pass from syllabic sound to rhythm. For it is clear that the effect of these artfully disposed syllables is suspended and swept forward in the larger and, on the whole, more potent effect of a rhythm. The raging disgust of Milton's fiends would not sound so notably in those harsh consonants and energetic vowels if they did not constitute a rhythmic sound.

Rhythm is the alternation, at recognisable though not necessarily uniform intervals, of any variations in a sound or succession of sounds. In language, rhythm may derive from three kinds of alternation in the syllables: alternation of long or short syllables, of stressed or unstressed syllables, of syllables high or low in tone. In modern languages, quantity and pitch are not felt to be decisive for the character of rhythm; they both enter into it in varying degrees, but rhythm is recognised by the accent or stress—the force bestowed on the utterance of syllables.

It seems impossible for language to avoid being rhythmical; any succession of noticeable variations in the stresses will be heard as a rhythm, and no natural utterance can help producing such a succession. But the rhythm may not be intentional. In the arguments of philosophers or scientists, in the statements of fact given by works of information, we may indeed hear a rhythm; but we feel that the rhythm of the words does not matter. The philosopher's argument gains no more from the rhythm it forms than the black-

The Sound of Words

smith's forging does from the rhythm we hear in his hammer-strokes. Here, for example, is one of the greatest moments of modern philosophy:

> Conjunction is the representation of the synthetical unity of the manifold. This idea of unity, therefore, cannot arise out of that conjunction: much rather does that idea, by combining itself with the representation of the manifold, render the conception of conjunction possible.

There is a certain rhythm in those words, if we care to attend to it; but we do not: it is as much as we can do to attend to the process of the reasoning, and we know that the success of the process does not in the least depend on the rhythm of its words; that success being our intellectual conviction, which is all that such language as this intends. But now hear a specimen of language which intends something quite different, and uses rhythm designedly to further the success of its intention:

> O eloquent, just and mighty Death! whom none could advise, thou hast persuaded; what none hath dared, thou hast done; and whom all the world hath flattered, thou only hast cast out of the world and despised; thou hast drawn together all the far-stretched greatness, all the pride, cruelty, and ambition of man, and covered it all over with these two narrow words, *Hic jacet.*

This is not the language of intellectual argument. It is the expression of a mood; of that moment of lofty and intense imaginative experience, in which Sir Walter Ralegh, bringing his *History of the World* to an end, collects his whole burning sense of the worth of human affairs. The words are rational, indeed; but they are also intended to stir imagery and emotion in us. And it is unmistakable that a notable part of this intention is entrusted to the rhythm. We do not have to listen carefully for it: we take it in, and accept its effect, as frankly as the meaning of the words. For the rhythm contributes part of the whole significance of the language. If, while the sense remained, the rhythm were changed, the language would not be the same expression.

It is language of this kind that we should specifically call rhythmical. Poetry, which must employ every appropriate power of language, will always be rhythmical: we shall presently see wherein rhythm is always appropriate to the purpose of poetry. But it need not always be the same sort of rhythm. As a rule, the rhythm of poetry is of a kind markedly different from that used by Ralegh in the famous passage I quoted just now. Ralegh's rhythms, though designed, are yet *free;* they do not accommodate themselves to the repetition of any definite pattern. They satisfy our sense of rhythm, but they will not tolerate a formula for their movement.

The sense of rhythm is not easily defined. We seem to have in our minds certain ideal possibilities of rhythm; and as soon as we hear a succession of sounds in which we can recognise the nature of any ideal type, even though the actual sound does not reproduce it, we feel the satisfaction of rhythm; we hear the succession of sounds as an orderly continuity. It is clear

The Sound of Words

that the natural rhythms of speech have an immense range of variety; but so long as the alternations of the accents may be clearly referred to some ideal type, however frequently and completely the type may change, we feel that we are accepting rhythm. Of this kind is the rhythm of prose, which is free in the sense that it is at liberty to change the type of its accentual alternation according to the natural utterance of the words: the skill being to choose such natural utterance as will result in rhythms valuable in the whole significance. Indeed, if the rhythms are expressive, they must be variable rhythms in order to keep pace with the varying sense of the words.

But the feeling for rhythm is exceedingly elastic. It is possible for a very wide range of variation in the succession of the actual sounds to be referred to a single type of ideal rhythm; and when, however the natural rhythm of the speech may alter, it is always recognised as according with one persistently repeating pattern or set of patterns, we have the special kind of rhythm which is called metre. And for metrical rhythm it will always be possible to state a formula and enunciate rules; not a formula, nor rules, for the actual sounds, but a formula of the pattern to which the ideal reference is to be made, and rules which make it possible to refer actual variation to ideal constancy. This is the *scansion* of metre; and it will be seen that scansion can have no abstract authority, but must depend on individual understanding of verse.

The difference between the free rhythm of prose

and the metrical rhythm of verse concerns, then, not so much what is actually heard as the way this is idealised in the mind. The difference is certainly very decisive; and verse has often been assumed to be a necessary specification for poetry. But where everything else required by poetry is present, the use of free rhythm cannot be considered as implying the lack of something which poetry must possess, but rather as the use of one means of expression for another. To say nothing of the Bible, many passages in the prose of Sir Thomas Browne, Treherne, Lamb, De Quincey, Francis Thompson, must be admitted to be *poetry* as clearly as anything in verse. But when prose-rhythm is employed not merely for momentary poetic purposes, but for the achievement of whole *poems,* then indeed we do feel a certain insufficiency in such rhythm; as will presently be noted more exactly.

Aristotle, who first pointed out that metre is not a necessary mark of poetry, was satisfied with this negative. But clearly this is not the conclusion of the matter. Sir Philip Sidney gives it in his brilliant *Apologie for Poetry.* "It is not riming and versing that maketh a poet, no more than a long gown maketh an advocate," he says; "it is that fayning notable images of virtues, vices, or what else, which must be the right describing note to know a poet by." But he goes on: "although indeed the Senate of Poets hath chosen verse as their fittest rayment." Metre may not be necessary to poetry, but it is a form of rhythm incomparably more suited to the purposes of poetry than free rhythm. And there can only be one reason for this: metre is more expressive than free rhythm. Whatever expressiveness can be gained by rhythm will, in the immense majority of occasions, be most effective in metre. I need not go to the Senate of Poets for a specimen of what metre can do; I will take a poem by John Clare, the exquisite pathos of which we should surely feel, even though we could not account for it by knowing that it was written after Clare had been finally locked up in the madhouse, where two hard-headed doctors had sent him because he had been "for years addicted to poetical prosings." Prosings! What artist in prose, had he such subtle power over his instrument as Laurence Sterne himself, could come near to the delicate yet irresistible poignancy of expressiveness in metre like this?

> Come hither, my dear one, my choice one, and rare one,
>   And let us be walking the meadows so fair,
> Where on pilewort and daisies the eye fondly gazes,
>   And the wind plays so sweet in thy bonny brown hair.
>
> Come with thy maiden eye, lay silks and satins by;
>   Come in thy russet or grey cotton gown;
> Come to the meads, dear, where flags, sedge, and reeds appear,
>   Rustling to soft winds and bowing low down.
>
> Come with thy parted hair, bright eyes, and forehead bare;
>   Come to the whitethorn that grows in the lane;
> To banks of primroses, where sweetness reposes,
>   Come, love, and let us be happy again.

We cannot but note there the two factors already mentioned as essential to metrical rhythm; and their interaction will explain why such rhythm is so extraordinarily effective. First, throughout the poem repeats a definite pattern of accentual rhythm. Secondly, this pattern, though definite, is yet not rigid; it gives to the impact on it of the natural accentual utterance. We feel a constant pattern maintaining itself through many variations. These two things, constancy and variation, are the essential things not merely in this metre, but in the very idea of metre. In free rhythm we have only one of these factors: variation. But in metre, variation takes place against a perceptible constancy, and is therefore infinitely more noticeable: the slightest variation becomes momentous, with keen and certain effect. And all the while there is also operating in metre that which compels the variation to be so remarkable there—the constant repeating pattern, operating on its own account; and a repeating pattern of rhythm, as man has recognised ever since the invention of the drum, is one of the most powerfully affecting things in the world.

We see, then, that while free rhythm owes its expressive power to variation alone, metrical rhythm employs two expressive forces operating simultaneously —variation and repetition; and the force of each is enormously enhanced by the contrasting presence of the other.

The systematic study of verse or metrical rhythm is called prosody, and we now have the general principle which must govern it: metre is the modulated repetition of a rhythmical pattern. The rules given

The Sound of Words

in prosody are valid only in so far as they show how, in this metre or that, variations of speech-rhythm may conform with the ideally constant pattern, and what variations are capable of so conforming. The sole authority for this is the practice of the poets; prosody can do no more than exhibit their practice in analytic form, by means of scansion. Beyond this there are no prohibitions to be set up, and consequently no licences to be permitted; but it comes within the province of prosody to account for any failure of verse to be expressive. Evidently, verse may so fail in two ways: the constant pattern may be maintained at the expense of the natural variations of speech, or these variations may so dislocate the pattern as to destroy it.

For the expressiveness of verse is given equally by its two essential factors. Conformity with the ideal pattern ought to be so certain that one merely has to read the words with their full natural accentuation in order to perceive it. But if one reads them with such emphasis on the pattern, as to force them into mere unmodulated reproduction of it, then they are deprived of that invaluable animation which is given by the ever-varying rhythms of living speech. The same result may, of course, be the fault of the poet: with the best will in the world, it is impossible to read the verse of *Ferrex and Porrex* or of Alexander's "Monarchicke Tragedies" with anything like life in the rhythm. In such verse, a purely mechanical understanding of metre has disposed the accents as regularly as possible into exact repetition of the pattern; and the effect, far from being expressive, is stupefying. On the other hand, when Byron puts for blank verse such rhythms as these:

> Unless you keep company
> With him (and you seem scarce used to such high
> Society) you can't tell how he approaches;

the pattern has ceased to exist: not so much because the variation is excessive, as because the poet has not troubled to manage it. There is as much variation of rhythm, perhaps more, in these lines of Marlowe's; but it is variation so contrived that the pattern sounds in it irresistibly:

> Bags of fiery Opals, Saphires, Amatists,
> Iacints, hard Topas, grasse-greene Emeralds,
> Beauteous Rubyes, sparkling Diamonds.

There is, of course, a very great range in the degree of mutual accommodation possible between speech rhythm and pattern rhythm in metre. On the whole, the history of English prosody shows a progressive absorption of more and more varieties of speech rhythm into metrical forms of one kind or another. It is to be noted that a distinctly metrical effect may survive a considerable loosening of the pattern. That the perfectly strict maintenance of a pattern may allow of very wide variation in the spoken rhythm is proved by the verse of *Paradise Lost* or Shakespeare's middle period; but the later work of both Milton and Shakespeare shows a tendency, not indeed to take *liberties* with the pattern—the phrase would imply a serious misunderstanding of the function of the pattern in metre—but to use the furthest deviation from it in the actual rhythms that can possibly be referred to it: so that lines like

> And made him bow to the gods of his wives;

or

> Is goads, thorns, nettles, tails of wasps

are, in their context, equivalent to such a line as

> Or where the gorgeous East with richest hand.

But Milton in *Samson Agonistes* goes further even than this, and dispenses with reference to a pattern of uniform length. There is, therefore, strictly speaking, no repeating pattern underlying the actual sounds here; but there is preserved, with astonishing art, a constant ideal *character* of movement, to which all the variations, not only in the placing of accents, but in the combination of accentual elements into line-lengths, are plainly to be referred. And this is enough to make the metrical effect absolutely decisive. Not much has been made hitherto of the many developments in English prosody suggested by the lyrical parts of *Samson Agonistes*. Matthew Arnold made some interesting experiments, but could not always keep his varying measures from dissolving into free (that is, prose) rhythm. The late work of T. E. Brown contains some singularly charming instances of the effect of irregular line-length; the resulting rhythms convey a comment of extraordinarily delicate feeling, and the reference to a constant type of movement is so assured, that the very tone of easy colloquialism has been captured into unmistakable metrical form.

As for what it is that metre expresses, our difficulty is that it cannot be expressed otherwise. If you do not feel that metre *is* expressive, description will do nothing for you. But it is possible to point out where the peculiar virtue of metrical rhythm may be found. Rhythmical expression is certainly emotional. Nothing can consciously occur in the mind without some accompaniment of emotion; and for conveying the emotional aura which must surround every moment of attention, language has no power to compare with the rhythm which envelops its words. Since poetry consists in conveying experience itself, undiminished in any vital character, out of the poet's mind into ours, it is plain that poetic language must always be language designedly rhythmical. So much we may say of the natural variations of speech-rhythm which form one essential factor of metrical rhythm; and so far it is on a level with the free rhythms of prose. But a poem, to be successful, must have been conceived as an *inspiration:* the whole of its matter must have been collected into one intense experience, which has then become the urgent motive working itself out through all the details of technique. Now such a moment of intense and rich experience cannot but have been accompanied by considerable emotional exaltation. This exaltation with which the poem was conceived will itself be part of the experience to be expressed; and the expression of it must therefore accompany the matter all the time it is being unfolded in language, with the possibility of unifying all its serial moments into a final impression in the reader's mind equivalent to the originating inspiration in the poet's mind. This, then, is what that constant repetition of a rhythmical pattern—the other factor essential to metre—has the duty of expressing: the exaltation which surrounds the poet's experience as a whole.

And now we are brought to a most important property of metrical rhythm: its continuity. As we read metrical language, we do not, when we come to the end of each sentence of the rhythm, or complete statement of its pattern, simply start afresh to build up another sentence. Just as each sentence of the meaning is carried over into the next, and so on until the meaning of the whole poem has been organised in our minds; so it is with the rhythm. Sentences of rhythm become integrated into inclusive movements of major rhythm, until we arrive at the sense of a large undulation embracing the whole phonetic process of a poem. Thus the final unity of impression is doubly assured by the simultaneous achievement of intellectual form and of instrumental form. We shall see in the next lecture the inestimable importance of this final unity of impression in the function of poetry. What we must note here is, that metrical rhythm, with its persisting pattern, is incomparably superior to the free rhythms of prose, in its power of combining into an inclusive major rhythm which may at last become instrumental or phonetic form, whereby a poem may be *heard* as a whole as well as *understood* as a whole. This is why poetry, if it is to perfect itself into the self-sufficient, self-authorised existence of *poems*, will always instinctively prefer metrical to free rhythm.

It is here that we must consider, very briefly, the function of that phonetic device which is so usual in modern versification: rime, with its consequence of rhythm disposed in stanzas. The accentual nature of modern metres is looser and less assertive than the quantitative system of classical verse. This has its advantages; but it is apt to make the larger movement of major rhythm somewhat uncertain without extraneous assistance. *Blank verse* is, indeed, capable of that inevitable and massive solidity of paragraphic structure which Milton achieved, mainly by the use of a most subtle device to which he himself calls our attention. Few poets have been able to make "the sense variously drawn out from one verse to another," supply the lack of "the jingling sound of like endings." It is this very jingling sound which has enabled the immense majority of modern poets to achieve some firm structure of verse larger than the particular pattern their verses repeat. For the riming of lines binds them into groups, whereby the formation of a major rhythm is obviously strengthened. The simplest case of this is the couplet; and Dryden's odd notion of rewriting a great part of *Paradise Lost* in rimed couplets enables us to watch

The Sound of Words

the peculiar structural effect of rime very clearly. This
is how Milton's Moloch speaks:

> My sentence is for open warr: of wiles,
> More unexpert, I boast not: them let those
> Contrive who need, or when they need, not now.

And this is what the speech becomes when Dryden has,
in Milton's contemptuous phrase, "tagged" the verse.

> My sentence is for war; that open too:
> Unskilled in stratagems, plain force I know.
> Treaties are vain to losers; nor would we,
> Should heav'n grant peace, submit to sovereignty.

What has happened is clear enough: the lines, which
were gradually and freely organising themselves into
a paragraph of major rhythm, have been decisively
coupled into groups; the structure of the lines into
larger rhythms has become more emphatic. In this
case, no doubt, it has also become more mechanical;
but then it is Milton who is setting the standard. The
insistence of rime in couplets too easily becomes tedious;
the compensation for this is the assurance of the structure it supports.

But the grouping and consequent constructive power
of "like endings" readily expands into the formation
of stanzas. These, then, are to be regarded as re-
ceptacles prescribed for major rhythm, very much as
the pattern of the line may be regarded as the receptacle for the natural speech rhythm of phrases and
sentences. The manner in which the varying major

The Theory of Poetry

rhythms of the metre accommodate themselves to and fulfil the requirements of stanzas, according to the disposition of their rimes, is in close analogy with the modulating effect of speech-rhythm on the recurring pattern of the lines. Stanza-rhythm is, in fact, something like metrical rhythm on a larger scale; its effect depends on the same two factors of constant pattern and varying movement. And a very slight variation may become notably effective when it occurs within, and is felt against, the accepted pattern of a stanza. The third stanza of the following quotation from an Elizabethan song is singularly plangent, especially in the fourth and seventh lines; the rhythms of the phrases are not specially marked, but they have an instant prominence and keen effect, owing to their occurrence within a stanza of such strict formality:

> At her fair hands how have I grace entreated,
>   With prayers oft repeated!
>   Yet still my love is thwarted:
> Heart, let her go, for she'll not be converted.
>   Say, shall she go?
>   O no, no, no, no, no!
> She is most fair, though she be marble-hearted.
>
> How often have my sighs declared mine anguish,
>   Wherein I daily languish!
>   Yet still she doth procure it:
> Heart, let her go, for I cannot endure it.
>   Say, shall she go?
>   O no, no, no, no, no!
> She gave the wound, and she alone must cure it.

*   *   *   *   *

The Sound of Words

But if the love that hath and still doth burn me
No love at length return me,
Out of my thought I'll set her:
Heart, let her go!   O heart, I pray thee let her:
Say, shall she go?
O no, no, no, no, no!
Fixed in the heart, how can the heart forget her?

To see how readily the same form of rimed stanza can adapt itself to rhythms expressive of widely different moods, we need only compare the graces and humours of Suckling's *Ballad upon a Wedding* with the grandeurs and raptures of Smart's *Song to David*. This is certainly the right stanza for Suckling:

Her feet beneath her petticoat
Like little mice stole in and out
As if they feared the light:
But O she dances such a way!
No sun upon an Easter day
Is half so fine a sight.

But is not this also the right stanza for Smart?—

Strong is the lion—like a coal
His eyeball—like a bastion's mole
His chest against the foes;
Strong the gier-eagle on his sail;
Strong against tide the enormous whale
Emerges so he goes.

We see, therefore, that the expressive effect of rime does not operate on its own account. It is to be looked for in the whole effect of the rhythmic structures which rime supports. That, at any rate, is generally true;

but very occasionally rime may be directly expressive in addition to its structural function. The greatest feat of riming in our literature is Dunbar's *Ballat of our Lady:* and such a reiterated chime as this, carried on through seven stanzas, does certainly infect our minds with the poet's rapt intensity of adoration:

> Hale, sterne superne! Hale in eterne,
>   In Godis sicht to schyne!
> Lucerne in derne, for to discerne
>   Be glory and grace devyne;
> Hodiern, modern, sempitern,
>   Angelicall regyne,
> Our tern inferne for to dispern
>   Helpe rialest rosyne.
> Ave Maria, gratia plena:
>   Haile, fresche flour femynyne;
> Yerne ws guberne, wirgin matern,
>   Of reuth baith rute and ryne.

A somewhat similar effect is clear in Shelley's *The Cloud.* It is to be noted that in such cases a good deal of the riming has been set free from its usual structural duty; and in this respect it resembles alliteration. Old English verse, and a good deal of Middle English verse, was composed on a principle radically different from that of modern verse, though we still find in it the essential elements of metre: constancy and variation. The difference consists in the nature of the element of constancy; instead of being a constant pattern of accents, it is simply a constant number of accents, balanced in pairs on each side of a pause. Now just as modern accentual verse may be uncertain

The Sound of Words

in its structure of major rhythms, and to give them
decision has brought in the grouping effect of rime;
so Old English accentual verse would have been uncertain in the metrical structure of its *lines* unless it
had brought in alliteration, binding, not line to line,
but phrase to phrase within the line, and thus empha-
sising the balanced numeration of accents which otherwise would hardly give a sufficient sense of basic constancy underlying the varying speech-rhythm.   For
alliteration here means the employment of the *same*
consonant, or of *any* vowel (which is as emphatic as
a repeated consonant), at the beginning of accented
syllables.   The expressive effect of alliteration in Old
English verse is therefore indirect; it is the metrical
rhythm as secured by alliteration which is expressive.
The more exact formality, and consequent superior expressiveness, of verse based on a definite pattern of
accentuation, at last brought the old alliterative verse
into disuse; but the habit of alliteration was frequently
carried over into the practice of the new versification.
Then it was found (as for example by the great artist
who composed the noble and lovely poem called *Pearl*)
that alliteration, now superfluous as a structural device,
was capable of yielding on its own account a remarkable expressiveness.   The habit of alliteration has gone;
but as an occasional device, no poet who is sensitive to
the qualities of syllabic sound, and eager to use all the
means of his art, will be indifferent to it.   To illustrate
the masterly use of alliteration for enhancing the phonetic expressiveness of language, not according to any

system, but simply as occasion requires, I will quote a stanza of Kipling's; but indeed, every other expressive effect of the sound of language which has been discussed in this lecture—metre, stanza-rhythm and rime, syllabic symbolism—might be illustrated by such superbly assured craftsmanship as this:

> 'Less you want your toes trod off you'd better get back at once,
>   For the bullocks are walkin' two by two,
>   The *byles* are walkin' two by two,
>   The bullocks are walkin' two by two,
> An' the elephants bring the guns!
>   Ho! Yuss!
> Great—big—long—black forty-pounder guns:
>   Jiggery-jolty to and fro,
>   Each as big as a launch in tow—
> Blind—dumb—broad-breecht beggars o' batterin' guns!

Let that serve to remind us that no poetic theory, however it sharpens its analysis, is ever likely to come to an end of its topic: there must always remain a mastery unexplained.

VI

THE POETIC WORLD

I AM now to collect the chief results of these somewhat desultory studies into some sort of a summary.
With a caution that every one may not commend, I
have so far avoided committing myself to any direct
answer to that formidable old question, What is poetry?
I cannot put it off much longer, but I have still some
evasions left: evasions which, however, I hope may at
last appear to have so prepared the way for my answer
that it will seem unavoidable. It has been my concern
to discuss *how* poetry conducts its business; this being
matter which we can take hold of without making ourselves liable to serious disputation. I am now to inquire what, from the means employed and their effect,
we must suppose to be the general scope and nature of
this business. And in order to make it as broad and
conclusive as possible, I will put the inquiry in this
form: What are the main characteristics of the *poetic
world*—of that condition of experience which the usages
of poetry promote?

Condition of experience: that is the first point. The
poetic world does not refer to special *kinds* of experience. Many people, who will readily admit that, considering the huge variety of matters which have proved

The Theory of Poetry

themselves suitable for poetry, it would be hopeless to think of defining a poetic subject, nevertheless retain the opinion that there are certain topics which the poetic world will not tolerate. We hear it said that the everyday lives of undistinguished people in this industrial age of ours afford no matter for poetry. That, no doubt, is a vulgar notion; but I do not believe there is any presumed unfitness for poetry in a topic which could not be as decisively refuted as this has been by the genius of Mr. Gibson, who has made not only colliers and fishermen, but shopkeepers and clerks, unquestionable inhabitants of the poetic world. This vulgar notion itself might be the subject of quite engaging poetry; something very like it, at any rate, inspired some delicious lines in Theocritus. Nay, there is no reason why a proposition in Euclid should not be a topic for poetry. It certainly would not be the proposition as Euclid states it: there must be something distinctive about poetry. But suppose a man's whole current of life were to be changed by an accidental reading of the Forty-Seventh proposition of the first book: suppose that this sudden revelation of a new world, the world of mathematical truth, produced a rapture of intellectual experience which soared into spiritual conviction of man's immortal dignity as the vehicle of that divine thing, reason; would not Euclid have become poetical? Yes, and the very unpoetical philosopher of whom the story is told, Hobbes, himself becomes in it excellent matter for poetry: for he, like Euclid's proposition, appears in the story under a cer-

The Poetic World

tain condition. It is the condition, not the thing, which we recognise as poetical.

And so in general. If we follow the indications given by the *methods* of poetry, we shall conclude that the poetic world which those methods are designed to serve is ready to accept anything, so long as it is brought in under a certain condition. It is a general idea of this condition, then, which we have now to construct, in order to form some valid idea of the poetic world, and thus answer the question, What is poetry?

It is sometimes made a difficulty, when we come to this stage of the discussion, that the poetic world may be looked at from opposite sides: from the side of the poet who creates it, or from the side of the reader who receives it. No doubt, looking at it from the reader's side, we accept with a good deal of equanimity what cost much intellectual and spiritual agony; nor can our most delightful appreciation equal the joy of creation. On the other hand, if we try to put ourselves on the poet's side, and interpret his work by our knowledge of his life, we may be tempted to value the work for what we suppose it must have cost. But the poet is the only person who can really count the cost. What the actual experience in Shakespeare's life-history may have been which set him on to write his Sonnets, we cannot tell. Speculation about it is a harmless entertainment, so long as it does not seduce us into believing that the speculation, even if it were true, can enhance the value of the sonnets as poetry. For it is not this actual experience which the sonnets express, but the imaginative experience into which the actual deepened and widened and was utterly transformed. And as to what this imaginative experience is we do not need to speculate; there it is before us, complete and radiant, in the sonnets.

The difference between the poet's and the reader's attitude to a poem does not, in fact, concern us here at all. Poetry cannot help expressing *imaginative* experience; for whatever the event may have been which prompted the composition of a poem, whether it was in his inner or in his outer life, the poet, in order to put it into language, had to make his sense of the event continue after the event itself had happened. He had to keep it held before him and look at it: that is, he had to imagine it. And this very necessity of turning his sense of the event into an imaginative act, enabled the poet's mind to know and feel the event to the utmost, to distinguish all the nicety of its peculiar character, and to enrich it with the fullest comment of association; and thence to make it an occasion of that beauty and significance which we require in poetry, and into which we are now inquiring. By means of this transformation into imaginative experience, moreover, the event is removed from all dependence on the poet's life-history. In order to understand it, we do not have to relate it with any actions or behaviours recorded in the poet's biography; without ceasing to be personal, it has become independent of circumstances, and its individual quality has become a property not of any particular life, but of human nature. The poet's spirit, without losing its identity, has become capable of transferring itself to any other spirit; or rather, it has become capable of conferring its identity on any other spirit. This is the case, at any rate, when the imaginative transformation has been complete; and the more complete it is, the more absolute its expression must be as poetry.

It is because this is so that poetic technique can exist at all. The nature of technique need not be further elaborated; it is enough to mention once more its governing principle, which is *communication*. The poet devises his technique for the purpose of putting his audience in possession of something which he himself possesses. Clearly, then, the ideal of technique in poetry must always be to make of language a stimulus so penetrating, and at the same time so controlling, that any one who accepts it may end with a final impression as like as possible to the inspiration with which the poet began his business. This obviously supposes that a poet's inspiration is not bound up with those secrets of a man's life which his biography hopes to elucidate, with no likelihood of success. It must, on the contrary, be something in which every one can share to whom the opportunity comes. The poet's technique is that opportunity. The poetic world, therefore, is to all intents (allowing for the inevitable subjective differences) the same whether we take it as the world of the poet when he is inspired to write poetry, or the world of the reader when he is in tune to appreciate poetry. From whichever side we view it in order to discuss it, the theoretical result should be the same;

and I shall take it now from this side, now from that, according to convenience.

If it were possible to regard technique, and its primary results, as a sort of surface, it would not be difficult, within such a limitation, to describe the poetic world, nor to answer in consequence the question, What is poetry? For the first thing to note about the things we experience in poetry is the extraordinary richness of the impression they make on us; and poetry, regarded simply as the technique of language, may be defined as the simultaneous employment of every available and appropriate means of expression which can be got out of language. Poetry, by adding to the direct meaning of words the fullest and nicest use of verbal allusion, and, while these are operating, complicating their effect by the subtle suggestions of syllabic sound and the excitements of metrical rhythm, can give us in one complex impression the image of a thing distinctly seen and heard, with allusion thrown off to other sensuous experiences, accompanied by an elaboration of mood, and an instant certainty of understanding relationship, which, if we had them at all in everyday life, could only be had by reflection and studied inspection.

But as soon as we have noted the richness and intensity of the impression which the things of the poetic world make on us, we become aware of something even more characteristic; and when we note this, we seem to pass from the *means* of poetry to something at least of its *purpose:* from technique to its motive, from the surface of the poetic world to its inner nature. The

The Poetic World

poetic world is a world without prejudice. The writ
of those moral and practical judgments which we feel
compelled to exercise elsewhere, does not run here.
We have even left behind those judgments as to reality
and unreality without which we cannot elsewhere feel
safe. But here an impression has only to be vivid
enough in order to justify itself. This is the world
in which Macbeth, on the brink of his crime, alarms
us with the fear that his wickedness may not succeed.
This is the world in which the villainy of Iago delights
us with its refinement and resource. This is the world
in which Ariel and Titania, Circe and Armida, Poly-
phemus and Fafnir, Satan and Prometheus, are figures
which we accept as easily as the man next door; and the
instant we ask ourselves whether such figures really
exist or can exist, we are aware that in the very act
of asking that question we have come clean out of the
world of poetry. Just so, if we rely on the verdict in
which morality reprobates Iago, then instead of accounting for his part in the poem, we have destroyed
it. It is precisely as a villain that we enjoy him; we
can even detest him, so long as we enjoy our detestation. We know he is a bad man; we see the destruction he causes; but in the poetic world, badness, like
every other quality, and destruction, like any other occurrence, can only have positive valuation. The admirably bad is no paradox there, but as heartening as
the admirably good: no paradox, because there can be
no contradiction in a valuation for which there is no
reason, but only an immediate intuition.

The Theory of Poetry

For the value of things in poetry is the value of experience simply as such: the value which living spirit must feel in every vivid motion of its life. This is why the art of poetry is so much older than every other deliberate use of language. Long before it was worth man's while to express his reasoned or moralised view of things, it was worth his while to express his sense of being a spirit delighting in its powers and faculties, and in whatever will call them into use; and it was worth his while to manage words for that purpose with such art that he could delight in an added mastery—in knowing he could impose his own peculiar delight on the minds of others. The energy that finds expression in poetry must exercise itself in infinitely various moods; but let it be in rage or in hatred as well as in love or in exultation, there is a joy in it; the core of it is the spirit's primitive relish for *experience*. And whatever can be accepted without arguable valuation, frankly as experience, is matter for poetry; it bears its value on the face of it, a value which is instantly decisive, which will not alter, and cannot be stated in any arguable verdict; for it immediately declares the essential virtue of spiritual life—the virtue of delightedly conscious activity. What is there that cannot be so accepted? It is even possible for trains of reasoning and moralisations to be so accepted; and for this it is not in the least necessary that they should convince us. What is necessary is that we should be able to enjoy the excitements of exercising the power of reason, without having to ask ourselves whether we are intellectually in agree-

154

ment with its results. How many of us agree with Dante's reasoning, or Milton's? Those moments of close scholastic reasoning in *The Divine Comedy*, of animated forensic reasoning in *Paradise Lost*—do we *value* them as moments of philosophy? By no means; but, on the contrary, precisely as we value moments of imagery and emotion: as parts, namely, of an immense whole of self-sufficient experience, including in its scope every faculty by which spirit can put forth its vigour. No doubt intellectual matter is the most intractable thing poetry can deal with. "How charming is divine philosophy!" But the Milton of *Comus* did not venture to exhibit its charm. The passage which prompted that remark is actually the very antithesis of philosophy; for it is a chain of magnificently unreasoned assertions. A great deal of what goes for philosophy in poetry is of this nature; but though it may be usual, it is not necessary for philosophy to give itself up when it enters the reign of poetry. The older Milton could even afford to be syllogistic; for he could make logic serve in the whole result a purely imaginative purpose, and invest it with the emotion appropriate to the grand achievement of his purpose. And if any one were to give us the Forty-Seventh proposition of Euclid's first book, not merely so as to *prove* the proposition, but so as to infect us completely and unmistakably with the rapture, say, of Hobbes' delighted *experience* of that train of thought—would he not be giving us poetry?

But it is not enough to say that the poetic world is

a world of immediate values; there is a further condition to be noted. It is a world in which these values are always *significant*. It is very common, in discussions round about the nature of art, to bring in this useful word *significant;* and it is too often used as though the mere syllables of it had a magic force to resolve difficulties. We must try to form some tolerably precise notion of poetic significance, and it is clear, from what has been said already, that it must be the notion of a significance that does not require to be argued in order to be effective. But it is also clear that there is something in our valuation of things in poetry for which we have not yet accounted. I mentioned just now, in order to emphasise the unprejudiced nature of poetic values, one or two instances of matters which we eagerly accept in poetry, but which outside poetry we should feel compelled to detest. Now it is true enough that in common life we have an unregenerate faculty of enjoying notable wickedness and calamity; and poetry no doubt takes some advantage of this. Our first interest in Iago may be of this nature; but as the poem develops, and especially as it ends, we must feel that our interest has gone far beyond this. We enjoy the villainy of Iago not only because it is a superb specimen of villainy, but because it is villainy in which we find significance.

I do not propose to meddle with that vexatious problem, the *meaning of meaning*. It is enough for us to note that, when we find a thing significant, we certainly do not profess to look down on it from above

The Poetic World

and assign to it some mystical import outside the world of things here and now; by whatever process we arrive at it, the significance of a thing takes us no further than some relationship with other things. The sense of significance, in fact, is at bottom nothing else than a sense of clear and close relationship. A thing is insignificant to us when it does not belong to our way of living: when, that is, we cannot relate it with anything else we know. Unless we can make out some kindred for it, we decline to be interested in it. Indeed, it discomforts us, and we ignore it if we can. But the more richly, the more intricately, the more evidently a thing claims relationship near and far among our ideas, our moods, our sensations, the greater our sense of its significance; and the keener our interest in consequence. Now the whole texture of the experience we have in poetry is of this closely and vividly interrelated nature; nothing stands alone there; rather, by reason of the unusually delicate and precise adjustment of verbal suggestion surrounding the obvious meanings, the connexions between one part of an experience and another are far finer and more numerous than we can commonly perceive. Moreover, that elaborate diction of poetry, with all its simultaneous variety of expression, in sound and in sense, brings out a pressure of significance behind every detail of the imagination which is more than the nice connexion of one part with another. For the intricate subtlety of allusion and association in poetic diction gives us the constant impression of a world in which nothing can be touched without setting up a widening harmony of things round about it; everything that comes to us in the poetic world is vivid not only in itself but in many-sided relationship to the rest of that world. Now to say that such a world is, for this reason, more significant to us than the world of common affairs, is to say that it is a world of which we are more completely conscious than we are of the common world. The very fact, that everything here comes to us in an unusual radiance of significant allusion to moods and images all round it, means that in everything here there is more to be conscious of than is usual. And poets habitually employ devices which have no other purpose than to make our consciousness of their imaginative world as rich as possible. For besides the constantly implied allusions in their diction, they love to bring out the relatedness of the things in their world by openly insisting on the *likeness* of one thing to another. They have an instinctive inclination for metaphor and simile, the employment of which often produces a remarkable complexity of interrelated meanings. But the purpose is always the same: it is to enhance our sense of the significance of the things we are to imagine; that is, to enrich our consciousness of them. Thus Milton describes how, just before "the great consult began," the fiends thronged the courts and porches of Pandæmonium. They have throughout been visualised, in spite of their wings, as human figures; and this is emphasised by an allusion to the armies of chivalry. But to bring before us how the countless hosts

The Poetic World

Thick swarm'd, both on the ground and in the air,
Brusht with the hiss of russling wings,

Milton sets out an elaborate simile:

As Bees
In spring time, when the Sun with *Taurus* rides,
Poure forth their populous youth about the Hive
In clusters; they among fresh dews and flowers
Flie to and fro, or on the smoothed Plank,
The suburb of their Straw-built Citadel,
New rub'd with Baume, expatiate and confer
Their state affairs. So thick the aerie crowd
Swarm'd and were straitn'd.

The comparison with the familiar spectacle of a bee-hive simply helps us, it may be said, to *see* clearly and exactly what the sublime daring of Milton's imagination had created. But surely the simile does much more than make us *see;* or *hear* either. The care with which the business of the hive is brought before us, apparently for its own sake (what have "fresh dews and flowers" to do with Pandæmonium?), compels us to recollect the enigma every one must have felt in that inscrutable earnest bustle of the bees' common-wealth; and at once we transfer that feeling to the vision of the fiends: we *feel* ourselves spectators of the vision, as though it were objectively present; as though we had suddenly come upon it, and were marvelling what it is that can animate that horde of mysterious winged creatures, a feeling as "realistic" as if we had found ourselves in the presence of an excited mob in a foreign town. For the feeling of enigmatic business

The Theory of Poetry

in the hive, and the transference of this feeling to the vision of the fiends (with its objectifying effect on the vision), are both encouraged by the terms of the simile: the *simile* is to compare fiends with bees, but the bees in the simile are themselves described in *metaphors* of human city life. The result is, of course, a moment of extraordinarily enriched consciousness; fiends suggest bees, bees suggest men, and so back to fiends, with a new range of suggestion brought in at each stage.

So, too, Shelley, bringing mood and sensation before us in a metaphor, straightway proceeds to expound the metaphor by inserting a simile:

> My soul is an enchanted boat
> Which, *like a sleeping swan*, doth float
> Upon the silver waves of thy sweet singing.

Modern taste has developed unnecessary scruples about this kind of thing; scruples derived no doubt from the too narrow notion that the function of simile and metaphor is only to intensify and clarify imagery, usually visual. Such complexity as Shelley gives us leads rather, it has been complained, to confusion than to precision of imagery. And it is often regarded as self-evident that mixed metaphors (that is, an *incongruous* mixture of comparisons) must be poetically faulty. Ancient taste, however, seems to have been less disposed to cavil at such things; and I should suppose that, so long as ludicrous incongruity be avoided, the mixture of likenesses in one complex expression is still eminently defensible, since it has the virtue of enlarging the significance of the moment and enriching our consciousness of it.

Now, though it has taken some argument to make out the exact nature of significance in poetry, it is clearly not a significance which requires any argument to make it effective there. We have not gone beyond experience taken at its face-value. On the contrary, the significance I have been describing is automatically the property of experience whenever we are completely conscious of it; when we have it, for example, brought before us by means of such a many-sided instrument as poetic language. For just as each item of the experience is valued immediately and intuitively, so the interrelatedness of the items is valued; and this latter inclusive value (inclusive, but equally immediate) is our sense of the significance of the experience—a sense of face-value significance which, just because it is immediate, is much more satisfying than any intellectual construction of significance.

So far, however, we have not been considering the significance of an experience as a whole, but simply as it proceeds piece by piece. We have been referring to *poetry*, not to *poems*. Of poetry, we may indeed now venture to give a definition: It is the expression of imaginative experience, valued simply as such and significant simply as such, in the communicable state given by language which employs every available and appropriate device.

But if this is the nature of poetry, we must go on now to study the perfection of its nature; when, that is, it is made completely self-sufficient, and isolated in the single purpose of achieving the fullest possibility of its nature: when poetry exists as an individual poem. We must extend our notion of poetic significance. We have not yet accounted for such a crucial instance as the significance of Iago's villainy. As it is revealed to us moment by moment, the argument so far will certainly apply to it. But this piecemeal significance is slight compared with the final impression it makes on us when we have in our minds the poem as a whole.

It is, however, very easy to give the required extension to the notion of poetic significance which we already have. For it is only an extension; the notion is exactly similar, and may be arrived at in an exactly similar way. We formed our notion of the significance of things as they appear in the texture of poetry, by following up the indications given by the technique of its texture: by, that is to say, the technique of diction. But in order to enable poetry to exist in individual self-sufficiency, the poet, as we have already seen, must add to the technique of diction the technique of form. Now this simply means that, however complex and diverse the things may be which make up the substance of a poem, the meaning of the language which exhibits these things has been so exactly organised that, seconded by the rhythmical continuity of the language, the final impression is one of a harmonious unity of all the parts. For the form of the poem is the means whereby the imagination in it is at last fused into a unity, or rather expresses itself as a unity, similar to

The Poetic World

that which it must have had in the poet's mind in order to be the motive actuating the whole composition: what we have called the inspiration of the poem. The significance of a poem as a whole, therefore, is simply one way of apprehending its form: it is the sense of that vital interrelationship of all the elements in it by which they achieve their final harmony.

This sounds simple enough; and indeed it is simple. But it is nevertheless incomparably the most important effect which poetry can produce; and it is to this we must look for the function of poetry. It is infinitely more decisive and compelling than the significance which diction exhibits. That enriches our consciousness of things, indeed; and such experience is eminently desirable and beneficial. But it is more than desirable, it is an absolute necessity to us as spiritual beings, that we should experience such significance as is given to us by poetic form; and nowhere else is it given to us so penetratingly or so ineluctably.

For this is not the sense that everything would betray, were our perceptions only keen enough, some sort of relationship with other things; it is the sense that this matter and that matter, however apparently diverse from each other, actually are and must be related, by the mere fact of existing in our world. Iago's villainy, Desdemona's innocence, Othello's nobility—each of these, as it is unfolded to us, is enriched by an infinite subtlety of allusion and association; it is our good luck that we have them in such splendour of revelation. But we do not call it our good luck that the

163

poem as a whole brings these three things into such disastrous relationship with each other; we feel, on the contrary, that the poem has thereby revealed mere unavoidable necessity. These three things could not have existed except in this disastrous relationship. Do we deplore such a revelation? By no means; rather it gives us a profound satisfaction. We have seen evil doing its worst: we have seen it destroy that which we loved and admired; but we have also seen it operating not as a licensed intruder, but in strict obedience to the inner necessity of things. This is not evil which disturbs our sense of harmony in the world; rather, without ceasing to be evil, it has confirmed that sense.

What is it we most seriously desire our world to be? Is it a world without evil? That is not serious; it is a fairy-tale, a notion to amuse our vacant moments. What we do desire, and what we cannot spiritually exist without endeavouring to have, is a world into which nothing, not even evil itself, can come except in the interests of the whole, as a tone necessary for the establishment of fullest harmony. Our best efforts, intellectual, moral, or practical, are directed to the realisation of this world—of the world which admits of no exception to its order, the world of perfectly coherent and indestructible interrelationship: the world, in fact, of completely secure significance. We can never succeed in realising this world; but we can completely achieve an ideal version of it, if we will rely on experience taken at its face-value, without seeking to argue it into significance. Every poem is an ideal version

of the world we most profoundly desire; and that by
virtue of its form. A poem has no form unless everything in it unites into a single complex impression; and
in that impression we take, by immediate apprehension,
an instance of the world we require: for it is an impression of many things existing in perfect co-ordina-
tion, an impression that everything in the poem is there
in assured significance. It is natural to emphasise those
cases in which evil is thus mastered by the condition of
poetry; and indeed such poems—*tragedies*—are the
most striking examples of the way experience is idealised in poetry. Evil itself, without losing its nature,
has become what we require everything to be: the antithesis of everything desirable has submitted to our
desire. This is why tragedy is regarded as the highest triumph of poetic art. But every kind of poem,
from Herrick's song to Shakespeare's tragedy, from
Paradise Lost to *The Jolly Beggars*, takes us into the
world in which not only is experience immediately valuable in itself, but is, still without having to appeal beyond itself, inevitably significant. By what law things
are thus significantly related we do not need to inquire;
it is enough for us that in poetry things manifestly *are*
so related—that there we inhabit a world in which nothing irrelevant is known, but all is perfect order and
secure coherence.

But our account of the poetic world has an obvious
gap; so far we have ignored the quality which, I dare
say, most people would ascribe to it before any other.
For is it not the world of *beauty*? I have left this

quality to the end, because it does not seem properly understandable until we have clearly in our minds every other main quality in poetry. The beauty of poetry is a quality of another order than those we have been considering. It is not a quality which poetry sets out to achieve; at least, the desire to achieve it does not directly govern the choice and management of its methods. It may do so indirectly, however. Suppose that the impulse to compose poetry is an impulse to accomplish certain things; and suppose that the accomplishment of these things necessarily produces in us a certain effect. Now the poet may have had in his mind the production of this effect; but it will not itself have regulated his composition, for it can only emerge as the result of achieving his first purpose. That is the view of poetic beauty which I must now briefly put forward. Poetic beauty is the effect produced in us by the accomplishment of certain things—those things, in fact, which I have been broadly describing as characteristics of the poetic world. If this be so, it is fair to say that the governing purpose of poetry is not to be beautiful; but that the beauty of poetry is the sign that it has achieved its purpose.

If, however, we attempt to bring in the idea of beauty at the beginning of any theoretical account of poetry, it is difficult to avoid fixing the idea within preconceptions too narrow to be serviceable for long. It is impossible to maintain, in the face of poetry itself, that the subjects of poetry must be beautiful in themselves. We can only suppose, then, that they are bound to become beautiful when poetry takes hold of them, whatever they were before. How can that be? Clearly, it must be the beauty they acquire from the expression poetry gives to them. But how are we to define the beauty of poetic expression? We can only do so by defining poetic expression itself; and beyond saying that it must be *complete* and *just*, every case of poetic expression must be taken on its own peculiar merits. If we attempt to apply any preconceptions as to what poetic expression ought to be, we shall soon find ourselves in difficulties. When Browning published his *Soliloquy of the Spanish Cloister*, there were those who found it an offence against their idea of beauty. We can imagine Browning's reply: "What do I care for your idea of beauty? It was the Monk I was after; and I think I have got him." He has; the Monk is irresistible; the poem is a superb instance of complete and just expression. Is it not thereby beautiful? Those who condemned it might have appealed to Sophocles or Ronsard or Spenser; but why not to Aristophanes or Villon or Donne? There is no need, however, for a counter-appeal. To reject *The Spanish Cloister* as unbeautiful is (it must be on purely subjective grounds) to deny beauty there to the very thing which is accepted as beautiful elsewhere. For apart from beauty of subject, that which in any poetry we judge to be beautiful is—in Ronsard as in Villon, in Spenser as in Donne—nothing but some unequivocal success of expression.

There is, indeed, besides beauty of subject, another

The Theory of Poetry

kind of beauty which may possibly occur in poetry—
an accidental kind, as of an ornament unnecessary to any
purpose: and this is the natural beauty of the sound
of language. This must not involve meaning, for then
we should be back again in expression; and for the same
reason it must not be sound employed in the service
of the larger meaning which we call suggestion. We
come near to something like a purely ornamental use
of verbal sound in some of Milton's passages of proper
names:

> Nymphs of *Diana's* train, and *Naiades*
> With fruits and flowers from *Amalthea's* horn,
> And Ladies of th' *Hesperides*, that seem'd
> Fairer than feign'd of old, or fabl'd since
> Of Fairy Damsels met in Forest wide
> By Knights of *Logres*, or of *Lyones*,
> *Lancelot* or *Pelleas*, or *Pellenore*.

Or again:

> And all who since, Baptiz'd or Infidel
> Jousted in *Aspramont* or *Montalban*,
> *Damasco*, or *Marocco*, or *Trebisond*,
> Or whom *Biserta* sent from *Afric* shore
> When *Charlemain* with all his Peerage fell
> By *Fontarabbia*.

Everything that choice and arrangement can do, Milton
has done in order to make us notice the lovely sound of
such words. But of course they are not merely syllables; if our wits are alert enough, every proper name
comes burdened with splendid allusion, and nobly

serves to expand the meaning of the lines. But there seems to be a certain superfluity of sound in these passages; the beauty of the syllables is more than can be accounted for as expression. We come still nearer to the merely natural beauty of sound in language when we read that tremendous geographical survey in the Eleventh Book of *Paradise Lost:* simply because most of us have not the knowledge which can respond to such a cataract of names. We take it almost entirely as a passage of gorgeous sonority.

But it is easy to see that mere sonority does not account for the beauty peculiar to poetry; for mere sonority is not beautiful at all for long. Language which is not expressive soon becomes simply tiresome; syllables as pure sound will not hold our attention. Schliemann is said to have been captivated in his boyhood by the sound of Homer's hexameters; but he did not remain thus captivated any longer than he could help: he learned Greek as soon as he could, and the natural beauty of Greek syllables then became merged in the poetic beauty of sound that is *understood.* The instance of Swinburne is useful here, in order to show from another point of view how closely poetic beauty is bound up with expression. Swinburne began by discovering an extraordinarily individual technique, the beauty of which can hardly at its best be anywhere excelled. He then proceeded to repeat, over and over again, the devices which his youth had discovered. And why? Because he delighted in their beauty, and thought he had only to repeat them in order to repeat the achievement of beauty. Intent on preconceived beauty, allowing it to govern his technique directly, he lost that astonishing expressiveness his beloved verbal tricks had when he first found them out. The result is that, as his career went on, he failed more and more to write poetry, for he became more and more unreadable. His devices at last were not even beautiful; expression had deserted them, and left only a sonority that pleases for a moment, and then sinks into tedium.

But if we analyse what is happening in our minds when we read poetry: if we ask ourselves what any phrase which we judge to be beautiful is accomplishing for us while that judgment is effective, we shall surely feel bound to reply, that it is expressing something to us. This is the nature of the beauty peculiar to poetry. It is the judgment we pass on language which achieves, within the sphere appropriate to poetry, complete and just expression. It is the judgment of delighted approval, when language, by every power it possesses as sense and sound, compels us to live in experience which has its value manifest on the face of it, and which without argument securely establishes its significance.

The Idea of Great Poetry

LECTURE I

DICTION AND EXPERIENCE. MOMENTS OF GREATNESS

§ 1

THE title of this course of lectures—*The Idea of Great Poetry*—sufficiently indicates its purpose. I do not, however, by any means intend to lay down *a priori* the qualities which I suppose poetry *ought* to have in order to deserve the epithet "great"; my endeavour will simply be to enquire what *are* the qualities most noticeable in the poetry which has, as a matter of acknowledged fact, been recognised as great. I assume, you see, that great poetry is somehow recognisable; and I go on to ask what that recognition involves, and how it is made. Without that assumption, I could not, of course, begin to talk about great poetry at all. But that it is an assumption on which I can safely ground my argument seems tolerably clear from the habit of holding centenary celebrations, which has lately been growing on us. These outbursts of praise in accordance with the calendar, this dutiful connexion of enthusiasm with multiples of a hundred, may look a little factitious. But the habit at any rate shows how unmistakable, in the long run, the great poet becomes.

173

The Idea of Great Poetry

We have lately taken centenary occasions to celebrate the greatness of Shakespeare, Dante, Keats, Shelley and Byron; we have busied ourselves, if not on our own account, then vicariously in the newspapers, with the appreciation of these poets in their several qualities. Would it not be useful if, from this centenary habit of ours, we proceeded to ask ourselves, What exactly do we mean by a great poet? How, when we call Dante and Shakespeare great poets, do their remarkable differences come to be classified under one title? And what are we relying on, when we call Shelley a great poet, but not so great as Shakespeare? Suppose the almanac had been even kinder, and had added to our list other names equally convincing—such names as Homer, Milton, Goethe, to say nothing of Leopardi and Heine, Sophocles and Racine. What sort of similarity can it be, which the world perceives in such a miscellany of talents and achievements? But if we can make this similarity out, would it not improve our understanding, and therefore our enjoyment, of these talents and achievements—not only by appreciating their common function, but in the result sharpening also thereby our sense of their individual qualities?

There are those, I know, who deny that greatness has, properly speaking, anything to do with poetry. These are the sticklers for what, by a rather noticeable begging of the question, they call *pure poetry*. If a poem is the essence of what a poem should be (they make themselves the judges of that, of course), if a poem is as good as it can be, they say, what else mat-

Diction and Experience

ters? Perfection is what we are to look for; the scale of the achievement bears no relation to its *poetic* success. If it is strictly a question of poetry and of nothing else, why must we prefer Shakespeare's plays to his songs? This concern with greatness—what is it but obedience to a mere vulgar prejudice?

Well, let it be that. *Homo sum:* this vulgar prejudice, then, is my topic. It is a prejudice, at any rate, of some standing; the idea of greatness in literature is as old as criticism itself. It is no better for that, says our objector; is there to be no progress in our criticism, as in our other activities?—Let us hope so; but leaving on one side the question, what progress in criticism is, we may on our part ask, is there any reason why new notions should necessarily be better than old? *Change* is inevitable, no doubt, here as elsewhere; but it may sometimes be more profitable to change by re-stating old opinion rather than by replacing it with new. I think that must be the case here; for it can hardly be mere coincidence, that those who profess themselves superior to the notion of greatness in poetry, should be so markedly less interesting, in themselves and in all their habits and customs, than the poets and critics who accept it.

But I shall have enough to do without prescribing for that peculiar eyesight to which all stars are of the same magnitude. Who supposes that all poetry, even all the poetry which is to be called supremely good, must have all possible qualities? We may easily agree that poetic success as such is independent of scale.

The Idea of Great Poetry

Poetry may certainly be supremely good without being great; though I cannot conceive how it should be great poetry without also being good poetry. But there is in certain poems a quality which is recognised by common consent as *greatness*. I call it a quality; it may turn out to be a peculiar combination of qualities. But that makes no difference; it is then a quality of their qualities. Well, it is just this common consent, and the grounds of it, that I wish to investigate. But note that scale is certainly not the crucial thing even here. A long poem may as easily miss being great as a poem of molecular size—the smallest poem which can exist as such. Can a short poem, however, possess the quality of greatness? That is one of the questions we are to investigate; always remembering that a poem may be inestimably precious for other things besides greatness.

But I ought not to leave this modern notion of *pure poetry* without examining a little further its supposed power of damaging the old idea of *great poetry*. I have seen it argued that when Homer or Dante or Shakespeare is praised for the greatness of his poetry, it is not really the poetry that is being praised, but the man. And, though this kind of reasoning implies an intolerable and quite artificial limitation of the idea of poetry, there may be some excuse for it. Too often the poetry which is accepted as great has been praised for its ideas, its passions, its characterisation, without any appreciable regard for the conditions which enable these (or any other) qualities to exist as *poetry*. We are invited to admire them as if it were a matter of in-

Diction and Experience

difference, that they are elements in a work of art. What does that mean? It means, ultimately, that they have the importance, not necessarily of logical, moral, or practical validity, but simply of notable experience —the immediate interest of experience which cannot be entered without delighted excitement of intellect, emotion, or imagination, and which need not justify itself outside that excitement: its validity is self-evident: it is its own standard. And, in the art which we are now considering, we can only be urged to enter into such experience by the provocations of language wrought up to a consummate force and nicety of expressiveness.

Yet it is quite easy to see why this should come to be ignored, in many analyses of the greatness of poetry. It is not the magic of language itself which accounts for greatness, but that which comes to us through and by means of magical language. Nevertheless, to ignore this means is to leave out the characteristic fact, the fact that it is *poetry* we are dealing with. The omission is, accordingly, protested; and the pendulum swings right across to the notion that magical language is the only thing that matters. But no one can stop there. Language can only be magical when there is a purpose in its magic. No sort of language can exist for its own sake. But when is its magic most apparent? Clearly, when what is effected cannot possibly be distinguished from what is effecting it: all we can do is to acknowledge the enchantment. This, then, will be *pure poetry;* as thus:

The Idea of Great Poetry

Come unto these yellow sands
  And then take hands,
Curtsied when you have and kist
  The wild waves whist.
Foot it featly here and there
  And sweet sprites bear
The burthen—Hark!—(Bow-wow!)
The watch-dogs bark!—(Bow-wow!)
Hark, hark I hear
The strain of strutting chanticleer
Cry cock-a-diddle-dow.

But if you have to search appreciably beyond the skill of the language in order to find its final purpose, if you have to go to ideas, passions, characters, significances, which can be distinguisht and discussed apart from the language which pointed you to them, then (they say) you are dealing with adulterated poetry, with poetry which has admitted some mixture of what is alien to its own peculiar magic; and if great poetry takes you in this direction, then it takes you *away* from the essential nature of poetry. Poetry only preserves its purity so long as it resides in those prime immediacies of sense, feeling, imagination, which, once poetry has *said* them, leave us nothing to say *about* them.

That is the argument; and there is nothing wrong with it except that by *poetry* it means *lyrical poetry*. One may perhaps prefer lyrical poetry to all other kinds; but the didactic heresy itself was not more arbitrary or illogical than the attempt to confine the scope of poetry within its lyrical effort. Who disputes that poetry, to be supreme in its own nature, must be pure

Diction and Experience

and unadulterated? But what is pure poetry? What but the poetry which expresses pure experience? And that simply means—*experience itself:* experience valued merely as such, in and for itself, without having to rely on any external judgement of truth or morality or utility. The flowering of a cherry-tree, the dancing of a child, the attitude of a mountain, the sound and motion of waves, the sense of youth and love and mortality—we all know how these, and the like of these, dispense with any ulterior judgement, and give us the momentary, unconsidered rapture of *pure experience*. But where are its boundaries? There are none. Nothing whatever which the human spirit is capable of receiving, is incapable of being received simply as a pure experience, valued without needing any verdict of an ulterior judgement, appreciable simply as a particle of active life. And the really characteristic thing about the art of poetry is its power to present the whole conceivable world—the world not merely of sense and fantasy, but of severest intellectual effort, of subtlest psychological understanding, of the highest ardours of mutinous or consenting passion—to present anything which any faculty of ours can achieve or accept, as a moment of mere delighted living, of self-sufficient experience.

So now, after these preliminaries, I begin my attempt to build up roughly, but as substantially as I can, the *idea of great poetry*. I mean to imitate in my building the most elementary of architectural forms, the pyramid. I shall take first, as the broad foundation, squaring them to the purpose of the whole design, those obvious and necessary qualities which *all* poetry must have; and successively impose on these the qualities which, in this particular valuation of *greatness*, raise poetry higher and higher—but which occur more and more rarely—until at last we reach the narrow apex, the qualities of supreme greatness.

Of course, when we discuss poetry quality by quality, we are proceeding more in accordance with convenience than with truth. Poetry does not consist of separable qualities; if it exists at all, it exists as an indivisible whole. Unless, however, we were to allow ourselves, here as elsewhere in life, the liberty of analysing, criticism could never get much farther than exclamations of "well done!" and "ill done!" The disadvantage is, however, that when we come to the superstructure of our argument, we may seem to be ignoring the fundamental qualities on which it necessarily rests. I hope it will be allowed, during the later stages of our discussion, that nothing which is there said to make for *greatness* has been admitted except under the conditions which make it *poetry*, though these conditions may not be expressly mentioned: for they will, in fact, have been mentioned once and for all as the foundations of everything else.

§ 2

What, then, is the first thing which we require of all poetry—not merely in order to be great, but to exist at all? It has already been indicated. I will call it, compendiously, "incantation": the power of using words so as to produce in us a sort of enchantment; and by that I mean a power not merely to charm and delight, but to kindle our minds into unusual vitality, exquisitely aware both of things and of the connexions of things. This, of course, cannot be taken as a detachable craftsmanship; try to do so and, like chipping varnish off woodwork, it flies to pieces: we can make nothing of it. Nevertheless, the exceptional way words in poetry will command our minds is the first thing criticism can lay hold of: the first thing we come to know distinctly, as soon as we begin to study our delight. We do not require an absolute enchantment in every phrase we read, even in the finest poetry. The poets have an art of making us expect the magical phrase; and when it comes, it casts its enchantment over the whole surrounding texture of language. But unless it does come, and come often enough to keep our minds invigorated by its release, even from common words, of uncommon energy of meaning, we begin to murmur: "This may be very sincere and painstaking, but it is not *poetry*."

When Theseus, in *The Knight's Tale*, cuts down a whole wood for a funeral pyre, Chaucer disclaims, very minutely, any intention to describe the business. And no wonder! Who wants description when he can have incantation? Every detail, which Chaucer mentions as something he will not describe, is mentioned in such magical words that it flashes out at us like the light of a diamond. Let a single instance suffice. The dense wood has been all cut down, and the havoc cleared away; and Chaucer says he will not tell us how the nymphs and the fauns, the beasts and the birds, fled away in fear:

Ne how the ground agast was of the light.

Well might he disclaim *description!* And if we wish to account to ourselves for our delighted astonishment in that line, surely the first thing we should lay hold of would be the astonishing and delightful efficacy of that one word *agast*. Why, with that word, the line becomes such an incantation, that we feel what the very ground itself was feeling: the ground has become alive and sentient in our minds. Words have not *described* a fact, they have re-created in our minds the very fact itself.

Where was this fact originally? In Chaucer's mind: but he found the words which could transfer, perfect and unimpaired, this piece of his mind into ours. So did Herrick, when his gliding Julia passed, sumptuously languishing, before his admiration:

> Whenas in silks my Julia goes,
> Then, then (me thinks) how sweetly flows
> That liquefaction of her clothes.

Herrick's Julia, after that, is every one's Julia. And it is not Herrick *describing* what he loves to admire: our minds have become a moment of Herrick himself, admiring and making harmless love. As with Herrick and his Julia, so with Casca and his lion: it is a unique

Diction and Experience

moment of life that enters our minds when Casca tells us how, during the night of prodigies in Rome, he met the lion,

> Who glazed upon me and went surly by.

There was never any other lion quite like that. And the sight of its mysterious demeanour has been made over to us in perpetuity. The very sense of Casca's appalled encounter is absolute in us; Shakespeare's art has so enchanted us, that we become, for a moment, what he became.

There are, naturally, infinite occasions for the poet's incantation; but its purpose is always the same. It may be giving us simply a moment of sensation: but it will make the moment individual, exquisite, unique. If I told you I had seen a scatter of rose leaves floating on water, you might guess the sight had pleased me; and you would no doubt call up in your minds some vision fairly corresponding with mine. But when the poet writes:

> And on the water, *like to burning coals*
> *On liquid silver*, leaves of roses lay:

it is a quite special vision of floating rose leaves that is imposed on us. Such delicate extravagance of diction gives a personal distinction to the image; and chiefly by distinctly charging it with the poet's vivid and singular delight. The distinction of the moment will, no doubt, be even more noticeable, if the sensa-

183

tion comes to us not merely alive with appropriate feeling, but complicated with some unusual peculiarity of mood and allusion: something quaint and fantastic, perhaps, as when the same poet—Giles Fletcher—sees the first light of dawn strike the pines on the mountainside, and says of it that the trees

> Dandled the morning's childhood in their arms.

Or it may be something remote and mysterious, like the obscure sympathy which Keats divined in the very stones of his landscape, when

> Crag jutting forth to crag, and rocks that seemed
> Ever as if just rising from a sleep,
> Forehead to forehead held their monstrous horns.

Whatever it be, the poet's words not only make the whole fact start alive in our minds; they are electric with the subtle distinction of the moment in which the fact occurs, stored with those delicate and profound reverberations which make the fact unique. For the facts we are speaking of are experiences; and experiences are always unique: they occur in some particular person's mind, in some particular sequence of other experiences. Now poetry is the translation of experience into language; and the translation has not properly been made at all, unless, along with the stuff of the experience, goes a rendering of its peculiar moment, instinct with the moods, implications, references, influences, which made the moment unique. My in-

Diction and Experience

stances have been mainly visual—whether actual or imaginary makes, of course, no difference. But whatever the nature of his topic, the poet's business is always the same. He must, out of the subtly adjusted sound and sense of words, contrive such a texture of intensities and complexities of meaning, of unsuspected filaments of fine allusion and suggestion, as will enable these gossamers to capture and convey into our minds just those fleeting, gleaming qualities of experience which elude the hold of every-day straightforward language. For these are the very qualities which give to each moment of experience its unique distinction; and the words that can securely convey them are magical words, for they are truly creative. They have that incantation in them which can create in us, over and over again, the complete and many-coloured sense of a notably individual experience: the poet's experience. It is, indeed, *our* sense of it; and in becoming our sense of it, it no doubt undergoes inevitable modulation. But that does not lessen its individuality as an experience.

I have been speaking so far of the momentary phrases of enchantment: the phrases on which the spirits of imagination assemble as incalculably as the scholastic angels on the point of a needle. But when poetry is a continuous creation in us of the poet's habit of mind and its peculiar commerce with the world, then that poet, we say, has achieved *style:* that is, *his own* style, the habit of language nicely corresponding with the characteristic mode of his life. In any case, the magical infection of our minds with the poet's mind by means of language, is the first thing poetry must be capable of, in order to exist at all; and to accept the incantation—the re-creation in us of another man's experience,—is to make our first acknowledgment of the presence of poetry. I do not mean, however, by adopting this use of the word "magical" (common enough nowadays), to suggest that poets do not know very well what they are about, and just how to effect it.

Poetry is an art singularly privileged. It penetrates deeper, and mixes more intimately into our lives, than any other art, because the vehicle of its power is language; and language is the very faculty of spiritual existence in this world, as well as the means whereby human ability transacts its affairs. But poetry has to pay for its privilege. Men exist in nations; and the affairs of no nation can be quite like the affairs of another. Poetry is the most local of the arts. Dante, as is well known, scornfully refused to expound his poetry to "Tedeschi e Inglesi," to whom, he says, his art could never reveal its beauty. And he went on to utter his solemn protest against its translation:

> E però sappia ciascuno, che nulla cosa per legame musaico armonizzata si può della sua loquela in altra trasmutare, senza rompere tutta sua dolcezza e armonia.

There is no disputing this judgement. You cannot carry the fine interactions of the words of one language over into another; and this means, that you cannot transfer from one language to another the nice indi-

Diction and Experience

viduality of the poet's experience: the very thing, namely, that gave to his words the status of poetry. The moment which his language has exquisitely distinguisht is likely to become, in a translation, common and unnoticeable. Such lines as these may seem nothing extraordinary in their diction; but try to translate them, and see what happens:

ὑμεῖς δ' ἃ φράζω δρᾶτε, καὶ τάχ' ἄν μ' ἴσως
πύθοισθε κεἰ νῦν δυστυχῶ σεσωσμένον. . . .

denique tanto opere in dubiis trepidare periclis
quae mala nos subigit vitai tanta cupido. . . .

a questa tanto picciola vigilia
de' nostri sensi ch' è del rimanente,
non vogliate negar l'esperienza. . . .

The best that can happen is that the translator may be poet enough to provide out of his own life and art some substitute for what has vanisht. How splendidly this may happen, let the Authorised Version of *Job* or *The Wisdom of Solomon* remind us; but the result will be, in effect, a new poem. Sometimes, indeed, in what is called a translation, the original has been the mere stimulus of a wholly new creation: the famous instance is Fitzgerald's *Omar Khayyám*. What is most likely to happen is, however, that the translation will be not merely out of the original language, but altogether out of existence as poetry.

Yet something may survive, in either case: in diminisht efficacy perhaps, or perhaps not as poetry at all.

The Idea of Great Poetry

And of all qualities, the quality of greatness is most likely to survive somehow. Let Dante witness against himself. No poet ever made words mean so much; no poet ever made language the means of such distinction and intensity of individual experience. In any translation, *The Divine Comedy* must seem, moment by moment, to have suffered an intolerable loss; and yet the greatness of the whole will substantially survive. And so, too, when the translator substitutes for the original a poetic craftsmanship peculiarly his own. Chapman's Homer is quite unlike Pope's, and neither Chapman's nor Pope's Homer is like Homer himself. Yet unmistakably the greatness of both Chapman and Pope is Homer's greatness: this, in either paraphrase, is the surviving thing.

It would come in plausibly here, to object that, if greatness can survive the loss of poetry or a change of poetry, it can be no necessary or original part of poetry. But this would imply a thorough misconception of poetry's nature. Poetry exists as the perfect expression of experience, within the possibilities of language. In translation, the perfection of the expression is likely to go, because there is no exact equivalent of one language in another. The living reality can never be transported out of its native language; but a serviceable indication of the living reality may nevertheless survive. It will be crippled, diminisht, truncated: an experience vainly demanding to live in the words of the man who experienced it, since only he can know what words will enable it to live completely and hap-

Diction and Experience

pily. But the nature of the experience may be plain enough, nevertheless; even though it be degraded to the mere topic of the experience. It may be not only plain, but still alive. If you are not a traveller, you may see in a menagerie the sort of beasts that live in foreign lands. You do not see them there living their ordained and distinctive lives; for they are abstract beasts, remote from their native reality: they are, in fact, translations of beasts, and woefully incomplete. But they are still alive. Or, if you go to a museum, you may see the same beasts even more brutally translated. But as well say that tigers are no necessary part of tigers' lives, because the mere beasts themselves can be seen caged or stufft a thousand miles from India, as say that the greatness which can survive translation is shown thereby to be no necessary part of poetry. Whatever poetry has to express is a necessary part of it; for it is by virtue of expressing this that it exists at all. The common mistake in these matters is the confusion of experience itself with the matter of experience. Poetry differs from the rest of literature precisely in this: it does not merely tell us *what* a man experienced, it makes his very experience itself live again in our minds; by means of what I have called the incantation of its words. If you want to live in Dante's experience, Dante himself, in his own language, is the only person you can go to. But any decently competent translator can tell you *what* Dante experienced. He can never, however, tell you this completely or quite satisfactorily; because the matter of an experi-

189

ence is nothing but an abstract of reality—of the experience itself.

This question of translation has not taken us into a digression which is wholly without bearing on our present purpose. Our concern is, to discuss the quality of those experiences which give greatness to the poetry designed to express them. Now, if *poetry's* greatness could not survive translation, still less would it be *poetry's* greatness which would be capable of discussion: for that must require a much more complete abstraction from its original existence. It can only be usefully discussed as something which did exist as poetic art; but obviously, the greatness (or any other quality) of poetry will not be the same thing in discussion as it was in the art which prompted the discussion. The most conspicuous difference will be, that it is a less satisfactory thing: criticism is even more like a museum than a menagerie. But the fact that the animal on view there may be subjected to all sorts of methodical comparisons and examinations, and placed in a sedate series of resembling animals, does not affect the fact that it was once a live animal. Indeed, it is only in order to improve our understanding of the live animal, and its peculiar activities, that we study our dead preparations of its species at all. [1] And the museum of criticism has this advan-

[1] By "a species of poem" is sometimes meant what would be better and more simply called a *kind* of poem—lyric, epic, elegy, satire, etc.: rough distinctions which have no validity except occasional convenience. It is, however, in quite strict analogy with biological classification to call any particular poem—*The Divine*

tage, that its doors are always open, and immediately outside them is wild country, full of the living creatures that are but preserved specimens within-doors. In a word, the living experience we have had in poetry becomes in criticism the mere matter of experience. That is a remarkable difference, never to be forgotten: and I am wholly in agreement with any one who says, that it is not only a difference, but a degradation, as plainly as the museum-specimen is a degradation of the divinely alive beast. But only so can we take accurate account of our experience; and perhaps the accurate man is the only kind of man whose existence is excusable. The thing is, that we can, in our topic, pass at once from the account of experience back to the living experience itself; and if our account has indeed been accurate, in depth as well as in breadth, we go back to an experience which we find has enormously enricht and invigorated itself. That, at least, is the apology for studies such as these.

§ 3

But why should we delight in other people's experience? For if we delight in poetry, that is what it comes

Comedy, or *Paradise Lost*, for example—a species: a species made up of an indefinite number of variable individuals. A poem exists as an individual in the mind of each person who reads it; but in its possibility of multiplying these individual existences without losing in their variation a consistent and characteristic uniformity, it exists as a species; and it is as a species that we usually refer to it.

to. Have we not enough life of our own, that we should go to the poet for his? Indeed, no; we can never have enough: especially we can never have enough of the life that is most truly alive—intensely and delightedly conscious of itself, exulting in its faculties and in the world which calls them into use. We certainly do not need for this any uncommon or astonishing matter. Some of the most captivating moments in poetry are precisely those that render the most ordinary things. When Cowper takes his early morning walk in winter, surely the incident that must please us most is the sight he catches of his own shadow. The "slanting ray" of the sun, he says,

> Slides ineffectual down the snowy vale
> And, tinging all with his own rosy hue,
> From every herb and every spiry blade
> Stretches a length of shadow o'er the field.
> Mine, spindling into longitude immense,
> In spite of gravity, and sage remark
> That I myself am but a fleeting shade,
> Provokes me to a smile. With eye askance
> I view the muscular proportioned limb
> Transformed to a lean shank. The shapeless pair,
> As they designed to mock me, at my side
> Take step for step; and as I near approach
> The cottage, walk along the plastered wall,
> Preposterous sight! the legs without the man.

There is no occasion for any conspicuous verbal magic here; but there is enough to make the incident alive. And what a pleasant incident it is, the sight we catch of our legs (for Cowper's legs as we read become our legs) thus parodied beside us on the bright ground,

Diction and Experience

absurdly opening and shutting like a crazy pair of scissors, and then surprisingly jerking upright on the cottage wall, "the legs without the man!"

And yet, does it need a poet to give us an experience so simple as this; so trivial, one might think, as to be hardly worth noticing? But that is it: nothing is beneath a poet's notice. What pleases us here is the thing that pleases us (and a good deal more than pleases) in every experience that poetry can invest us with: not so much the substance of the experience, whether commonplace or far-fetched, as the quality of it. The poet (assuming that he is justifying his title) has been as keenly alive to it as if it was the novelty of the world. Let it be the order of the stars in heaven, or the shadow of his legs on the ground: whatever, when he is indeed a poet, catches his attention, catches it entire and engages his whole spirit in the experience of it. It is in this sense that the experience capable of producing poetry is something extraordinary: in that it is an experience on which a whole personality has been focussed with peculiar intensity and delight: experience, we may say, exceptionally conscious of itself. Poetry, we often hear, is ideal life: and so it is, as I shall, later on, have to argue more largely. But poetry does not need to decline the actual in order to be ideal; it is ideal in the *manner* of its experience—an image of the ideal way of experiencing this present world of here and now.

Well, this is true of poetry in general. How much nearer has it brought us to the idea of great poetry?

The Idea of Great Poetry

Here I must return to my original assumption—the assumption that great poetry is *recognisable*; for, once more, my only purpose is to enquire what the world means when it calls this or that poetry *great*. But to make our recognition secure, we must set up some sort of contrast. Read, for example, *The Knotting Song*, by Sir Charles Sedley:

> Hears not my Phillis how the birds
>   Their feathered mates salute?
> They tell their passion in their words:
>   Must I alone be mute?
>   *Phillis, without frown or smile,*
>   *Sat and knotted all the while. . . .*

And so on! A delicious moment! And is there not an exquisitely personal distinction in it? And could anything be better as art than the precision and proportion of its rendering into language? But no one would suggest that Sedley's version of unpropitious love has anything of the quality we call greatness. Contrast it with the half dozen lines with which Swinburne evokes the spirit of Sappho. After Sedley, there may seem a suspicion of rant, but there is surely the accent of greatness, in the torrent of simile and metaphor that throngs into the passion of Swinburne's imagination:

> The intolerable infinite desire
> Made my face pale like faded fire
>   When the ashen pyre falls through with heat.
> My blood was hot wan wine of love,
> And my song's sound the sound thereof,
>   The sound of the delight of it.

194

Diction and Experience

"Why," you may say, "the difference is already accounted for, when you admit that there is *passion* here. Sedley's elegance makes no pretence of passion; but Swinburne's vehemence exists for nothing else. Why look further?" But we must look further: for this really tells us very little about what we are trying to find. You cannot make out that greatness in poetry always depends on this sort of passion. Besides, what exactly is passion? And why should it make poetry great? For note that poetry cannot give a passion direct; we can only get it indirectly, from the imagery that embodies it. Is it the kind of the imagery, or its extent, or its complexity, or what, that gives us a sense of greatness?

We must, at any rate, try to find, in our sense of such a difference as that between Sedley and Swinburne, something broad enough to account generally for the accent of greatness: for the fact which we are investigating is just this—that extraordinarily divergent instances of poetry may all deserve the epithet "great." How do they come to deserve it? Clearly, there must be something common to them all; and clearly the value of it cannot be discussed until we have decided what it is.

After Swinburne's Sappho, let us contrast Sedley with Sappho herself. Certainly, the full sense of her greatness can only be given in her own magical language; the impossibility of rendering the many-coloured splendour of her diction is notorious. But even in the blurr of a translation, there survives unmistak-

ably the character of that for which the incantation of
her language was designed. The unknown incomparable critic, to whom we owe the preservation of *The
Ode to Anactoria*, said that it was not so much a passion as a concourse of passions. This is often quoted;
and the keen insight of that phrase, "a concourse of passions," brings us near to what we are looking for. But
the critic had more than this to say. It was not only
the concourse of *passions* which he noticed; it is a marvel, he says, how Sappho fuses together "soul, body,
ears, tongue, eyes, colour. Uniting contradictions, she
is, at one and the same time, hot and cold, in her senses
and out of her mind, fearfully alive and almost dead."
And he completes his brilliant analysis by adding the
essential thing: the singular excellence of this poetry,
he says, is that all these form in it "a combination into
a single whole." [1]

Now here we have got to something broader and
deeper than the mere existence of passion in a poem.
This puts poetic greatness on universal ground. Poetry
is always the communication of unusually vivid
experience, charged with an unusually personal delight. The sense of the greatness of poetry is nothing
but a sense of the *richness* of each moment of the life

---

[1] He does not mean the "single whole" of the complete poem:
the phrase (ἡ εἰς ταὐτὸ συναίρεσις) simply refers to the fusion
of all these passions and sensations into a single momentary complex of experience. Accordingly, he quotes, not the whole poem,
but just enough of it to show this. Unfortunately, therefore, the
whole poem no longer exists, and we can only illustrate from it the
greatness that exists in notable moments.

Diction and Experience

which is being communicated to us. But we must note carefully what this implies. Momentary richness of experience means also an intensity of experience. It will not be a richness that runs out in diffusion nor one that is amassed in confusion: it will come out of a life the conscious vigor of which may in any single moment be sensuous, emotional and intellectual all at once; all distinctly imagined, along with their fine radiations of significance and allusion, yet all combined in an inextricable harmony. That is why I emphasise the *personal* quality of poetic experience, in the elucidation of its greatness. For only a life centred in a white heat of exultant personality and power of self-knowledge *could* accept and fuse into single moments of experience—into single intuitions—the infinite wealth offered to it by the occasions of great poetry, lavisht on it by every faculty of sense and mind and spirit. That which any one moment of great poetry concentrates into its harmony would, in ordinary experience, be dispersed through a whole series of moments. And this is why the language of great poetry must always be notable for its enchantment, for its power of collecting many kinds of meaning round a single phrase; yet this richness and intensity of experience explain also why even a prose translation of great poetry will be worth reading: however much is lost, there is still more that must survive.

Now how do we stand as regards our contrast with Sedley? Taking them simply as versions of experience, *The Knotting Song* and *The Ode to Anactoria* may be equally successful. We praise the intensity of Sappho's art; but the mood which Sedley's delicate nicety of art renders so perfectly has all the intensity it will bear. We praise the splendour of Sappho's diction; but Sedley's is just as exquisitely adequate to its occasion. The thing simply is, that there was incomparably more in any moment of Sappho's experience than in any moment of Sedley's. In any moment, therefore, her life had to collect itself into a far brighter and more ardent intensity of focus than his; the command of her personality must immeasurably transcend his. But, as far as adequacy of art is concerned, we must not say that Sedley is below Sappho; we should rather say that, in order to be as adequate as Sedley's, Sappho's art was bound, moment by moment, to achieve beyond any comparison a keener and fuller expressiveness, a more magical incantation, than his.

This is what we mean, and all we mean, when we call *The Ode to Anactoria* greater poetry than *The Knotting Song*. To make it still clearer, let me bring in another though similar contrast with the latter: an early ode of Dante's, written in his unregenerate days, and certainly one of the greatest of his lyrics. Passion is still the theme; and passion disappointed—nay, enraged. But the passion is so richly and solidly substantiated, that even a bare summary of the poem may convey some notion of its greatness. After preluding about his scornful lady's impenetrable mood—her mind is as hard and as cold as jasper, he says—all she has made him suffer starts up before him into the towering presence of a vision: he sees the armed Spirit of Love striding terribly and triumphantly over him—Love imagined as a malignant god exulting in cruelty. He has been thrown to the ground, and he feels himself there in bodily prostration under the threat of that blinding sword; the stroke descends and pierces him, and he can but lie there motionless, so tired with agony that his limbs are incapable even of shuddering. But while he is lying there, helplessly gazing up at that pitiless spirit, even then he is, in the very midst of his terrified anguish, feasting his imagination on the vengeance he will take on his lady for all his sufferings; and first he is gleefully revenging himself on the detested beauty of her hair.

All this is given to us in that strain of impassioned intensity and majestic grace

> That bloom'd to immortalize the Tuscan style.

The perfection of Dante's diction here is one of the marvels of poetic art; but merely to give you, as I have done, an abstract of the poem—and an incomplete abstract at that—is enough to indicate, past mistake, the nature of its greatness. For at the climax of the poem, consider what a throng of feeling and sensation has been poured by Dante's imagination into a single moment of consciousness. He feels the posture of his agonised fear, prone on the ground, frozen there in immovable rigor; he sees the dreadful face of the god blazing malignity at him, and the sword in act to strike; and still, right at the heart of his agony, burns his own confident hope of revenge, already calculating its delight, intent on his mistress' hated loveliness, relishing the cruelty and lust he promises himself. That all this should be experienced in a lucid and coherent harmony of distinguishable elements is obviously the work of an astounding power of self-knowledge and organised self-command; and Dante's supremely capable art transmits this faculty to us. Only in an exceptional intensity of conscious living, of active personality, could such a complex of riches make up a single moment of experience; and, by virtue of the enchantment of language, this personal mastery of an infinite wealth has become our possession too, and every one's.

Here we have, I cannot but believe, the general characteristic of all the poetry which strikes us as *great:* not only of that which is, as we say, subjective, but of the greatness of dramatic, narrative, reflective poetry also. The differentia is evidently one of degree only, but it is decisively noticeable. What we recognise in great poetry is this unconfused complexity of rich experience, this confluence of all kinds of life into a single flame of consciousness, triumphantly asserting its luminous unity over all the manifold powers of its world. With Dante still in my mind, I take, to illustrate my theme further, and in objective substance, the first incident that occurs to me when I think of *The Divine Comedy:* an incident the more to my purpose for being so well known. The superb Farinata, as Dante approaches him, lifts himself erect out of his agony among the damned, "as though he had hell in great scorn"; and abruptly and contemptuously greets the poet with the question, "Who were thy ancestors?" At Dante's answer, he raises his eyebrows a little and says, "They were my fierce adversaries, and I broke them twice." And what a compound of the immortal grandeur and folly of human pride lives before us there! It is in this sort of life, in this concentrated wealth of simultaneous impression, with its allusion all round to all sorts of experience, that we move continually throughout *The Divine Comedy*.

And note, that it is not merely the rich vitality of the incident which gives us the sense of greatness, but the harmony which fuses the wealth of matter into a single compound of impression. That is the characteristic thing everywhere in *The Divine Comedy*; and is it not, as far as our recognition of greatness is concerned, the characteristic thing also throughout the *Iliad*? Take one instance only. Hector hurrying out to battle in radiant armour meets Andromache and the nurse, with his baby in her arms. Andromache sees the inevitable end—Hector killed, herself in abominable slavery. Hector sees it too; better even than Andromache, he knows what the Greeks will do to her. But not even that anguish can weaken him. If these things must be, what can we do but endure them—nay, go out erect to meet them? Then Hector reaches out his arms to his little boy to kiss him good-bye; and the baby is frightened at his helmet, and cries. And we instantly realise that Hector, the man-slaying terror of the Greeks, is a

The Idea of Great Poetry

Hector the baby has never seen before; he has only known the daddy that played with him in the nursery. So Hector takes off his helmet and sets it gleaming on the ground: and then the boy will come to him and be kissed. And Hector goes out to fight, and to accept his fate. And Andromache goes home, to await hers. Homer has there sublimed and compacted into a single living moment the whole lamentable infinite splendour of man's *courage*.

And exactly similar is the recognition of greatness when the power of imagination neither concentrates inwards on itself, nor dramatises itself outwards in action, but meditates. When Shakespeare's petulant Achilles asks, "What, are my deeds forgot?"—his Ulysses has an answer for him which is one of the greatest things in the world. Yet it could all be reduced to the merest commonplaces of proverbial wisdom. But this worldly lore has come to new and individual life in Shakespeare's mind; it is being experienced there like a keenly appreciated event. It is something vividly happening, and all the powers of imagination come trooping together to join in. Common sense, without ceasing to be thought, turns also to a pomp of things seen and felt; and the language of the poet gives us a rich and instantaneous harmony of imaginative experience which is thought, sensation, and feeling all at once:

> Time hath, my lord, a wallet at his back
> Wherein he puts alms for oblivion,
> A great-sized monster of ingratitudes:

Diction and Experience

Those scraps are good deeds past,
Which are devour'd as fast as they are made,
Forgot as soon as done: perseverance, dear my lord,
Keeps honor bright: to have done, is to hang
Quite out of fashion, like a rusty mail
In monumental mockery. Take the instant way;
For honor travels in a strait so narrow
Where one but goes abreast; keep then the path;
For emulation hath a thousands sons
That one by one pursue: if you give way
Or hedge aside from the direct forthright,
Like to an enter'd tide they all rush by
And leave you hindmost:
Or, like a gallant horse fall'n in first rank,
Lie there for pavement to the abject rear,
O'er-run and trampled on. . . .

§ 4

But the greatness of this kind of poetry, you may
tell me, is due to the fact that it is distinctively and
specifically *imaginative:* its matter could not have been
presented at all, except by a lofty act of symbolic
imagination. For what is the real matter of this passage? Certainly not the *thought;* which, in itself, is
nothing remarkable. But as it is represented to us in
the poetry, in the noble procession of these images,
it is singularly remarkable. Why? Because it is not
presented to us simply as *thought,* but as the finely
emotional and subtly allusive experience of an individual mind *thinking*—of, precisely, Shakespeare's
Ulysses thinking. Only an exceptional power of capturing the intangible could have so exactly, so splen-

didly, given shape and feature to such fleeting significances: and there is no other power that can do this
but an exceptional *imagination*.

No one can doubt it; but our agreement need not
modify the conclusion we have so far arrived at. The
sense of poetic greatness is precisely the same here as
anywhere else: it is the consciousness of unusual richness and intensity in the life that is being communicated to us. Whether any kind or degree of poetry
can exist at all without proceeding from the imagination is a question I may not stop to examine; but when
great poetry is assumed to depend peculiarly on imagination, clearly that word is being used in a special sense.
This is the sense implied by the old and celebrated
distinction between *imagination* and *fancy*; and, I
think, as soon as the distinction is mentioned, you will
agree there is something in it—something pertinent,
too, to our topic. I cannot enter into the philosophy
of the distinction; I doubt if there is more to be made
of it than a critical convenience. But, if it is valid
at all, it should be recognisable, whatever the philosophy of it may be; and if it has any bearing on the
idea of poetic greatness, that too should be recognisable.

I suppose there is no passage more typical of the
work of sheer fancy than Mercutio's speech about
Queen Mab, her antics and her equipage:

> she comes
> In shape no bigger than an agate-stone
> On the fore-finger of an alderman,
> Drawn with a team of little atomies

Diction and Experience

Athwart men's noses as they lie asleep:
Her waggon-spokes made of long spinners' legs;
The cover, of the wings of grasshoppers;
Her traces, of the smallest spiders' web. . . .
And in this state she gallops night by night
Through lovers' brains. . . .

Who can resist this world of gay, miniature immortality, and the intrusion of its whimsies into the serious habits of mortality? We call this sort of thing *fancy;* let me now put beside it an instance of what, in contrast, we should, just as certainly, call *imagination.* My instance is the famous Anglo-Saxon poem known as *The Dream of the Rood.* The poet (in what he calls "the most precious of dreams") sees the Cross before him; it is blazing with the encrusted light of jewels. He is shamed by the splendour. Instantly, instead of jewels, the Cross is dripping with blood; and, mysteriously yet inevitably alternating, the Cross continues to be now a thing of dazzling glory, now a thing of loathsome horror. And then the Cross speaks. It recalls how it was once a happy tree on the edge of a wood; but men cut it down to make an instrument of torture. They set it on a hill, and the victim is brought. The Cross longs to hurl itself on His persecutors and crush them to the ground; but that is forbidden; and the shuddering Cross is compelled to give the agony of death to its beloved creator.

Fancy is not the word for that! But wherein lies the difference between the fancy of Queen Mab and the imagination of the living and anguishing Rood?

The Idea of Great Poetry

Essentially, in nothing but the range and depth and complexity of the emotion that is presented to us by the imagery. *The Dream of the Rood* puts us in possession of an incomparably richer harmony of experience than Mercutio's account of Queen Mab; and so far as the sense of poetic greatness depends on it, the distinction between fancy and imagination is simply another confirmation of the notion we have already attained to. Simultaneous riches of impression, a scope ranging from dread and pain to beauty and delight, and the harmony of all this—that is what we mean by greatness of poetic experience.

NOTE ON FANCY AND IMAGINATION

It is not easy to make out exactly what is or has been meant by the qualitative distinction between fancy and imagination. Coleridge professed his intention of settling the distinction once and for all; and after the most elaborate philosophical preliminaries, decided, when he could no longer postpone the crucial question, to take the advice of a convenient friend and leave the matter as vague as he had found it (*Biographia Literaria*, Chap. XIII). There can be little doubt that Coleridge's mind was set working on this matter by Wordsworth's early conversation; but Wordsworth had a special use for the word imagination; as he expressly says, he was driven to use it, for certain sublime exercises of intuition, "by sad incompetence of human speech" (*Prelude*, Bk. VI, 592-616). This seems to be the origin of Coleridge's "esemplastic" imagination. But he extended the meaning of that portentous phrase far beyond Wordsworth's mean-

Diction and Experience

ing; and the difficulty is to see just what this extended
meaning is—a meaning which, for all its immense
extension, must never even border on that of fancy: for
fancy and imagination are "two distinct and widely
different faculties." So that when Milton is said to
be imaginative and Cowley fanciful, the proposition
is not in the least concerned with any sort of *degree*
(in which case most people would accept it), but with
the use of two originally distinct *faculties*. Yet whenever Coleridge's "imagination" is at all intelligible, it is
either so narrow that, as a general doctrine for poetry,
Wordsworth himself felt bound to protest against it, or
so wide that Cowley comes in as easily as Milton. It
should be noted that Wordsworth's mature opinion,
in the admirable Preface of 1815, after first classing
them together as *one* of "the powers requisite for the
production of poetry," discriminates imagination and
fancy chiefly by their effects; and it comes to very
little more than Leigh Hunt's sensible definition of
fancy as "a lighter play of imagination . . . analogy
coming short of seriousness."

This was too simple for Coleridge. The two faculties, he allows, can co-exist in a poet; but they are
distinct for all that. If there is any meaning to be
attached to his "fancy," Shakespeare was fanciful when
he wrote Mercutio's Queen Mab speech. Now the
one positive thing that emerges from Coleridge's discussion of the difference between fancy and imagination, or from the discussion of any other maintainer
of the distinction, is this: that fancy, at bottom, is
something *irresponsible*. It is just because of its in-
variable reliance on this notion that the distinction
seems to me to have no validity whatever, except as a
matter of degree. For there is no such thing as irresponsible fancy, toying with imagery for the mere sake

of the images, like the tumbling about of coloured glass in a kaleidoscope. And if it is not that, if there is some significance in fancy's image-building, wherein does it differ from imagination, except in degree of significance? But there is always at least an emotional significance, and usually much more than that, in any game the mind may play with images. A really irresponsible game would be utterly unlike the way the human mind works. However lightly you may seem to play with images as if they were counters, there is always a mood standing by you, ready to put a value on the counters. Fancy is all one with imagination in function: in the shows of sense to symbolise mood— i.e., mood *at least*.

Take Mercutio's speech. "I talk of dreams," he says; and for the moment it seems easy to agree with him that these are "begot of nothing but vain fantasy." But just look what dreams they are. Every one is characteristic of the dreamer; by no means vain or irresponsible fantasy, but fantasy responsible in every case for a certain precise significance, the fantasy that is nothing but the shaping of habitual mood or ruling desire. And as with the dreams, so with their instigator—Queen Mab herself, that vision of a busy potent littleness, with her exquisite absurdity of an equipage, riding forth uncontrolled by any apparent law. Is she a mere irresponsible whimsy of the mind? How do the fairies continue to live at all, except by *meaning* something to us? Why, they are the symbol of one of the deepest, most universal longings that man is capable of nourishing. Anxious, accountable creatures as we are, compelled to exist in just one scale and no other, obedient to Ricardo's law of rent and the association of ideas—how could we endure ourselves if we could not now and then fantastically escape into the

Diction and Experience

life of fairies and happily despise our troublesome
necessities—"Lord, what fools these mortals be?"—
a remark which completely dissolves any qualitative
distinction between fancy and imagination: the fantasy
of Puck here proclaims itself utterly indistinguishable
from imaginative significance.

Or take another instance: Poe's *City in the Sea*. Is
this not a piece of sheer fancy—a glittering pile of
imagery enclosing a mere arbitrary conceit, and built
up simply for the pleasure of building in such ornamental stuff? Or perhaps it is on the borderline, or
—should we rather say?—*both* faculties are involved
in the poem: it began as an act of imagination, which
was handed over to fancy to be workt out. The meaning of the poem as a whole is clear enough, at any rate:
death is triumphant in it. The sense of his triumph
may have hardened into a conceit, an ingenuity, by
being localised in a city contrived to exhibit it; but
surely in the first instance it was *imagined*—nay,
"esemplastically" imagined. Surely, too, the whole
conduct of the poem is very far from being a go-as-
you-please of imagery: it is *designed* from start to
finish. Yet is not the design covered by an encrusta-
tion of merely ornate fancy, an arabesque of far-fetcht
whimsy planted on as a taking decoration? What, for
instance, have "the viol, the violet, and the vine" to
do with Death Triumphant?

I think, in such a case, the poet's mind works something in this way. It is like a man narrating his dream
at breakfast. The dream would anyhow make a story
sufficiently odd and striking; but as he tells it he cannot resist improving it, to make it even more astonishing and absurd, more complete in its matter-of-fact
improbability and nonsensical coherence. We say that
he *invents* these improvements—he is simply amusing

himself in them. But really he is no more doing that than his brain was amusing itself with the actual dream. The dream, we know, was a symbol: some obscure shapeless impulse from the depths of his nature was embodying itself in a train of imaginary sensation. And when this symbolic substance is consciously toucht up, deliberately improved to make it more entertaining, it is thereby actually improved *as a symbolism:* whatever the man thinks he is doing, he is really elaborating still further the transformation into imagery of his original impulse. He is, by continuing in the story of the dream, continuing in the influence of its origin and carrying on the tendency of its influence. And so it is with Poe's vision of Death Triumphant. However curiously and deliberately invented the detail may seem, as though the poet meant nothing but a wanton fantasia of ornamental figures, however he may seem to be carving "the viol, the violet and the vine" for the mere delight of doing so—actually he is, with every unexpected stroke, sharpening and securing the impression of the whole vision on our minds. And the more convincing the *substance* of the vision becomes by these apparently irresponsible touches—the light from the hideously serene sea, the diamond eyes of the idols, the gaily-jewelled dead, and the rest—the more securely the whole *mood* of the vision establishes itself. The initial inspiration never leaves go of the ingeniously elaborating imagery, but continues subtly to command it, however wayward and wilful it may seem to have become.

It is entirely allowable, and may be very useful, to call such poems as *The City in the Sea* fanciful. But if to call them so implies any derogation—if it implies any qualitative separation from *imaginative* work—then the word *fanciful* has, somehow or other, gone wrong: it has taken too much meaning on itself. It

Diction and Experience

has, in fact, assumed the right to label a distinct faculty. Now, the faculty of fancy does not exist: it is one of Coleridge's chimeras, of which he kept a whole stable. Fancy is nothing but a degree of imagination: and the degree of it concerns, not the quality of the imagery, but the quality and force of the emotion symbolised by the imagery. Poe's poem is a masterpiece; but the triumph of death in it has neither the force nor the quality of, say, Petrarch's *Trionfo*, not to mention *Othello*. Just as fanciful as *The City in the Sea*, and deserving the epithet for precisely similar reasons, are, for example, many passages in *The Divine Comedy*: such as the quarrelling demons in the *Inferno*, or the Earthly Paradise at end of the *Purgatorio*. There is no radical change from the process of imagination in such passages; but there is a certain limitation and agreeable specialisation of emotion in them. And that is what we refer to—but it is only that we refer to— when we call such poetry the work of fancy.

LECTURE II

GREATNESS OF FORM. REFUGE AND INTERPRETATION

§ 1

So far I have been mainly engaged in examining, for the signs of greatness, poetry in its momentary existence. For that is how we take it in—moment by moment: in poetry, as in everything else, we live first of all in the immediate *now;* and in order to build up our idea of great poetry, we must begin with its momentary condition. If we have succeeded in accounting for our sense of greatness in some signal moments of poetry, still we have done no more than make a beginning. So long as we are concerned with poetry as we take it in, moment by moment, we cannot expect to get anything more than the accent or manner of greatness: the suggestion of what we may look to have when the accumulating sequence of moments is complete. If we are to lay our hands anywhere on *greatness itself,* it will not be in the effect of poetry *while we are reading it;* but in the effect it may have on us *when we have read it:* when the orderly series of poetic experiences has been collected into one final and inclusive imagination which is the compact summation of the whole: that is to say, when not merely *poetry* has come into existence in our minds, but a *poem*.

The greatness we are looking for is, therefore, strictly a property of poems rather than of poetry. The distinction might be put in a more emphatic and perhaps more familiar way, which we may find useful. For this is nothing but the distinction, so common in discussions of this kind, between Substance and Form. It is sometimes misconceived. If we regard form as something *added* to substance, a mould arbitrarily imposed on the stuff of poetry from without, it would be unintelligible to say that greatness is a property of form. But if we take form to be simply the fore-ordained and finally resulting whole impression which sums up and includes an orderly sequence of contributory impressions, then clearly it is here, if anywhere, that the quality of greatness will reside. What we have while we are still reading a poem is its substance; but a substance which only exists for the sake of its eventual form. For the moments of a poem are only there in the interest of its design and whole intention; we read a poem for what we are to feel when we have read it. But if a poem has any effect as a whole at all, that must be because the recollection of the series of its moments impresses us as something complete in itself and self-contained, in boundaries effected by its own coherence; the recollection, that is to say, is of something which has *form*.

But, though we may agree that greatness in poetry strictly belongs to form, we must make out more exactly what this means. In any noticeable moment of poetry, we see that there is a certain set of words responsible for it. But when, at the end of a poem, we receive its final impression as a whole, there is no set of words that is directly responsible for that. It certainly comes to us as the result of all the words in the poem; but not directly. It is the organised accumulation of the whole series of momentary impressions: the impression made by all the other impressions united together. Often enough the series of impressions is so short, and accumulates into a self-sufficient whole so rapidly and simply, that the process is not noticed at all. The whole poem seems to form a single moment, and may legitimately be so described; and we seem to take its completed impression directly from the words. Here is a poem of Allingham's which is perhaps as simple an instance of the art of poetry as we could have:

> Four ducks on a pond,
> A grass bank beyond,
> A blue sky of Spring,
> White clouds on the wing:
> What a little thing
> To remember for years—
> To remember with tears.

We are scarcely conscious of organising these impressions into a whole. But how does, for example, *Othello* come to exist in our minds as a whole? Not so much by a unification as by a whole series of unifications. We take first from its enchanted language a procession of imagined experiences, and these we con-

dense into an impression of character, and of the interaction of character; and this interaction we then condense into an impression of plot; and the plot compacts
itself into the sense of a single complex event moving
inexorably onward: and our sense of this movement
we condense still further, when the play is at an end,
into a final summation of impression—some sense of
life corresponding (so far as we are capable of corresponding) with that piercing sense of the pitiable irony
of things which, stirred by an old story he was reading, gave Shakespeare the motive of his tragedy. It
is nowhere directly given; it could not be expressed
at all, except as the organic inclusive impression of
everything that has happened in the play. For the
play was designed for no other end than to express this:
and this final impression is the *form* which the accumulating substance has been forced to assume in our
minds by the art of the poet. In order to tell us what
his original intuition was, the poet has to expand it and
disintegrate it, and put it forth piece by piece in the
moments of his language; but he also had to be providing, all the while, for its eventual reintegration into
just the right harmony of total unified impression. If
he could have conveyed his original intuition instan-
taneously from his mind into ours, there would have
been no need for form, for unity would never have
been lost. When St. Lewis visited Frate Egidio, they
found it more satisfactory to converse directly, in a
silent ecstasy of communication, mind to mind, than to
discourse aloud; for that would have been, we are told,

"per lo difetto della lingua umana . . . piuttosto a sconsolazione che a consolazione."[1] But the art of poetry consists precisely in using "lo difetto della lingua umana," in order to get, in the final result, as near as possible to the effect of such immediate communication as passed without words between the king and the friar. If "lo difetto" did not exist, the art of poetry would not exist. Since language is the medium, the first thing that must happen is breakage of unity: and the final thing should be its restoration—as poetic form. And this is where we must look for the greatness of a poem.

There is a heresy, very prevalent nowadays, which goes clean against all this. It is the doctrine that poetry can only be lyrical; even epics and dramas, this doctrine supposes, can only justify themselves as poetry by their lyrical moments, their suddenly kindled raptures of imagination that detach themselves and escape from a non-lyrical purpose: a doctrine sometimes taken to its logical conclusion, that what we have been calling the form of such poems is properly to be regarded as a mere scheme for introducing lyrical moments, otherwise of no value as poetry. The opinion is not new; it was responsible for those odd compilations, once so popular in drawing-rooms, *Beauties of Shakespeare*, *Beauties of Spenser*, and the like. But it has lately taken on the airs of a dogma; and evidently it is related to the belief in "pure poetry," which I mentioned in my last lecture. We can, once more, leave out of

[1] *Fioretti*, XXXIV.

Greatness of Form

our discussion any temperamental preference for lyrics over epics and dramas; though we should expect that preference to follow, since the dogma can only allow form, in our sense of the word, when it is lyrical form.

It will be worth our while to look into this opinion; for it should enable us to see rather more clearly what it is we get, or are likely to get, from the *whole* effect of a poem as distinguisht from the incidental effect of its signal moments. I will take a very familiar instance of lyrical ecstasy soaring out of and, it may seem, away from a non-lyrical—in this case, a dramatic—purpose. Faustus, in despair of satisfying his heart with earthly pleasure, after the whole range of it has been offered to him by his infernal servants, summons the phantom of Helen. Every one knows how he greets the vision:

> Was this the face that launcht a thousand ships
> And burnt the topless towers of Ilium?

And so on: a flight of twenty lines into the supreme regions of poetry. Most noticeably, a lyrical moment! How it leaps out of its context, and makes a place of its own in our minds, sufficiently existing in its own perfection! If you learn those lines by heart, you can repeat them over and over again with endless pleasure, valuing them simply for themselves, as if they were a separate poem. Or apparently so: but is the passage really detachable from its context? Can you, for example, ever really forget that it is Faustus speaking to Helen? If so, surely you cripple the meaning; but if you remember that, surely also you go on to remember that it is Faustus adoring the beauty of a phantom with his feet on the brink of hell: the man who has sold himself to enjoy every bodily delight, every intellectual rapture mortality is capable of, finds that, for all the satisfaction his bargain has brought him, he might as well have stayed with *"on cai me on"* among his books; he it is who tries to lose his despair and "glut the longing of his heart's desire" by abandoning himself to beautiful illusion; and it is too late —Helen herself cannot distract him from the approaching doom.

No, you may say; this is to read too much into the passage. In the lines as they stand, secure in their own perfect achievement, Faustus has become Everyman; this lyrical moment simply exists as an instantaneous perfection of man's worship of woman's beauty. I would answer, that certainly, at this moment, Faustus has become Everyman; but without ceasing to be Faustus. For how is it that I can read all this into the passage as it stands in its own achievement? Why, because I also know how it stands in the achievement of the poem as a whole. The lines are magical in themselves; but they are much more magical in their place—in the particular context designed for them, for which they were designed. When the whole poem has completed itself in our minds, we have had their lyrical moment in all the splendour of its imagery and the intensity of its mood—in everything it can give us in itself, if it could be detacht; but super-added even to that, the moment has given us further beauty and significance by the way it has harmonised with the rest of the story. You cannot account for everything the lyrical moment accomplishes by regarding it simply as an individual moment, existing for its own sake; the exact rightness of its contribution to the whole event of the poem, itself adds a meaning to the moment; beauty and significance are reflected back into it by the passions and affairs to which it is linkt. To regard such a poem as *The Tragical History of Dr. Faustus* as justified merely by detachable lyrical moments, however splendid these may be, is to take the means for the end, to put substance above form; and that is to ignore a vital part of what the lyrical moments themselves have to say to us: for you cannot see all they mean until you can see their place and function in the whole poem. They exist for the sake of the poem's final impression; and by existing for that end they are impregnated by something more than their own individual and immediate beauty: they catch a glamour from the final organic beauty of the whole poem.

§ 2

This indicates more exactly the state of things we mean when we speak of a poem having form. We mean that, in the final impression made by the whole, every moment of the poem has become something more than its immediate self: every moment has affected us not only as itself, but as it contributes to the presiding characteristic unity of the whole. In this sense, every complete poem is some sort of a microcosm—its own peculiar sort: it is a perfect system of its own interrelationships: nothing is there that does not belong to everything else there—each for all and all for each: every element in the poem is a note or tone unmistakably helping to establish and characterise the full harmony of the poem as a single complexity of things. Ordinarily, if we follow up relationships in the world of everyday actuality, we find ourselves led endlessly on and on, out into interminable deserts. We find no finality, no terminal satisfaction, in our desire for *significance;* for the significance of a thing is nothing but the degree and manner of its relationship with other things. But in a poem, our sense of the significance of things comes full circle, and, while we remain in the poem, is complete. We possess a self-sufficient and self-contained satisfaction, and we are delighted with the consciousness of a world which is in boundaried and rounded perfection of accord with itself.

And thus, though every poem must be its own peculiar microcosm, it must also, by virtue of what we call its form, be some aspect, large or small, of a world eternal and universal: the ideal [1] world. For nothing can come under the rule of poetic form in an incoherent, and therefore an insignificant, manner: where everything is interrelated, everything must mean some-

---

[1] The word, of course, is not used in its strict philosophical sense: the ideal world here is universal because it is the world of a universal desire. But this does not exclude the philosophically ideal and universal; for it also is the world of the idea of law.

thing in terms of the whole. Chance, which is essentially incoherence and insignificance, can have no place there: we experience nothing that is not measured and orderly and lawful; and that is the experience which answers to our profoundest desires. When *poetry* achieves the perfection of its nature by becoming a *poem*, it cannot but be some revelation of the ideal world.

This is the world, then, in which the greatness of poetry will be found; and it is a world which is ideal in its condition rather than in its matter. We have seen what sort or condition of matter it is which gives us, in the *moments* of poetic experience, the accent or tone of greatness: it is matter so concentrated and organised as to effect an unusual richness and intensity of impression. Greatness itself must therefore be some establishment of the ideal world by means of such matter as this. When we have some notable range and variety of richly compacted experience brought wholly into the final harmony of complex impression given us by a completed poem, with its perfect system of significances uniting into one significance, then we may expect to feel ourselves in the presence of great poetry; and the greater the range, the richer the harmony of its total significance, and the more evident our sense of its greatness. A similar effect may be given by a *series* of poems, when some connexion of theme, in idea or mood, some relatedness in the kind of harmony effected over things, enables our minds to fuse the several impressions into one inclusive impression; but the effect can hardly be so decisive as when our minds are, without interruption, dominated by the single form of *one* poem.

We can see now what the length of a poem has to do with its greatness. Length in itself is nothing; but the plain fact is that a long poem, if it really is a poem (as for example *The Iliad* or *The Divine Comedy, Paradise Lost* or *Hamlet,* are poems), enables a remarkable range, not merely of experiences, but of *kinds* of experience, to be collected into single finality of harmonious impression: a vast plenty of things has been accepted as a single version of the ideal world, as a unity of significance. As far as unity is concerned, no less than as far as splendour of imagination is concerned, a sonnet by Wordsworth may be just as unmistakably an aspect of the ideal world; and it is a marvel, the range of matter in, for example, the sonnet to Toussaint l'Ouverture. But as for greatness, think for an instant of *The Iliad* as a whole, or *The Divine Comedy.* The thing simply is, that Homer and Dante can achieve an inclusive moment of final unity out of a whole series of moments as remarkable as that single one of Wordsworth's: obviously, then, irrespective of poetic quality as such, that final intricate harmony of theirs will be far richer, and so greater, than his—though by means of a unity far less direct than his, and a form less immediately impressive and therefore, no doubt, less lovely. [1]

[1] I might therefore have quite justifiably used a sonnet (one of Wordsworth's, for example, or Meredith's *Lucifer in Starlight*) as

Greatness of Form

§ 3

Just as the accent of greatness, then, is recognisable in those moments of poetic diction which give us the impression of unusually rich experience, so greatness itself will be a harmony effected by poetic form out of an unusually rich accumulation of such moments. It will be, that is to say, an unusual range and variety of experiences transmuted into a version of the ideal world —the world of things known and felt in perfect and satisfying significance. Such a version will, however, only differ from other versions in degree; all we can say at present is, that the greatest poetry will be that which represents something like the whole gamut of possible experience, and that this will become in our minds a single infinitely rich chord of harmony.

But there are two main moods, very different in kind, which may urge us thus to idealise our experience of life—to exalt the things of this world into the condition of a more desirable world, where nothing is out of relation with the rest and all is of assured significance to us. And poetry, in its larger scope, has chiefly accommodated itself to the requirements of these two moods; and has given us, in the result, what we may call the poetry of *refuge* on the one side, and of *interpretation* on the other. We have to decide now which

an instance in my first lecture of *momentary* greatness; just as the argument would have indemnified me for so using the *Ode to Anactoria* if it had existed as a whole, or Dante's *Cosí nel mio parlar* if I had used it as a whole.

The Idea of Great Poetry

of these two kinds is the more likely to effect greatness.

In either of them, we put our consciousness of life and of the world beyond the power of that senseless disaster, Chance: for there can be no feeling of chance in the experience which gives us what we long for above everything—manifest significance. But in this present world of everyday actuality, chance—the mere incoherence of things—plays, as far as we can make out, an unpleasantly important part. We may, therefore, wish to enter into poetry's perfected version of the world simply in order to *escape* from the harsh caprices of actuality. If so, we are not likely to welcome there any sharp reminder of those humiliations of our hopes and desires which make the events of life so strangely at odds with our sense of what ought to be; though, like captured enemies, they may certainly make a very satisfactory appearance, if they can be somehow robbed of their power. On the contrary, our sense of their power ought to be enhanced and intensified if, instead of requiring a world the perfection of which is to enable us to *forget* them, we require a world the perfection of which consists in enabling us to *understand* them—to force them to yield a *meaning* for us. Thus, the poetry which gives us an experience of things beyond the reach of misfortune, may either do so by offering us a *refuge* from it, or by offering us an *interpretation* of it.

Examples will best explain my meaning; though the aim of providing a refuge from the sense of the evils of life may seem to need little explanation. It has

Greatness of Form

often been deliberately adopted; and never more deliberately than by Boccaccio when he wrote his *Decameron*, which, for the purpose of such a discussion as this, can only be regarded as a poem—indeed, as one of the first poems of the world. It certainly starts off with a masterly and appalling description of pestilence: but that is only by way of an emphatic symbol of the meaningless griefs and injuries which rule the world we are leaving behind. And we go with the band of young men and maidens, escaping from the infected, disordered city, into ten days of delight in quiet gardens—feasting, singing, lute-playing, dancing, strolling and, above all, story-telling: and the world of bitter reality is effectually shut out and forgotten. Does that mean that we forget there are such things as sorrow and horror? By no means: many of Boccaccio's finest stories deal expressly with them. But he has the art to make them harmless. He induces in us a state of mind like that which Coleridge keenly notes in himself when, after a catalogue of the beauties of an evening landskip, he adds:

> I see them all so excellently fair;
> I see, not feel, how beautiful they are.

So, in Boccaccio's tragical stories, we *see* how terrible they are, but we do not *feel* it—or not very seriously. The sheer art of narrative is with him so stringent—he keeps so intent on the exquisite linkage of events, he draws the pattern of incidents with such delicious and alert precision—that even his ostensibly sorrowful tales are, like the comic and fantastic ones—*entertaining*.

But go from this *Decameron* world to the world of his younger contemporary, Chaucer, and you enter a region in which the art of poetry has taken on a different function. If Chaucer has a tragic story to tell, he uses no art to disinfect it of distress, to make you see sorrow without feeling it; his art is rather to make you feel what you see with unexpected poignancy—indeed, to make you feel more than you can possibly see. He may, in the end, reconcile you to the wound; but you are to feel the stab of it first.

But poetry is hardly an escape from the insistence of our everyday world when, instead of being concerned to make painful things pleasant, it seems rather concerned, if painful things must be dealt with, to sharpen the edge of them anew. But do they therefore remain merely painful? They do not: that is the important fact. Their emotional effect is not, as in the poetry of refuge, skilfully deflected towards an agreeable sense of things. On the contrary, it is kept ruthlessly and piercingly direct. And yet they occur in a world which, as a whole, including them and all the distress they carry, is somehow profoundly satisfactory: more satisfactory, perhaps, than any world can possibly be from which sorrowful things are excluded, or in which they are rendered harmless and entertaining. And it is satisfactory because these misfortunes have, within the nature of poetry, been given a meaning. This, then, is the poetry which

Greatness of Form

accepts the evils of life because it can interpret them.

But many of the most famous triumphs of poetry have been in building cities of refuge. That has not always been the poet's intention. *The Faerie Queene* may seem the very type of seclusion from the world. In no other poem can one so completely lose oneself in enchanted safety from the actual. Spenser certainly did not intend that; but his genius would not obey his intention. What he gave us is not, of course, really a poem at all, but rather an immense mound of poetry; for it is incomplete, and the form he intended for the whole can only be guessed at. Each book, however, is practically self-contained; and the sort of world he can transport us into is unmistakable everywhere. It is a serious world; when we take refuge in it, we are by no means giving ourselves over to careless fantasy. Few poets, indeed, have been able to modulate their verses into such a plangency of wistful pathos. And yet somehow it is all harmless; beauty and virtue in distress do not, in Spenser's images of them, really wound our emotions. For they are only images, not persons; they are the figures of an allegory. It is often supposed, that the allegory is so vast and complicated, and the imagery of its embodiment so delicately charming, that enjoyment would hardly survive the trouble of understanding it: we must look on the events simply as a magical phantasmagoria. That is not quite true. Certainly, when we hear of valour sending the groaning ghosts of his enemies to direful death, our interest is merely chilled when we understand that these are only the ghosts of moral abstractions allegorised.   And when we are able to see

> One in bright armes embatteiled full strong,
> That, as the sunny beames do glance and glide
> Upon the trembling wave, so shined bright
> And round about him threw forth sparkling fire,
> That seemd him to enflame on every side;

when we can watch the dazzling approach of this nobly-mounted knight, who

> prickt so fiers, that underneath his feete
> The smouldring dust did round about him smoke;

how have we improved our pleasure, by learning that this handsome figure is the emblem of a classified vice? Nevertheless, no one can read Spenser with any liveliness of attention and ignore his allegory altogether. That is where the universal sense of his incidents is placed.   It is always a moral sense; but the scale of moral values which he keeps so continually in use brings no sense of inexorable and necessary judgement, majestically presiding over human affairs.   It is a serious world, but there is a spell on it: a spell that effectually seals up any deep disturbance of our emotions, and leaves us free to enjoy, simply and equably.   Yes, in *The Faerie Queene* we can even enjoy moral values!

But the poetry of refuge has no need to keep clear of serious, or even of tragical matters, so long as the poet has the art to make them harmless.   The loveliest world poetry has ever attained to is the idyllic world of

228

Greatness of Form

Theocritus; a world which, after so many futile attempts to imitate it, we may judge to be inimitable. It was Theocritus who discovered the golden age. Before him, men had only heard about it; Theocritus discovered it in the only possible way: he created it. And the extraordinary thing is that he made it a *real* world. It is a world of reality enchanted. They are real people, these shepherds and goatherds who, the instant they meet at the spring, or under the pine tree, must challenge each other to a singing match. The art of their singing is faultless: not, we feel, because they are mere disguises of the poet, but because that is a talent real people have in the golden age. And their songs capture more of the joy of life, the inexplicable relish of earthly things, than any songs before or since. But seas and mountains and copses and flowering meadows and streams are not the only things that are familiarly radiant in their minds. They have seen the one-eyed giant sitting on the cliffs and lamenting his ugliness; they have seen the sea-nymph of his hopeless love rising mischievously out of the glittering shallows to pelt his dog with apples as it runs barking at the waves. And just as everybody to-day knows of Barbara Allen and Jemmy Green, and of her "Young man, I think you're dying"; so everybody in those days knew how Aphrodite herself, with the smile on her lips and the cruelty in her eyes, came to mock at the dying Daphnis. But they are real country people, for all that: they know their trades, and there is a rough side to their tongues. What is more to our purpose just now, they have their sorrows. But what sort of sorrow? Does it bring any discord into this enchanted world? Listen to the serenade of the distressed goat-herd:

Now I know Love. A cruel god is he: a she-lion's breasts
He sucked, and in a forest his mother nurtured him,
Since with slow fire he burns me thus, smiting me to the bone.

. . . .

O Misery! what will be my fate, poor wretch! Will you not
 answer?
I'll strip my cloak off and leap down to the waves from yonder
 cliff,
Whence Olpis the fisherman watches for tunny shoals:
And if I perish—well, at least that will be sweet to you.[1]

Doubtless he will not really kill himself; but he really is sorry for himself: his hopeless love has real and bitter pangs for him. But it is all of a piece with the world he is in—a world in which there is nothing but the beauty of things and the unending astonishment of beauty. Who would not wish to live in a world in which sorrow itself has become merely another form of beauty? There is no need for any reconciliation to it there; for it is sorrow which has been, like everything else in this world, enchanted; it has become harmless.

One more instance: escape from this too actual world of ours is not to be mistaken when it is a purely fantastic existence poetry catches us up into: some such dazzling region as that which Shelley contrived for his Witch

---

[1] R. C. Trevelyan's translation: for English felicity, and for closeness to the Greek, by far the best known to me.

of Atlas to play in. What power has the world of commonplace distractions over us, so long as we remain in a world where we can possess *an aviary of odours,*

> Clipt in a floating net, a love-sick fairy
> Had woven from dew-beams while the moon yet slept;
> As bats at the wired window of a dairy
> They beat their vans———?

But note: fantastic though it be, this version of the ideal world does not altogether omit the troublesome problems of our present world. Shelley was always a reformer, and his Witch must be a reformer too:

> And she would write strange dreams upon the brain
> Of those who were less beautiful, and make
> All harsh and crooked purposes more vain
> Than in the desert is the serpent's wake
> Which the sand covers—all his evil gain
> The miser in such dreams would rise and shake
> Into a beggar's lap;—the lying scribe
> Would his own lies betray without a bribe.
>
> .   .   .   .   .
>
> The soldiers dreamt that they were blacksmiths, and
> Walked out of quarters in somnambulism.
> Round the red anvils you might see them stand
> Like Cyclopses in Vulcan's sooty abysm
> Beating their swords to ploughshares;—in a band
> The jailors sent those of the liberal schism
> Free through the streets of Memphis; much, I wis,
> To the annoyance of King Amasis.

But the Witch's zeal for reform rouses in us no great sense of the scandals of actuality. It is all part of the dream; the Witch must have her pranks. Shelley, however, can give us an equally perfect instance of the other kind of poetry—the kind which I say interprets life. If ever there was an ideal world, it is the world of *Prometheus Unbound:* for it is a vision of the world purified. But the poem does not allow us to forget the shames and wrongs that infest this actual life; it enforces them on us; in order to reach the vision of their banishment, we have to pass through the magnificent agonies of the First Act. Here, if anywhere in poetry, we may experience *ideal evil:* in a symbolism which condenses the whole possibility of evil into an elemental and original malignity:

> *Prometheus:*   Horrible forms,
>   What and who are ye? . . .
>   Whilst I behold such execrable shapes,
>   Methinks I grow like what I contemplate,
>   And laugh and stare in loathsome sympathy.
> *1st Fury:* We are the ministers of pain and fear
>   And disappointment and mistrust and hate
>   And clinging crime: and as lean dogs pursue
>   Through wood and lake some struck and sobbing fawn,
>   We track all things that weep and bleed and live. . . .
> *Prometheus:* Can aught exult in its deformity?
> *2nd Fury:* The beauty of delight makes lovers glad,
>   Gazing on one another: so are we.
>   As from the rose which the pale priestess kneels
>   To gather for her festal crown of flowers,
>   The aëreal crimson falls, flushing her cheek,
>   So from our victim's destined agony
>   The shade which is our form invests us round
>   Else we are shapeless as our mother Night.

In very few poets has imagination towered to such a height of speculation as the First Act of *Prometheus Unbound.* But what is it that urges Shelley's mind

thus to concentrate into living form the sense of everything he hates? Prometheus is the power of love:
Prometheus Bound is the world as it is—love helpless
in the power of evil. The conclusion of the poem is
the resolution of this discord into the perfect harmony
of love triumphant and the power of evil destroyed—
Prometheus Unbound. Here is the reformer, not now
escaping from his own impotence into day-dreams of
the Witch of Atlas and her pranks, but piercing himself with a white-hot sense of all the injuries and im-
becilities life must suffer, for the very purpose of convincing himself that a reality above all this must surely
be destined to descend at last into being, and replace
these purposeless miseries. It cannot be (he tells us
in effect) that life is to be forever so hideously pestered; since what chiefly suffers in it is the very power
that can cure all ills: let but love awake, and remember
its strength, and all the infinite persecution man has
suffered from the world will fall away like the terror
of a dream:

> The loathsome mask has fallen, the man remains
> Sceptreless, free, uncircumscribed, but man
> Equal, unclassed, tribeless, and nationless,
> Exempt from awe, worship, degree, the king
> Over himself; just, gentle, wise: but man
> Passionless; not yet free from guilt or pain,
> Which were, for his will made or suffered them,
> Nor yet exempt, though ruling them like slaves,
> From chance and death and mutability,
> The clogs of that which else might oversoar
> The loftiest star of unascended heaven,
> Pinnacled dim in the intense inane.

The Idea of Great Poetry

That, at any rate, is the main theme of the poem; and it will serve as an instance of what I mean by the poetry of interpretation. Why do I call it that? Is it because it is the poetry of a reformer, who offers some explanation of life's evils, and a remedy for them? In that case, the value of the poem would depend on the value we attach to the explanation and the remedy; if we cannot agree with them, then clearly Shelley, as far as we are concerned, is no interpreter. But no one need accept his belief that love will prove a sufficient cure for human imbecility, nor even his belief that human imbecility is curable at all. And the notion that mortal affairs will ever be "perfected," in the sense that evil will cease to contaminate them and will leave man as he ought to be—"just, gentle, wise": this is a very romantic notion. The beliefs which inspired Shelley have, in fact, no more (though also no less) importance than Milton's resolve to "justify the ways of God to men" in *Paradise Lost*. Milton can scarcely be held to have made out this justification; that resolve of his has merely an historical or psychological interest. And yet the poem which it inspired is one of the greatest and noblest interpretations of life that have ever been achieved.

But in looking for such power of interpretation as poetry may be allowed to have, we must not be led outside the nature of the art: we must not let it depend on the validity of any doctrine, idea, or explanation of life. Many poets, indeed, set out to tell us, dogmatically and decisively, what life means. But what a poet may set out to do is no great matter to us; our concern is, what he actually did. Shelley has his doctrine, and passionately expounds it. But to what result? That need not depend on our belief in it; it need not even depend on the fact that his doctrine is pleasant enough to be accepted provisionally. A similar result is just as notable in the poetry of Leopardi: the result of an equally passionate exposition of a doctrine which few would call pleasant.

About the time when Shelley was making Prometheus the symbol of man's eventual perfection through love, and of the sacred spirit in man which meanwhile, tortured but unsubdued, endures the alien tyranny of evil; Leopardi was making of Prometheus quite another sort of symbol: the symbol of man's baseless pretension to goodness or even to any importance at all, and the symbol of Leopardi's own bitter amusement at man's regard for himself. The muses, he tells us, had offered prizes in heaven for the most useful inventions; and the prizes had gone to Bacchus for wine, to Minerva for oil, and to Vulcan for a brass saucepan. These were awards which the gods could understand. But to everyone's surprise, Prometheus complains that no notice has been taken of *his* invention—Man. He puts an extraordinary value on this darling invention of his; and to make it out, carries Momus as referee down to earth on a tour of inspection. But the truth about man does not quite come up to Prometheus' assertions. I give the first incident of the tour, and the last, as specimens of

The Idea of Great Poetry

Leopardi's image of life. The celestial travellers land first in the new world, to inspect man as the noble savage. They find a chieftain outside his hut, surrounded by the ceremonial reverence of his tribe. Prometheus pleasantly asks him, what he is doing.

Chieftain: Eating, as you may see.

Prometheus: You have something good to eat?

Chieftain: Passable: a trifle of flesh-meat.

Prometheus: Butcher's meat, or game?

Chieftain: You might call it butcher's meat: a domestic animal, anyway: my son, in fact.

Prometheus: What, was your son a calf?

Chieftain: A calf? No, a son like any other man's son.

Prometheus: You can't mean that? Are you eating your own flesh?

Chieftain: My own flesh? No, I'm eating my son's flesh. It was just for this I got him, and took care to feed him up.

Prometheus: In order to eat him?

Chieftain: What's surprising in that? And his mother too, as she must be past child-bearing by now, I expect I shall be eating her soon.

After a little more of this, Prometheus notices the amorous way the noble savages peruse his own limbs, and thinks it advisable to inspect some more cultured kind of men. Momus, of course, is highly delighted: and continues to have the same sort of pleasure during the whole tour; for Prometheus' invention does nothing but let him down. At last they arrive at the climax of civilisation, London. A crowd in front of a house rouses their curiosity. They go in, and find, in a room full of police and lawyers and servants, a man lying on a bed with his two boys beside him. They learn

that the man first shot the boys and then himself.
Prometheus is interrogating a footman:

Prometheus: Killed himself and his children, you say? What terrible misfortune had befallen him?

Footman: None that I know of.

Prometheus: He had squandered all his money, perhaps, or was universally despised for something, or disappointed in love, or had lost his place at court?

Footman: Not at all: as wealthy as you please, and very well thought of; love was nothing to him, and he stood high at court.

Prometheus: Then what made him do such a desperate thing as this?

Footman: He was bored—tired of life, according to a letter he left behind him.

Prometheus: And he had no friend or relation to whose care he could have bequeathed these unhappy children, instead of slaughtering them?

Footman: O yes he had; in fact, to the person who was most nearly related to him, he did bequeath the care of his dog.

That is the gamut of life, in Leopardi's version of it. Natural man breeds children for food; civilised man shoots his children to secure them from a life which is, possibly, good enough for dogs. This is the prose—the exquisitely ferocious prose-comedy—of Leopardi's image of life. In his poetry, the same governing idea prevails; and in a grandeur and dignity of utterance hardly to be equalled outside Dante. In his astonishing chorus of mummies, the quiet of death is only stirred by vague memories of that nightmare, life; in the moonlight song of his Scythian Shepherd, the ceaseless workings of the things of heaven and earth, always returning in their circular motion to the

The Idea of Great Poetry

starting-place, is as useless and fruitless as the vapid circulation of human affairs. And so on. There is nothing of Leopardi's which is not governed by this idea of *pessimism*, as it is usually called—of disillusioned clairvoyance, as it might be called. English critics, unable to resist the splendour of Leopardi's art, think themselves bound to reprove the idea which rules it. But we have nothing to do now with the truth or untruth of his idea; what concerns us is the use he makes of it. How can this be said to be in any way similar to the use Shelley makes of *his* doctrine?

Why, the thing simply is, that whatever we may think of Shelley's and Leopardi's idea of life, the poets themselves each passionately believed in his own idea. Nay, they lived in it: it was the manner of their consciousness. By means of it, they collected and organised the multitudinous confusion of life in this world into an ordered harmony of experience; and out of their vivid sense of this harmony sprang their poetry.

And this is the poetry of interpretation. To understand why it is that we need not trespass beyond the nature of the art. There are poets who cannot endure to think of the evil in life without feeling themselves able to say why it is there: such poets as Milton and Dante. The value of this for us is that it enables these poets to take up the whole generality of life into their poetry. But there are also the poets—Shakespeare and Homer are the instances now—who can do that without, as far as we can make out, needing any explanation at

Greatness of Form

all. In either case the result for us is the same. When, by whatever means, some sense of the whole possibility of life—its good and its evil, its joys and its misfortunes—is presented under the condition of poetry, it becomes *thereby* an interpretation of life.

And that must be understood in a way independent of any particular explanations, moralisings or consolations: understood in a way strictly within the conditions of poetic art. The poet, by the incantation of his language, makes his world ours: his experience becomes ours; and if this has achieved the perfection we call a poem, it has become some participation in the ideal world. For it will have achieved a perfect coherence and interrelation of its parts, however various, into organic unity; nothing is there which is not necessary to the whole; nothing can happen without reference to all the rest: the sense of this inheres in the very manner of our experience. This is the kind of experience which we most desire; for it is wholly an affair of measure and order and law. Nothing is in it which does not carry significance; for everything *means* the whole of our consciousness: and the significance of the whole is the designed and finite harmony, the focussed shapeliness of the whole.

Now when the matter of such experience is something like the whole possibility of life, then we have the poetry of interpretation: then we have the experience which, without needing explanation, can make the evil of life as well as the good, its sorrow as well as its joy, somehow satisfactory: for evil itself must then

The Idea of Great Poetry

come to us in some profound and necessary relation with everything else: its presence is altogether in accordance with the law of the whole. Or, if the poet has an explanation, that is only his means of organising his sense of the utmost range of life into steady unity.

It must now be quite clear, that the poetry of interpretation cannot but be greater than the poetry of refuge; for the harmony it effects cannot but be a fuller and richer version of life. The poetry of refuge need not exclude the sorrowful side of things; but it must make of this a mere innocent apparition. It is always therefore a version of life made under a certain selective imitation. But no poetry can be said to interpret life, unless it includes the afflictions as well as the delights, and urges them into their fullest emotional realisation. The poetry of refuge harmonises life by leaving out or modifying the discordant tones; the poetry of interpretation brings them in and insists on them, because it can resolve them into an ultimate harmony. The world of poetic interpretation is, then, the world of great poetry; and it is more than a jingle of words to say, that the greatness of poetry is the greatness of its significance. For this means that its greatness is the greatness of the scope of its unifying harmony.

There are degrees of this, of course. Why is not Shelley's poetry as great as Shakespeare's, Leopardi's as great as Dante's? The answer is simply this: both Shelley and Leopardi employ, for focussing the whole range of life into shapely coherence, a certain limited definiteness of idea; and in consequence their representative version of life is neither as large nor as richly substantiated as that of the poet who can achieve as harmonious a result with less selection. We must therefore now go on to a more detailed examination of the way in which poetic harmony of experience may be attained.

LECTURE III

IDEAS AND PERSONS

§ 1

I said that Shelley and Leopardi, with their astonishingly different ideas of life, both achieved, by means of them, a similar result: and that was a certain unity of experience, which enabled their poetry to present, as a single rich harmony of complete significance or manifest interrelation, something typical of the whole range of life, its evil as well as its good. This does not mean that such a unity is always of the same kind. Its similarity lies simply in the fact that it always makes on us some impression of greatness. But there may be as many different kinds of harmony as of individual minds; the kind will depend not only on the particular experiences it includes, but also on the kind of idea which enables it to be inclusive at all. Great poetry will always be individual in one aspect, and universal in another.

But the idea itself may vary infinitely. It may be a definite moral, theological or philosophical *explanation* of life; or we may be unable to define it as anything more than a dominant *sense* of life, an habitual mode of experience. It may also be something less definable still, in any intellectual terms, and yet, as we shall see, even more potently efficacious as an intensification of some large variety of life into harmonised singleness of vivid, complete, final expression, or *greatness*. But before approaching that, I wish to illustrate the way a presiding sense of life may exert its power of focussing the whole scope of a poet's experience. I will begin with the poet who was capable, perhaps, of a larger interpretation of life than any other in our modern literature—Wordsworth. To *The Prelude*, to which I shall chiefly allude, he gave, as second title, *Growth of a Poet's Mind*. From our present point of view we might call it *Growth of the Conditions of Great Poetry;* for the process it describes is the expanding mastery of a dominant idea, and its eventual power of holding everything life can offer in an organic interrelationship and coherence.

It is not my business to formulate Wordsworth's "philosophy." There may be something in him you can call a philosophy, though only if you rather stretch the meaning of the word. But there is obviously and very grandly in him a genius for living significantly, a power of presiding over a full harmony of things, of ordering everything he knows into one consistent and characteristic manner of experience: and of giving it irresistible expression in poetry. He did not, as Goethe did, regard nature as the garment of eternal spirit; nature was, for Wordsworth, the very life and action of eternal spirit. Once let humanity come in as part of nature, and nothing, in such a habit of experience, can remain discordant: all must at last resolve into final harmony. This is what we mean by Wordsworth's interpretation of life. I do not stop to enquire whether "pantheism" is the right name for his ruling idea; I do not ask whether, as philosophers, we accept it or decline it. My concern is with what it did for Wordsworth, and for the world it organised round him, and can continually organise: with the interpretation it effected for him and for us, within the bounds of poetry; that is to say, with the shapeliness of the design it induced his world to become, that satisfying and greatly ordered design which is its own significance, and a type of the ideal. I must illustrate in its gradual enlargement the kind of harmony which Wordsworth's ruling idea enables his sum of things to impress on us, when his language can enchant our minds with the finest and deepest motions of his spirit.

He must first become vividly *conscious* of the characteristic manner of life which his mind has insensibly assumed. He shows us this happening in a famous passage, in which like magic the subtlety of the art keeps its workmanship in that exquisite precision we call restraint. It happens in response to, and so overcomes, the shock of an early sense of disharmony in things: it is when his boyhood first realised the presence of death in the world, and the blank ending of such vigors and delights as his own. This is not when he saw the grappling irons bring up the drowned corpse, and

Ideas and Persons

> the dead man, 'mid that beauteous scene
> Of trees and hills and water, bolt upright
> Rose, with his ghastly face;

the mere spectacle of death to him, "a child not nine years old," was nothing appalling: his inner eye, he tells us, "had seen such sights before." No; it was when he brooded over the grave of the boy he had known so well and played with so often: then it was he realised the depth of his own marvellous feeling for the living earth, and consciously took possession of it, by projecting it into the memory of the lost companion:

> There was a Boy: ye knew him well, ye cliffs
> And islands of Winander!—many a time
> At evening, when the earliest stars began
> To move along the edges of the hills,
> Rising or setting, would he stand alone
> Beneath the trees or by the glimmering lake.

Then follows the thrilling description of the owls hooting—"quivering peals and long halloos and screams"—in answer to the boy's mimicry: and how the "concourse wild of jocund din" would suddenly fall silent:

> Then sometimes, in that silence while he hung
> Listening, a gentle shock of mild surprise
> Has carried far into his heart the voice
> Of mountain torrents; or the visible scene
> Would enter unawares into his mind,
> With all its solemn imagery, its rocks,
> Its woods, and that uncertain heaven, received
> Into the bosom of the steady lake.

The Idea of Great Poetry

This boy was taken from his mates, and died
In childhood, ere he was full twelve years old.
Fair is the spot, most beautiful the vale
Where he was born; the grassy churchyard hangs
Upon a slope above the village school,
And through that churchyard when my way has led
On summer evenings, I believe that there
A long half-hour together I have stood
Mute, looking at the grave in which he lies.

But his boyhood knew of discords in its world stranger and perhaps even more penetrating than this: discords with the accent in them of a nameless primitive terror, suggesting in the midst of his familiar delight some insufferable discrepancy. One summer evening, he was rowing on the lake: in recounting the incident, Wordsworth characteristically notes that it was "an act of stealth and troubled pleasure." The careless reader might suppose this to be the moralist speaking; but of course it is the psychologist—the profound and subtle psychologist who had just achieved that misprized masterpiece, *Peter Bell*. Without doubt, the mood in which the affair began had a good deal to do with its sinister ending: the grown-up psychologist could see the necessary coherence where the imaginative boy felt himself mysteriously haunted; and it is only with the boy we are concerned. He is rowing with his eyes fixed

Upon the summit of a craggy ridge,
The horizon's utmost boundary; far above
Was nothing but the stars and the grey sky . . .
When, from behind that craggy steep till then
The horizon's bound, a huge peak, black and huge,

246

Ideas and Persons

As if with voluntary power instinct,
Upreared its head. I struck and struck again,
And growing still in stature the grim shape
Towered up between me and the stars, and still,
For so it seemed, with purpose of its own
And measured motion like a living thing,
Strode after me.

The impression was so strong on him that, he tells us,

for many days my brain
Worked with a dim and undetermined sense
Of unknown modes of being; o'er my thoughts
There hung a darkness, call it solitude
Or blank desertion. No familiar shapes
Remained, no pleasant images of trees,
Of sea or sky, no colours of green fields;
But huge and mighty forms, that do not live
Like living men, moved slowly through the mind
By day, and were a trouble to my dreams.

These nameless fears could be nothing but benefit
in the end; they could only urge his strengthening
mind to enlarge the habitual manner of its experience,
and thus dissolve all sense of fearful incoherence in
nature. Unknown modes of being? It is all an unknown mode, in the sense of being inexplicably *here:*
but it is all *one* mode, it all belongs unmistakably to
one vast coherence of being, it is all everywhere alive
and sentient with the single spirit of the whole of
things:

To every natural form, rock, fruits, or flower,
Even the loose stones that cover the high way,
I gave a moral life: I saw them feel,

247

The Idea of Great Poetry

Or linked them to some feeling: the great mass
Lay bedded in a quickening soul, and all
That I beheld respired with inward meaning.

"I gave a moral life": by what authority? Is it only the personal mind that confers its specious unity on the else unreasoned multitude of things? So Wordsworth's mind turns in upon itself, and engages with the mystery there. And to save him from failure in this crucial test—from failure to maintain an harmonious experience just when a completely inclusive harmony was most required—"rose from the mind's abyss" *Imagination,*

the Power so called
Through sad incompetence of human speech;

the imagination which is the mind's ambassador to *infinitude,* "our destiny, our being's heart and home": which is our sole commerce with that which cannot be limited even by its own existence, but is "something evermore *about to be.*" In the power of this imagination the mind is

blest in thoughts
That are their own perfection and reward,
Strong in herself and in beatitude
That hides her, like the mighty flood of Nile
Poured from his fount of Abyssinian clouds
To fertilize the whole Egyptian plain.

And so we find it: the full diapason of this imaginative power follows, in a strain of sublime confidence in the harmony of earthly things which cannot easily be paralleled. It is Imagination, the authentic interpreter, that has brought all the brute turbulence of things into the living shapeliness of a single masterful manner of grandly ordered experience. In the Alpine pass, absolute illumination suddenly possesses him; this earth is the very presence of eternal spirit: *that* is the unity of nature:

> The immeasurable height
> Of woods decaying, never to be decayed,
> The stationary blasts of waterfalls,
> And in the narrow rent at every turn
> Winds thwarting winds, bewildered and forlorn,
> The torrents shooting from the clear blue sky,
> The rocks that muttered close upon our ears,
> Black drizzling crags that spake by the wayside
> As if a voice were in them, the sick sight
> And giddy prospect of the raving stream,
> The unfettered clouds and region of the Heavens,
> Tumult and peace, the darkness and the light—
> Were all like workings of one mind, the features
> Of the same face, blossoms upon one tree;
> Characters of the great Apocalypse,
> The types and symbols of Eternity,
> Of first, and last, and midst, and without end.

But there can be no pause here. When the rapture of this attainment is quieted, the mystery of the earth has indeed been relieved, and leaves the mind free to enjoy tranquillity. But it is still nature—the life and beauty of the earth—which chiefly engages his spirit; the life of man is rather assumed to belong to this harmony than actually wrought into it, in

The Idea of Great Poetry

> that blessed mood
> In which the burthen of the mystery,
> In which the heavy and the weary weight
> Of all this unintelligible world
> Is lightened . . .
> While with an eye made quiet by the power
> Of harmony, and the deep power of joy,
> We see into the life of things.

But there must be no hint of discord between this beautiful harmony of nature and "the still sad music of humanity": else will the mystery roll thundering down again ten times more formidable than before. Man must be one with nature: there must be not only no discrepancy between man's life and nature's life, there must be no division between them, in the manner of the poet's experience of them. The whole effort of man, to evil no less than to good,—even "man arrayed for mutual slaughter,"—must, like nature, be the revealed presence of eternal spirit: so certainly, that it will be, for him, the mere utterance of a truism, to say "Carnage is God's daughter." It will be the end of youthful delights:

> That time is past
> And all its aching joys are now no more,
> And all its dizzy raptures. Not for this
> Faint I, nor mourn nor murmur;

ecstatic communing with the earth gives place to the more difficult joy of understanding man, and of taking the misery of his discordant mind up into an ultimate harmony:

Ideas and Persons

And I have felt
A presence that disturbs me with the joy
Of elevated thoughts: a sense sublime
Of something far more deeply interfused,
Whose dwelling is the light of setting suns,
And the round ocean and the living air,
And the blue sky, *and in the mind of man;*
A motion and a spirit, that impels
All thinking things, all objects of all thought,
And rolls through all things.

"The mind of man!"—that is the region to which the mature Wordsworth must return in order to have the whole possibility of his life ruled by his presiding genius, caught up into a single stedfast manner of experience,—"my haunt, and the main region of my song." He frees himself from all wistful regrets; those earlier raptures, when mountains became alive and rocks "spake by the wayside," are included in a larger ecstasy: his spirit has arrived at its loftiest, most dangerous, and most triumphant exultation in its own power.

For I must tread on shadowy ground, must sink
Deep, and aloft ascending breathe in worlds
To which the heaven of heavens is but a veil. . . .
All strength—all terror, single or in bands,
That ever was put forth in personal form—
Jehovah—with his thunder, and the choir
Of shouting Angels, and the empyreal thrones—
I pass them unalarmed. Not Chaos, not
The darkest pit of lowest Erebus,
Nor aught of blinder vacancy, scooped out
By help of dreams—can breed such fear and awe
As fall upon us often when we look

251

The Idea of Great Poetry

Into our Minds, into the Mind of Man—
My haunt, and the main region of my song.

Without this final mastery, his experience could not have completed the harmony of its world. Nay, all the ideal loveliness man ever conceived—"Paradise, and groves Elysian"—is conditional on this conquest of the mind; there is for Wordsworth no security of satisfaction, no certain banishment of "the fierce confederate storm of sorrow," until, in words "which speak of nothing more than what we are," he has been able to proclaim

How exquisitely the individual Mind
(And the progressive powers perhaps no less
Of the whole species) to the external World
Is fitted:—and how exquisitely, too—
Theme this but little heard of among men—
The external World is fitted to the Mind.

He never accomplished this noble purpose: indeed, in the prosaic tone of those last lines, we may *hear* his failure. He never achieved the poem to which he devoted his long and arduous contemplation: the poem which was to declare the World and the Mind as the two faculties of one being, the two real aspects necessary to ideal perfection: the harmony of infinite spirit with personal experience, of the things of eternity with the things of time. In that respect, if we make exception of one poem, Wordsworth must be considered to have failed. In moments, and in many moments, he is as great as any one; and when we re-

member them, we must certainly make him the third
of English poets. Owing to the peculiarity of his
genius, he reaches greatness chiefly by showing us, with
amazingly keen intuition, the conditions and sources
of his own greatness. Even so, I have had to choose
from several poems, in order to make out anything
like a full account of his achievement. He never
accomplished the complete existence of his characteristic harmony of experience in the impression of a
single work of art: as Shelley, relying on a much less
potent idea, did in *Prometheus Unbound*. That is to
say, he never brought to perfection the whole life of
his idea of things. But he came very near it once:
and perhaps this partial achievement of Wordsworth's
is the greatest thing in modern poetry; it is surely
the loftiest. Is there, outside Milton and Dante, anything really comparable with the *Ode on the Intima-
tions of Immortality?* The theme is a peculiarly spe-
cialised version of his dominant idea: but the form it
gives to the process of the idea's continually widening
power, and to the growth of its harmony over the
whole discord of personal life in an impersonal world,
makes it, at any rate, the height of modern poetic art
in English. Who else has found such security of harmony in such a range of experience? Who else has
mastered English to such breadth and yet such rarefac-
tion of power, to such a nicety and to such a grandeur
of proportion, as in the *Ode?* No wonder this poet
could, in *Michael* and *The Brothers*, in *Resolution and
Independence* and the beginning of *The Excursion*,

present the undeserved sorrows, the hopeless endurances of life, in such an aspect of deep serene significance.

§ 2

The *Ode* notwithstanding—for there, as I say, he considerably narrowed his idea of life—Wordsworth never achieved what he ought to have achieved. He can show us better than any one else what a great poet's governing sense of life should be, and how it should effect its government; and the result is supremely great *poetry*. What we miss in him is the supremely great *poem;* and we have only to mention Milton and Dante again to remind ourselves of what this means. We may perhaps admire Wordsworth's idea of life more than theirs: but, once more, it is not the idea itself, but what is done with it, that matters, as far as *poetic* greatness is concerned. Far less potent ideas than Wordsworth's have, by coming to the full perfection of their power in single poems, achieved greater *art* than anything of his except the *Ode;* for they not only focus into one intense impression the whole life of their idea, but also—and infinitely more important— the significance of everything that substantiates the idea: the significance that comes from the mere fact of existing in a single ordered coherence of experience —in the *form* of a poem.

An idea need not be universally admirable in order to have the power of collecting into the harmony of its own complete expression such a range of things as is required for the quality of greatness in a poem. A good instance of this is *The Wisdom of Solomon*. Many interesting things could be said of it outside our present purpose. It is the work of an Alexandrian Jew—a Jew, that is, who lived in Hellenism: and there is continually in it either the fusion or the hostility of two cultures. The difficulty of translating poetry which weds the cloudy storms of Hebrew imagination to the finest subtleties of Greek literary craftsmanship perhaps accounts for a certain deliberation in the splendours of the Authorised Version here: we feel a consciously achieved magnificence, or at least a carefully wrought distinction, very different from the spontaneous grandeur of the English Old Testament. The rhythm of the original, a sort of free verse, belonging to no assignable pattern, yet always forming itself into distinct and noticeable cadences, also no doubt represents a fusion of two nations, and an extraordinarily interesting one: it is everything Whitman's free verse wanted to be. But what is more important for our purpose is the fact that the rhapsodical abundance of the Oriental is throughout governed by Greek lucidity and reason. The prodigal energy which seems always in revolt against capture into exact expression, the passion for parallelisms and amplifications, the explosions into lyrical and homiletic digression and lampooning apologue, cannot dislocate the strong outline and continuous process of the whole: it is Greek in being a work of art, a thing of symmetry and ordered design:

The Idea of Great Poetry

it gives, in fact, to its turbulent matter that singleness of complex existence which we call a poem.

And it is out of the co-existence of two nationalities in one mind that the motive of the poem proceeds. The Jew is steeped in Greek civilisation. He accepts and relishes the method of Greek speculation, he delights in the loveliness and nobility with which Greek language has empowered his spirit. But always at the core of his Alexandrian citizenship he remains a Jew, conscious of the divine election of his race. He cannot, like his Palestinian brother, ignore the force of the Greek ideal, nor the beauty and reality of its success. And yet, as one of the chosen people, in the midst of it he is an alien; and he cannot avoid the contrast between the Jew's sense of God's election and the gentile sense of success in this world. Why do not the people of God's choice thrive, in the world He has made, like the mere gentiles? His answer is, that the gentile success is nothing but a misunderstanding: "unnurtured souls have erred"; the more completely it works itself out in their lives, the more completely they devote themselves to ultimate destruction.

For what is the central fact in the world of the gentiles? It is death. But "God made not death." It belongs to the mere appearance of things. But the heathen, by believing in death, made it real: they "made a covenant with it, because they are worthy to take part with it." If death be the prime reality of the world, the heathen values follow as reasonable and even necessary. "Let us fill ourselves with costly wine and ointments: and let no flower of the spring pass by us." It becomes, indeed, worth while to make a success of this present world; but to do so, Might must be Right, and the just man must be the powerful man: "let our strength be the law of justice: for that which is feeble is found to be nothing worth." And this uneasy ethic must be quick to defend itself: "let us lie in wait for the righteous, because he is not for our turn, and he is clean contrary to our doings . . . He is grievous unto us even to behold."

By making his values depend on death, the gentile admittedly makes the most of this mortal world, if this world be all. What can the Jew oppose to it? Some idea, evidently, in which this world is not all. The author finds this in the idea of Wisdom. Those who make Wisdom, and not death, the prime reality of the world will find themselves at last vindicated. Not that they will be preserved from death; but short life in the knowledge of Wisdom is better than long life governed by values adjusted to the false reality of death. The servants of Wisdom may be few and oppressed, but their triumph will come; and their success is not to be measured by the way it occupies the time of this world. The heathen shall at last see that and confess it; and death, by deceiving them, will then indeed be the calamity and damnation they sought to avoid. The superb visions of Jewry triumphant and the heathen in perdition bring the preliminary matter of the poem to an admirably effective close, and at the same time prepare us, in the manner of perfectly assured art, for the full development of mood and idea in the noble wealth of imagery and the swiftly changing emotions that follow.

Wisdom is no perfection of the intellectual man; it is no sort of exercise of human nature at all. It is an energy pouring into the world from beyond it, vivifying it and disposing it: "more moving than any motion." When it visits the mind of man, it is not merely government there, but the bestowal of knowledge of itself, as "the breath of the power of God, the brightness of the everlasting light." Wisdom is sometimes the name for the spirit of divine activity, sometimes for man's sense of this; and often the two meanings combine. When he is speaking of Wisdom as the executant of God's will, the poet can summon up a picture as direct as anything in Homer:

> For while all things were in quiet silence, and that night was in the midst of her swift course, thine Almighty word leaped down from heaven out of thy royal throne, as a fierce man of war into the midst of a land of destruction, and brought thine unfeigned commandment as a sharp sword, and standing up filled all things with death; and it touched the heaven, but it stood upon the earth.

But the grandest and most characteristic passages are those whirlwinds of vision which leave us almost bewildered by the fury of their surprising imagination, and yet in clear possession of the author's impassioned sense of Wisdom always manifesting itself in human nature and human events. The Jews, as the children of Wisdom, need not condemn this world, for all their disadvantage in it, as mere deceit and illusion. God has chosen their race to be his friends; and therefore they have Wisdom, and know what his actions mean— the actions which we call the world; they know that these actions are not all there is to be known: they have an intimacy with the Person behind and within these actions—the intimacy which alone can make them intelligible and coherent. Only because they have been so chosen for the friendship of God can they possess his Wisdom; and only because they have his Wisdom in their minds can they understand his actions. But the heathen can never really understand his actions. At best they are like the common run of ordinary folk trying to make out the character of a statesman. They have nothing to go on but the mere spectacle of his public life; but they make a sort of synthesis of this after their own fashion and call it his policy; and from his policy again, and the purpose they suppose in it, they deduce the man himself, and make to their own satisfaction an image of his personal character; and it is all ludicrously and hopelessly wrong, as those few know (and only they *can* know) who have been admitted to the statesman's friendship and know him in his private life.

There is such a thing, in fact, as natural religion; and it is this sort of thing. It is the religion of the best of the gentiles; but it is nothing more than a painful synthesis of God's public acts, and can never yield a true knowledge of God himself—a sense of the personality of God. Is it the gentiles' fault? The poet is not concerned with that; he is sometimes quite astonisht that natural religion should fail so completely, however sincere and reasonable; but all he is concerned to know is that his people alone have been chosen by God to be his friends; and therefore they alone have Wisdom, and the secret of God's personal purpose in the world. There is, indeed, along with natural religion, a natural wisdom; it is no more than an honest skill in the mere matter of things, but eternal Wisdom has a certain sympathy for it. It is the best thing the gentiles possess, but as far below the Wisdom of the Jews as natural religion is below election to the friendship of God. The poet instances boat-building and seamanship; and in a strain of ferocious amusement contrasts this natural wisdom with the capital imbecility—and that is as much as to say the capital sin —of idolatry. If a man must say his prayers to woodwork, why not choose such beneficently skilful woodwork as a seaworthy ship, rather than the skilful folly of a coloured figure? And his satire proceeds to give, still with amused contempt, and perhaps for the first time, a rational explanation of idolatry.

So, after largely expounding what Wisdom is, and the understanding of this troublesome world which it confers on the chosen people, the poet goes on to expound what Wisdom does, and the fortune it confers on the chosen people by its management of events. The magnificent rhapsody on the history of Jewry shows all this nameless poet's astonishing power. It is, as it were, the secret history of things; it shows us not the process of events as the gentiles see it, but as the privileged Hebrew understanding sees into it; for only the Jewish mind inspired by Wisdom as divine instruction can see how mysteriously Wisdom, as the divine energy of things, favours the Jewish nation. A noble metaphor, at first only suggested, and at last proclaimed with unforgettable force, elaborates this. Just as death, the calamity of the heathen, is a blessing to the Jews—"in the sight of the unwise they seemed to die . . . but they are in peace,"—so "the whole creature" might be changed, "serving the peculiar commandments, that thy children might be kept without hurt. . . . Where water stood before, dry land appeared . . . and out of the violent stream a green field." Things are made harmful and appalling to the enemies of the Jews even while the Jews are going unscathed through the midst of them: "for them the bitings of grasshoppers and flies killed, neither was there found any remedy for their life; . . . but thy sons not the very teeth of venomous dragons overcame. . . . For the creature that serveth thee, who art the Maker, increaseth his strength against the unrighteous for their punishment, and abateth his strength for the benefit of such as put their trust in thee."

Wisdom holds the world like a psaltery, and on its elements and forces can play comfortable or terrible chords. The instrument is the same, and the player is the same; but the mood of the player changes with those for whom he plays; and from the same events he may bring fearful music for the heathen, and then, turning to the Jews, melody like heaven opening. The grand type of this, and of all Wisdom's disposal of the affairs of men, is given in the account of the plagues of Egypt: language, whether we look at the English or the Greek, has seldom conveyed such complicated sublimity of imagination as this.

My abstract of this extraordinary poem may seem to have made it chiefly an affair of *thought;* but that is only because it was important to my purpose to extricate the governing idea of the poem. The value of the poem is certainly not in the logic of its thought, but in the passion and imagination of its thought: that is to say, in the vivid experience of the world to which this thought gives its governance and its form. I wisht to bring before you the immense scope of this idea of life, of this intricately organized manner of experience; and to give you some notion of its unifying power. In itself, no doubt, the idea is so harshly sectarian that it must be decidedly repellent. This is what the fierce and baffled prejudice of a Jew sees; yes, but he is a Jew who sees the whole fact of life, and sees it as a perfectly designed order of things. We acknowledge the greatness of the poem even while we dislike its idea; for the idea has irresistibly come to life in our minds; and in so doing has given us a sense of necessary harmony, whatever the particular version of it may be worth, somehow prevailing through the whole vast riches of human experience, through evil as well as through good, and uniting it all at last into the shapely significance of the world we so profoundly desire. To that end we are ready to accept any means.

§ 3

Something similar is to be seen in *Paradise Regained*. The ruling idea is much less obviously harsh and repellent, though it has some awkward difficulties, and at one point forces Milton to say things which should have been repugnant to him. What we admire in it, however, is its power of firmly holding an ample comprehension of life in the scope of its organization, and of thereby impressing on us its harmony of things as a type of the ideal world of perfect interrelation and significance.

The Quaker Elwood took to himself the credit of suggesting *Paradise Regained* to Milton, as the sequel of *Paradise Lost;* but the suggestion was superfluous. It appears that Milton had for long been attracted by the notion of a short discoursing epic, for which he cites the *Book of Job* as a model—a debate between opposed principles on the ultimate values of things. The characteristic thing in Milton's idea is the absolute and irreconcilable nature of the opposition. Satan as the maintainer of worldly values, and Christ representing spiritual values, can stand on no common ground: one or the other must be a usurper in existing at all. Either set of values supposes in its success the destruction of the other. This is in striking contrast with the idea of *The Wisdom of Solomon,* in which the

263

The Idea of Great Poetry

apparent opposition between worldly and spiritual life only needs to be understood in order to resolve the discord: this world being, so to speak, merely the public policy of God, which brings no sense of contradiction to those who are in private intimacy with his spirit. The contrasts between the entangled complications of *Wisdom* and the lucid shapeliness of *Paradise Regained,* and between the styles of imagination in the two poems—the scarcely governable frenzy of the one, and the noble ease of the other—these contrasts require no remark. Milton, it seems, when he arrived at the composition of *Paradise Regained,* had but to sit back and think, and his thought assumed instinctively the intricate symmetry of a work of art; he had but to talk at his ease, and the simplest language became enchantment and majesty. This, of course, is the illusion produced by craftsmanship when it has become second nature. Certainly Milton needed all his craftsmanship here, where the gorgeous elaborations of *Paradise Lost* would have been improper, and where an idea so simple and inelastic as the hard division of values into worldly and spiritual had to be transformed into the condition of poetry.

It has often been noticed that the Satan of *Paradise Regained*—Satan as the spirit of worldly success—is the spirit of vulgarity: spiritual success, for Milton, could only be aristocratic. That is one of the means which Milton uses to make his idea come to life in our minds; but it is also his way of enlisting our sympathies on the right side, and of making us rejoice with him

in spirit's victorious issue from its duel with the world.
Satan himself is a most mannerly disputant, and his
values always have an air of dignified reasonableness—
until they are contrasted with the values Christ main-
tains against them; and instantly then we recognize
the unconscious and incurable instinct which Satan represents. Each temptation would, if it had succeeded,
have been a victory for vulgarity. The very first bout
of the contest makes this unmistakable. After the
dreams of Christ hungering in his sleep,

> Sometimes that with *Elijah* he partook,
> Or as a guest with *Daniel* at his pulse;

it was a pitiable vulgarity in Satan to rely on such
gorgeous ostentation of power over the whole world's
edible resources, course after course of pompous cook-
ery, with music sounding and handsome attendants
inviting and all manner of luxury accompanying, in
order to break down Christ's fasting strength. The
passage is one of singular beauty; precisely because
Milton could not make his effect, unless the feast had
been delicious to every appetite of the flesh. Therein
consists Satan's misfortune in this duel; the more he
displays, and the more loftily he displays, the power
of the world, the grosser its contrast with spiritual
values. Does he insist that spirit is helpless in the
world without wealth, since wealth is power? But
power over the world has no sense without the power
which

> Governs the inner man, the nobler part;

that is the only power that matters, and nothing can assist it; for it is the power of the spirit. He may plead that glory and the praise of men make the proper motive of action. For how can nobility be selfish? Yet who gains by private virtue but the possessor? And how can even he be sure of his merit, without public approbation? He is answered, that noble action looks for no assurance outside itself, nor needs to stir the people, the "herd confus'd," the "miscellaneous rabble":

> To live upon thir tongues and be thir talk,
> Of whom to be disprais'd were no small praise:
> His lot who dares be singularly good.

So with the offer of either of the two empires that then divided the world: an offer made in that strain of vast panorama for which Milton has no rival. Rational purpose requires rational means: with Parthian militarism or Roman civilisation entirely at his command, Christ could do everything he wisht, and impose his spiritual values irresistibly. But what can spiritual effort have to do with the Parthians' "cumbersome luggage of war,"

> argument
> Of human weakness rather than of strength?

As little as it has to do with Roman "grandeur and majestic show,"

> though thou shouldst add to tell
> Their sumptuous gluttonies and gorgeous feasts.

Ideas and Persons

Whatever good there was in Rome originally has been stifled: and why? Simply because Rome did achieve worldly success; and that killed all its chance of spiritual success. There is no possibility of accommodation between the two sets of values: spirit can only live in matter by declining the whole authority of the material world.

Satan now becomes the embodiment of the business sense. Things offered free are, in his vulgar mind, despised: a price should always be asked. The price he now demands is, indeed, a nominal one, but sufficient to show that what he offers is worth considering.—Sufficient, certainly! For the price thus impudently named—that Christ should go through the form of worshipping Satan—is nothing but a symbol, that spirit *requires* for its success material means. If spirit were to admit that, it would cease to exist as spirit.

Rome now yields to Athens; and it is here that spirit's rejection of the world becomes unreal; something that Milton, "in the cool element of prose," could himself hardly have maintained. The spiritual life which rejects the empire of truth and beauty seems to empty itself of meaning. But the governing idea of the poem overrides these doubts: it is determined on its own complete victory.

And now, after the night of terrors, which serves as an artillery attack on morale, comes the final and the most dangerous assault. Let Christ *prove* himself the Son of God, and show the world what he means by the claim. For who is not, in one sense or another,

the Son of God? Even Satan may be so called: the
title "bears no single sense";

> The Son of God I also am, or was,
> And if I was, I am; relation stands;
> All men are Sons of God; yet thee I thought
> In some respect far higher so declar'd.

What harm can there be, what possible degradation, in
proving to the world what else must remain mere assertion?

> Cast thyself down; safely if Son of God.

But spirit knows its own virtue, and is content with
that:

> Tempt not the Lord thy God, he said and *stood.*

Why should spiritual power prove itself at all? Its
values would gain no authority by convincing anything
outside itself, for only spiritual life is concerned with
them and can delight in them. In any case, to convince
the power of the material world would be to admit
the right of the material world to be convinced, whereas,
for spirit, it has no right to exist at all. With the defeat of this last and subtlest attempt to make spirit
submit to matter, Christ's victory is celebrated in a
passage which for once challenges comparison with the
most elaborated art—simile inlaid with simile—of *Paradise Lost;* and with a stroke of art more marvellous
still, conclusion is given to the whole poem in lines of
quietest simplicity: the vast affair we have lived in so

greatly and so intensely resumes the pathos of mere humanity:

> hee unobserv'd
> **Home to his Mothers house** private return'd.

§4

The distinction between "world" and "spirit," with the separation of values into two codes, is perhaps one of the most vexatious things man's mischievous intellect has ever invented: and here is a poem written to celebrate this very thing—a poem, moreover, which may plausibly be said to accentuate the troublesome nature of the distinction just where it seeks to give it an absolute sanction. All this may be said, and the poetic greatness of *Paradise Regained* is not thereby impugned. We do not have to accept Homer's ethical and religious ideas in order to acknowledge the greatness of the *Iliad*; why should we make any more difficulty over Milton's beliefs? It is what he did with them that matters. The idea of life which governs *Paradise Regained* is one which could not be brought into imaginative existence at all without involving a vast range of human experience; and Milton's poetry realises to the utmost the immense possibility of speculation which surrounds the idea. And all this comes to us under the strict and living governance of the idea; so that it exists in our imaginations not only as a noble wealth of life, but also as a firm organization of life: and in the things we know, we welcome that sense of perfect mutual relevance which we desire.

But now we come to a further stage of our enquiry. Why has common consent never allowed *Paradise Regained* to be as great a poem as *Paradise Lost?* Is it that the idea of the earlier poem is one of even larger comprehension than the idea of the later poem? Certainly the idea of *Paradise Lost* is one of the eternal ideas: no conceivable criticism can lessen its force. How can there be individual existence except as a kind of forlorn revolt against the general existence of the whole? And yet how can the general existence of the whole be thought at all except by an individual thinker? How can we have the sense that we are, in our own right, *ourselves,* and yet, just as unmistakably, also have the absolutely irreconcilable sense, that we are particles in one single unbreakable process of things? Fixt fate—free will: that is the inmost theme of *Paradise Lost;* with the rider, that the pride of the individual in his revolt against the general law is the essence of what we call evil, and yet is the sole source of his dignity as an individual. Original sin: that is the second eternal truth (it is merely another aspect of the first) which inspires and governs *Paradise Lost.*

That these are ideas superior in themselves to the motive of *Paradise Regained* will not be denied: and they are not only superior in themselves—a fact, for us, of quite secondary importance—but their complete substantiation requires an even grander range of thought, of feeling, of imagination, of knowledge. But a poem is not only great by reason of the richness of the experience it induces in us: equally important is the intensity of its impression. And *Paradise Lost* is as far above *Paradise Regained* in its intensity of imaginative life as in the richness of this. And who can mistake the reason? What is it that lives in our minds when *Paradise Regained* has completed itself there? It is the *idea* of the poem. But what lives in our minds when *Paradise Lost* has completed itself? It is the figure, the *character* of Satan—with all the significance of the poem surrounding him like the atmosphere of a personal prestige. How can the life of an idea compete in impressiveness with the life of such a person as the Satan of *Paradise Lost?*—a life as vast as anything the mind of man has ever conceived, and yet more vividly known to us as a person than any one we are likely to meet in the actual world; for indeed it is we ourselves who give, urged and governed by Milton's art, the life we know in this Titanic figure.

Now Satan is a very distinct personality in *Paradise Regained*. I called him the spirit of vulgarity there; and so he is. But of course he is much more than that: the spirit of a single quality can never be a *person;* and there could be no more convincing revelation of depths of personality than Satan's answer to Christ's formidably thrusting question:

> What moves thy inquisition?
> Know'st thou not that my rising is thy fall,
> And my promotion will be thy destruction?

Satan, "inly rackt," replies: "Let that come when it comes";—

> I would be at the worst; worst is my Port,
> My harbour and my ultimate repose:
> The end I would attain, my final good.

A keen and awfully ironic refinement, this, on his original manifesto—his famous exclamation of "Evil, be thou my good!" And we get a quite different insight into his personal quality when he reminds us of his later progeny, Mephistopheles, by the fit of gibing that takes him at Christ's disdainful rejection of glory, "the people's praise." This aristocratic contempt of glory, he says, ill becomes one who boasts himself the Son of God; for certainly, God is no aristocrat: "He seeks glory!"—

> Glory he requires, and glory he receives
> Promiscuous from all Nations, Jew or Greek,
> Or Barbarous, nor exception hath declared:
> From us his foes pronounc't glory he exacts.

Yet the difference between this Satan and the Satan of *Paradise Lost* is unmistakable. In *Paradise Regained*, he is wholly subordinate to the idea; the idea is the thing there, and Satan belongs only to one half of it, and that the least important half, as the poet conceives it. That is why Milton could here at last draw the spirit of evil in a style satisfactory to Puritan conscience: a thing which he can hardly be thought to have done in *Paradise Lost*. Needless to say, since

Ideas and Persons

we are speaking of an art so consummate as Milton's, that is exactly the Satan required for *Paradise Regained*.

But in *Paradise Lost*, Satan *is* the idea: the character of Satan is the presiding thing; he is the essence and force and scope of the originating motive; and in his character, in the immense consistency of his superbly personal energy, resides the significance of the whole poem; for he is the focus of it all, and out of him and his destiny radiates that mutual relevance of things, which is what we call significance. The whole informing power of the idea, with its wealth of accompanying imagination, and its gamut of emotions, has been concentrated and transmuted into the presence of a living person; and how else could such a profound sense of the basic, the metaphysical contradictions in human existence as Milton's, have been presented in any harmony of impression, unless as the complex harmony of a vast personal life? Here is the very quintessence of individual existence, with all possible pride in its ability to stand out against the mere universality of things, its determination, even in the midst of defeat and destruction, to be itself and its own law, in defiance of the Almighty law of the world; here, raised to its highest power, is the dual consciousness of individual life— of what it is and what it is against—which constitutes both its excellence and its original sin: here, in a word, is *Fixt fate—free Will*, the idea of *Paradise Lost*, come to life, and to such a potency of personal life, that it surrounds itself with a world that is one immense tragic harmony—everything that is symbolised by *the Fall of Man:*

> What though the field be lost?
> All is not lost; the unconquerable Will,
> And study of revenge, immortal hate,
> And courage never to submit or yield:
> And what is else not to be overcome:
> That Glory never shall his wrath or might
> Extort from me.

§ 5

The art of poetry, in its widest sense, can do nothing more impressive than the creation of human character. It is never so alive, it never makes such seizure on our minds, as when the result of all its verbal and imaginative technique is our entrance into the life of a character, into a vividly personal form of experience. And so it is with *great* poetry. It is never so great, because never so impressive in its quality of greatness, as when its harmony of some large range of experience comes to life in us in the form of a personal figure. And besides the superior command over our imaginations and sympathies which it then has, two other advantages in this may be mentioned. The idea which has turned into a person is far less liable to the impertinence of logical criticism than the idea which, for all the wealth of its substantiation, remains an idea: the essential thing, the impression of a harmony, is far less likely to be interrupted by disagreement with its means, when the harmony comes by sympathy with the life of a character, than when it must, to exist at all, somehow stir our philosophy. We are less likely to object to the impiety of Satan or the villainy of Macbeth than to the opposition of values in *Paradise Regained* or the pessimism of Leopardi.

There is a second and even more important advantage. By the creation of vividly personal and credible characters, impulses may be transferred alive into our minds which otherwise could not have been given to us at all. The range of matter is therefore larger—the scope of the technique is wider—and there is in consequence the opportunity of greater poetry, when its government is the sense of unity in a subtle and complex personal life, than when it has the more rigid unity of the intellectual life of an idea. Analysis will never exhaust all there is in the impression made on us by the character of Satan; but that which evades analysis is as lively in our minds as that which can be captured. Even Milton could not have told us in direct language all that moved him in the inspiration of *Paradise Lost*. But his language can create Satan's character in us; and in the whole behaviour of that marvellously personal figure, nuances too fine and feelings too deep for direct statement can come unmistakably to life in us.

We could, no doubt, if minute classification were here worth while, make out many degrees and kinds of greatness in poetry. But the world seems pretty well agreed as to what it requires in the supremely great poems. It requires the kind of significance which is given by characteristic personalities: by unique personalities which nevertheless live universally in our minds as representatives of main aspects of human nature: by Milton's Satan; by Job; by Prometheus; by Achilles and Hector; by Hamlet, Lear, and Macbeth; by Faust; even by such deliberately economised characters as Tartuffe and Harpagon; or by the still more peculiar effect, when the poet himself is the character his poetry creates. This last, however, must be postponed till we have seen more exactly what character in great poetry involves.

LECTURE IV

TRAGIC GREATNESS: THE HERO

§ 1

THE mere presence of vividly credible and richly endowed character in a poem does not necessarily make the poem great. If it did, we should have to call *Henry IV* one of the greatest of Shakespeare's plays, which is certainly not what we do call it. Who would think of comparing *Henry IV*, for greatness, with *Macbeth, Lear, Hamlet, Othello?* Yet is not Falstaff as great a character as the central figures in these plays? Has he not as demonic a power as they have of taking possession of our minds, and of compelling us to live in all the riches and intensity of his many-sided genius? Yes; he is great poetry; but only in the sense of being a great incident in poetry; not even he can make *Henry IV* a great *poem.* His creation was a magnificent superfluity; he is not needed for the theme of the play: or rather, he is a disproportionate exuberance of one part of the theme. In a sense, no doubt, he dominates the play; but in the sense that, while he and his fortunes are present, we *forget* the rest of the play—not in the sense that in him and his fortunes all the rest of the play is collected into a single unifying purpose.

Let me summarize for a moment. When poetry is

called great, it is not only on account of the *range* of its matter, though that is important: for we could not call poetry great which did not face the whole fact of man's life in this world, its wickedness and misery as well as its nobility and joy. But its greatness also consists in the *organization* of its matter—and that, remember, is the evil as well as the good of life—into some consistent shapeliness or coherent unity of final impression; so that, whatever means have been taken to effect it, we have at last the sense of belonging to a life in which everything is related to everything else, in which nothing can intrude by chance, but all is required, even the evil is required, in the interest of the whole: nothing can there occur which does not belong to, and assist into being, one inclusive, harmonious orderliness of existence; and this, in the very manner of our acquaintance with it, is therefore throughout significant to us: for everywhere there is meaning in it, since everywhere there is unmistakable connexion. To give us some distinct and keen experience of this way of existing is the true sign of greatness in poetry: and it can only be complete when the nature of poetry has been perfected into a poem.

The poet, in fact, has had some means of focussing all the energies of his imagination into a single composite ardour of ideal experience: it is because, profoundly delighting in some special sense of the instant values of things,[1] or in some habitual manner of feeling

[1] And I should add, if I wisht to be meticulous, sometimes also in the instant valuation of his values; but it would only be for

and understanding, he has been moved to give to this a life as full, as radiant, as many-coloured, as he can contrive; and thus his imagination has supplied not merely energy to urge his poem and keep it going, but also government to manage it and keep it to one purpose. His ruling sense of things may have defined itself in his mind into a quite explicit idea of life; and in that case, when we feel everything in his poem contributing to its complete and vigorous vitality, it is not so much the idea itself that impresses us as its power of digesting and organising the mass of things. Nor is this really at all contrary to the poet's intention; for his peculiar sense of life, and whatever idea may have grown into definition out of it, are nothing but his mode of appreciating his own instinctive conviction of harmony in the whole of things. Thence the poet's idea of life arose, and to that his idea finally takes us in his poem.

But the poet's sense of life may also present itself to his mind, not as a definite idea, but as the vividly characterised experience of a person; and when by his art he hands over to us both the action which he sees and the inmost secret which he feels in his imagined impersonation of the significance of things, everything

the purpose of collecting all æsthetic valuation as instant and intuitive. Keats, for example, had his immediately intuited values of things, and rebuked Shelley for not sharing them, or for not being content with them. Shelley delighted in reasoned values; but it was a radiantly æsthetic delight in them; it was an intuited valuation of these rational values, the instant sense of his happiness in them, that his poetry so often expressed.

The Idea of Great Poetry

follows that has been asserted of the life of ideas in poetry: but with this addition, that now we acknowledge a life incomparably richer, more intense, more persuasive, and at the same time of a far wider and subtler reverberation. This is why the world has regarded as the supremely great poems those which collect their whole sense of life—and everything for which an idea of life may stand—into the behaviour and spirit of memorable personalities.

Think, for example, of the *Iliad*. Try to recollect its significance; and what do you find yourselves recollecting? Surely Achilles and Hector and Diomedes, Andromache and Helen. Achilles, no doubt, is the presiding figure: in him chiefly lives Homer's sense of the goodness of life. It is personal ascendancy. Homer has no need to explain what this is, nor to say why it is good. There it is, for him: heroic virtue, the one thing in life good past all mistake, the unaccountable and irresistible *prowess* which men like Achilles announce by their mere presence before us. The divine figure of Pallas Athene, towering beside him with her immortally blazing eyes, is not Homer's attempt to account for Achilles; it is his sublime metaphor of inexplicable virtue.

There are, of course, innumerable things to be praised in the texture of the poem; and we cannot praise them too much, so long as we remember that they *are* texture, and serve but to clothe the poem's action. There is, for example, the general sense which Homer conveys of the reality of his story to him; and this is important,

280

Tragic Greatness: The Hero

for it means that he never seems to be inventing, in order to embody the significance he feels in things: this always has the momentous air of being simply the real meaning of real things. He is recounting what, for him, actually happened, in the idiom which will best convey that (as, for instance, in the figure of Athene just mentioned); and his sense of the values of life emerges unproclaimed, from the mere manner of his story. This is the true epic quality: but nowhere else does such a gusto in the recording of actual affairs yield such an inevitable discovery of spiritual significance. On the other hand, there is the exquisite finish of the detail, especially in his similes: forest fires at night on the coastwise mountain, reddening the sea for miles; flocks of birds settling on the marshes; flies in the milking sheds; the curve of breaking waves; clouds in the night, opening out to reveal the unspeakable stars. No poetry, except Dante's, pours out such a lavish of exquisitely wrought treasure. And still it is only the texture of the poem; and to admire the *Iliad* for its texture is like admiring a mountain for its colour. The colour may be astonishing; but the really mountainous thing is the attitude of its mass. So with the *Iliad*; whatever else we admire in it, the thing most admirable must always be the shapely mass of the poem as a whole.

Now this notable form which the poem assumes when it is complete in our minds—what is it but the way Homer's sense of the heroic in life has moulded the whole matter of his story, from its height of exultation down to the bottom of its agony and despair, and mastered all the tumult of its events into one final and inclusive harmony? But why is it that the total impression of the *Iliad*—the whole pattern of its tragically noble world—has such an extraordinary power over our minds? It is because the agency by which it is effected comes to us in a form so absolutely commanding: for it comes to us in the form of radiantly living persons. We may make, if we like, some sort of abstract of it: we may even formulate the inspiration of the *Iliad* into a fairly definite idea. The goodness Homer sees in life, we may say, is the goodness man must make of things evil. Fate is the only disposer, and the ignominy of death is the only end. But man can make of these his own personal *danger;* and by so doing can give himself a sense of personal value. For he can face the danger, and be its master even if it kills him. War is the type of the evil of life; but it is also the type of the good man can make of it. In war, he has pre-eminently the joy of asserting his own value, and of seeing it reflected back to him by the honour of his fellows. But if, as happened with Achilles, the honour he has deserved is taken from him, life becomes shameful, for his prowess is despised, his ascendancy is useless. We may go on elaborating our abstract until we find ourselves describing the plot of the poem. But however accurately and faithfully we do it, we tell ourselves nothing of the force which Homer's sense of life really exerts on us. For it never comes to us as an idea at all; it comes to us as Achilles and Patroklos, Hector and Andromache, Agamemnon and Priam. It is in its creation of these superbly personal yet profoundly symbolic figures that the security of the *Iliad* lies, as one of the supremely great poems in the world.

Contrast this quality of effect with that of *The Dynasts:* the two poems have enough in common to make their contrast justifiable. In *The Dynasts*, too, war is the type of the evil of man's life; and it has, for Hardy, at least this good also: it forces us to face the essential things, it compels us to realise, in appalling concentration, the sort of existence we belong to—an existence, says Hardy, that takes not the least account of its individuals, but is simply concerned with going on, with keeping up its remorseless and purposeless elaboration of the destiny of the whole. And this is brought before us in the true epic manner, as the result of recounting solid reality, things that actually happened. Nor has the *Iliad* itself a greater range of matter than Hardy's chronicle of the Napoleonic Wars; and as this is compacted into tremendous unity of final impression by a singularly potent idea of life, the result is a poem which can only be compared, and will only be compared by the criticism of the future, with the great poems of Europe. For any true comparison in English literature we must go back to Wordsworth, or even, for the wholeness of its effect, to Milton. Yet the very nature of its idea prevents *The Dynasts* from exerting such an effect as *Paradise Lost* or the *Iliad*. For no kind of personal life could ever be its symbol; since the whole force of the idea is its denial of any personal life at all, except as the most trifling of illusions. As, from the circle of the Phantom Intelligences, we look down on the tormented earth, we see "innumerable human figures busying themselves like cheesemites"; we see transports and battleships floating before the wind "like preened duck feathers across a pond"; and three whole armies become "motions peristaltic and vermicular, like three caterpillars." And when to this mere height of vision is added the penetrating clairvoyance of the Intelligences, we see the whole multitudinous world as one of the Immanent Will's "eternal artistries in circumstance"; an artistry which here happens, "in skilled unmindfulness," to have produced in its pattern the perfectly futile decoration of life individually conscious—or, as Hardy fiercely puts it,

> the intolerable antilogy
> Of making figments feel.

But the Will of the whole, the Immanent Will, makes nothing of that; it is a sublimely entranced automatism, heedlessly operating its incredibly intricate handicraft:

> So the Will heaves through Space and moulds the times
> With mortals for Its fingers. We shall see
> Again men's passions, virtues, visions, crimes
>   Obey resistlessly
> The purposive, unmotived, dominant Thing
> Which sways in brooding dark their wayfaring:

a Will, however, which is only "purposive" in the sense that it has the purpose of going on, and continuing its own existence, "raptly magnipotent."

Tragic Greatness: The Hero

The grandeur of *The Dynasts* seems to me undeniable; and perhaps no better instance could be found of the greatness of poetry coming from the rigorous mastery of an idea over the whole unruly fact of life. But it is a mastery which, whatever its authority, can never possess men's minds like the presence of a Satan or an Achilles. The idea of life which will not allow individuals to be more than the "fingers" of universal Will has of necessity entered a self-denying ordinance against the achievement of supreme greatness in poetry: the greatness of the living symbolism of vividly personal figures.

§ 2

The poet, however, who goes to legend for his material is likely to find himself provided from the very beginning of his work with the first condition or rudiments of that achievement; for if it is a myth which he takes in hand, he certainly starts with a symbolic figure. Probably it is a figure of no very distinct personality; and probably too its significance is not very distinct either. The poet's art must be not only to widen and deepen and enrich the significance and make its force unmistakable (and he may even alter its direction); it must also effect that utmost intensification of this which comes of making it live as an absolute personality. Much criticism has been spent on Goethe's *Faust*, with varying result; and it seems clear that, while it is acknowledged to be, beyond question, one of the great European poems, it has not won common consent to a place among the few supremely great poems. It needs no remarkable analysis to show us the reason.

Like Hamlet and Don Juan, the figure of Dr. Faustus first makes his appearance as one of the myths of the Dark Ages. Faustus is something of a Prometheus for the Dark Ages: he is the vicarious sacrifice —not, like Prometheus, for life itself,—but for intellectual life; for he is the embodiment, the living symbol, of the idea, or rather perhaps the feeling, as old as man himself, that progress in knowledge is evil, or at least to be punisht. Well—in spite of the fact that Universities exist respected and perhaps revered—is not the intellectual appetite one of the evils of life? How comfortable and sedate life might be, if only intellect would keep quiet! And what do we gain from its meddling? Always some new disappointment—what Dante called "the eternal grief" of the philosophers! No wonder the Dark Ages (as we call them), discovering afresh both intellectual ambition and its doom— that it must always frustrate itself just at the moment of its success—in their sensitive simplicity took this as a positive torment. For intellectual progress consists merely of successive failures to be that which it exists by desiring to be—*certainty:* and the farther it goes the better it knows this. We cannot even nowadays be certain of our own uncertainty. All we know is, we can never get outside our own version of things and see whether it be right or wrong: and insatiably we long to do so, and to see things as they are. Besides, this intellectual ambition of ours, and our desire of knowledge for its own sake—what is it but a kind of revolt against the original earth of our being? And what else is evil but revolt? There is no evil in nature; for nature is obedience: only man has the power to rebel.

Yes, and it is just this power which is the dignity of man; and precisely in the unending exploration of science is its ennobling exhilaration. But who knows better than Faustus that progress in knowledge is good as well as evil? He sells his soul for it! And that enigmatic gesture, that piece of unmistakably human behaviour—*that* is how the myth formulates the vague cloud of aspirations and suspicions, desires and disappointments, which I have just been attempting to formulate in terms of thought, as some sort of an idea. The myth makes no attempt to collect them into an idea; suddenly, inexplicably, this mass of half-thought, half-feeling *lives* in our minds as the act of a man: Faustus sells his soul to the devil for some satisfaction of his lust to know. It is an act in which, inevitably, we recognise the virtue of a personality: it has only to be mentioned, to call up the man who was capable of it. And no less certainly we recognise the pressure of meaning behind the act. The price of knowledge is damnation: and it is worth the price. No idea could concentrate its significance so deeply and intensely in us as this concrete symbolism, this moment in the life of a man; and assuredly no idea could go home to us so instantly as this thrilling motion of characteristic human nature. The myth does not substantiate the person it supposes: there is little more personification in it than the single fact of the infernal bargain. But there is enough to make it apparent how the significance of the myth should work itself out in the logic of its personified symbolism. Suppose Faustus does somehow transcend the mere human version of things and acquire the immediacy of spiritual understanding. That is what we are to suppose by his *magic*. Yet what enterprise more desperate, more paradoxical, than for mortal intellect to aspire beyond mortality, only for its own mortal satisfaction?—That is symbolised by Faust's damnation.

Of this symbolic figure, Marlowe made a living person—"human, all too human." When Faustus at last has the power for which he has bartered his soul, what does he do with it? He plays tricks and japes; he astonishes ostlers and courtiers, and annoys the Pope. And yet he is still the Faustus who could think of such a bargain: and the knowledge of his own self-contradiction, which is all he has gained by the power of his magic, turns his life into a fever worse than the desire of his youth, before the dreadful remedy of Mephistophilis allayed it. He becomes a delirum of passion for a phantom; and it is time then for the devils to tear him to pieces—for Marlowe understands the logic of the mythical symbolism as well as how to please an Elizabethan audience.

Goethe added so much to this that he changed the whole sense of the story. The addition was gradual. In the first version of his tragedy he romanticised

Tragic Greatness: The Hero

Faust's damnation by involving it with a love-affair. Vulgarisation, compared with the single intensity of Marlowe's passion, obviously threatens. It was ingenious innovation, to shipwreck Faust in his ruin of Gretchen; but what has this ordinary disaster to do with that terrible aspect of man's destiny which is represented by Faust's business with Mephistopheles? It needs no formal bargain with the devil to be a seducer of girls. Faust's transaction supposes an ambition more remarkable than that.

Did Goethe feel this? His nature, at any rate, was, as he tells us himself, "too conciliating for tragedy." It seems, at first, an odd accommodation to such a nature, to make Faust survive Gretchen; that, one would think, would rather be a fearful addition to his damnation. We accept it, however, first because this is now merely *Part I* of Goethe's whole intention; secondly, because the story has otherwise been so modified, that even a love-affair now may justify itself in Faust's career. For the *Prologue in Heaven* has changed the sense of the legend. Faust is no longer the symbol of intellectual hunger alone. That may still predominate in him; but he has become the stake in the eternal wager between good and evil; and, very rightly, the ambition of his intellect has become the mere market or clearing-house of an ambition to have the whole possibility of life known and proved.

This is grandly carried out in *Part I* of Goethe's poem. Gretchen is no longer incongruous; she is not even superfluous. She is a stage in Faust's career, and he has become a person capable of representing in his own experience the whole range of life's emotion. The contest of good and evil lives in our minds as the fortune of an astonishingly vivid character. But it is obviously incomplete. When Faust leaves Gretchen crazy in her cell, we know there is more to come. The wager is still undecided; Mephistopheles, that brilliantly real emanation from the depth of Faust's desire, does not yet know whether he is to win or lose.

And the poem remains incomplete; it fritters away in the anthology of wise remarks and the icy allegories of *Faust, Part II*. I do not forget the magical opening of this second part, nor its soaring conclusion. I can remember with admiration the Helena episode, with its marriage, if not of heaven and hell, at any rate of classicism and romanticism. And every one respects the fifth act, with its justification of knowing not for itself, but as the means of doing. But what has happened to Faust all this while? He has simply faded away, deserted by his author for tedious reflection and ungainly satire. The person of Faust has ceased to exist; and so has his spirit of evil. *Faust, Part II*, is in its whole result a failure—and therefore the entire poem is a failure—because the personal symbol of it all has failed to go on living. Instead, we have a miscellany of notions. The incomparable legend of Faust has missed its artistic destiny. Twice it has become great poetry; perhaps, remembering Lessing and Lenau, more than twice. But it has been frustrated in its effort to become supremely great, as it deserved to be. For when Marlowe endowed the myth with a consistent and impressively personal incarnation, the scope of its meaning was still too rigid; and when Goethe gave it the required expansion, the figure in whose name this was done vanisht out of it—the figure who was to have caught it all up into his potent being, and turned the whole of it into the living unity of a person. Faust himself had disappeared.

§ 3

Would it be unfair to contrast the second part of Goethe's *Faust* with one of Shakespeare's great tragedies? That, at any rate, would be the way to realise what Goethe failed to accomplish. Who can mistake what it is that has issued out of Shakespeare's tragic art "conquering and to conquer"? Everything that can contribute to greatness of poetry is there; but what has taken possession of the world's imagination is the personal force of those figures into which the manifold art of his tragedy collects itself: Hamlet, Macbeth, Othello, Lear, and, in a slightly less degree, Coriolanus and Cleopatra. I say, the personal force of these figures: but in the force of each one of them lives a whole world of significance. In each of them, a sense of life, as profound and as unmistakable as Goethe's, and governing at least as large a range of fortune and misfortune, has focussed the whole order of the process by which it became a poem into one vividly personal history. This was the habit of Shakespeare's tragic art; and thus these presiding figures of his have a personal force which is indistinguishable from their symbolic force. I can only look at two of these figures; but this will serve, besides illustrating still further our main topic, to show also how our idea of great poetry relates itself with the idea of tragedy. First, then, what is tragedy?

This is a very old and a very formidable problem, this business of tragedy. We have been approaching it for some time: now it strides across our road, and we must face it. It is a giant notoriously disputatious and obstructive, and we had best avoid any altercation with him; for we can hardly expect to skewer him once and for all with our answer to his riddle. But perhaps we can find an answer which will enable us, while he is thinking of a reply, to slip past him, and proceed to our conclusion.

For, after all, is tragedy anything more than a special case of the matters we have been discussing? Poetry, we say, raises our experience of this world to the condition of ideal experience; and that not by its ex-purgation of things, but by its subtly vibrant connexion of things. So that, in the perfection of this art—in a poem—whatever the matter may be, we live in a distinct system of connexion so thrilling and complete that everything there is relevant to everything else; and the shapely order of our whole experience of this is an ideal experience, because everything in it, evil as well as good, is necessary to the *design of the whole*.

Now the peculiarity of tragedy is just this: it is,

ostensibly, a version of the mere evil of life. The *design of the whole* here is man in disgrace and misfortune: the power of wickedness over virtue, the blind collaboration of events to destroy innocence, death frustrating love,—some aspect of the world in which this, or the like of this, so predominates, that everything else there is coloured by sorrow or pain. I say, it is ostensibly this: this is what analysis of the matter will show. But clearly something has escaped analysis, if this is its whole result. For tragedy is not merely sorrowful, not merely distressing: it is also and at the same time profoundly satisfactory. That could not be achieved by retribution of the evil, supposing there were occasion for it, and it suited the poet's purpose to take the occasion: for retribution (as for example, "poetic justice") could only satisfy us *after* we had been distressed. But tragedy satisfies us even in the moment of distressing us. Satisfies? The word is not strong enough. Tragedy does not exist unless it is *enjoyed*. Define it as you please; but this, at any rate, is certain: if the notion of enjoyment does not somehow come in, you have failed to define tragedy at all, for you have left out a thing essential to its existence.

This is the real problem of tragedy: how do we come to enjoy what seems a version of the mere evil of life? Nay, how is it that tragic art gives us the loftiest, though the severest, delight we can have in poetry? It cannot simply be, because evil has become in it orderly and systematic. There might be a kind of maniacal æsthetic enjoyment in a vision of the world as an affair wholly organised for evil; but that would be nothing like the enduring satisfaction which is the ground of tragic enjoyment. Indeed, there is no surer sign of a healthy mind than the enjoyment of tragedy. There must, then, be good as well as evil in it; and out of the final harmony of the two, here, as elsewhere, will come the sense of the significance of evil overriding its injury—the sense that evil is no longer the intrusion of irresponsible and useless malignity, but the servant of universal law: which is the essence of the tragic satisfaction. Our æsthetic enjoyment of the spectacle of evil (which is certainly present in tragedy) is always accompanied by implicit assurance that we are not merely assisting at its triumph. But when we ask whence tragic poetry is to provide itself with good to match its evil, the answer can only be, that the good must arise out of the evil. This is what the peculiarity of tragedy comes to: out of things evil it must elicit good. That, you may remember, is what we found at the heart of Homer's valuation of life; for, indeed, the tragic spirit descends to us from Homer, as Aristotle said. And now we can see why the tragic idealisation of life has such a lofty delight for us: right in the very evil of life, in the thing most opposite to all our desires, even *there* experience has become desirable. May we not say, that man knows no height so superb above his mortal destiny as the art of tragedy—the height we live on when we assume the spirit of Æschylus or Sophocles, of Corneille or Racine, or of Shakespeare? But I am not now to discuss tragedy in general, and the various methods (as those names suggest) by which its peculiar nature may be established; I am only concerned with Shakespeare, and with him only in order to show how the method of his art falls in with our main argument.

Where, then, does Shakespeare's tragic art provide itself with good? Precisely where all the evil of his tragedy concentrates and organises itself; and precisely also where we are to look for his final harmony of good and evil: in the *character* which creates and endures the evil. Out of him, whether he is blameworthy or not, goes the impulse which sets events conspiring against him; and in the return it makes on him, the evil of the tragedy consists. It comes back to him with all the power it has collected in his world: the whole conspiracy enters into him and becomes incarnate in his personal life; and thereby becomes evil: *his* evil, because it is his implacable enemy. He is the evil he endures; and he is also the good which comes into being by reason of that evil, and his endurance of it. His personality drew destruction on itself; and in its resistance to destruction, in its assertion of itself against the hostility it has provoked—even though that assertion can be no more at last than exquisitely agonised perception of all the depth and subtlety of this enmity; —in the heightening of the first of all the virtues, the virtue of personal existence; in the white heat of man's most essential vigor, the vigor by which he is *himself against the world;*—here it is that Shakespeare places the good his tragedy requires. It was this method of deriving good from evil (not peculiar to him, but by him most remarkably used) which enabled Shakespeare to be supreme in greatness of achievement above all other tragic poets; for it enabled him to make tragedy of the utmost extremity of the evil of life, and to embody both the evil and the mastering of it in single personalities which have imposed themselves on the whole world's imagination. It enabled him, for example, to turn sordid motive and habitual crime into the tragedy of Macbeth; and to make the whole of that tragedy consist in the life, the potently individual life, of its hero.

Macbeth starts off by bringing before us the very powers of evil themselves, personified in figures of grisly vivacity, hideously blithe in their confidence of success: a confidence the more shocking because the witches, in that snatch of their infernal conversation with which the play opens, do not even allude to their hopes. It is merely their tone that instantly sets the key for all that is to follow. Ten lines of lyrical dialogue, and the action is in full career. No other play sweeps our imaginations at once into the full strength of its current like this.[1] From the very first word of it, we know, or at least feel, that the powers of evil are to have their will with the life of a man. Their

---

[1] And in the most elaborate of recent editions of the play, this opening scene is set down as *spurious;* expressly on the grounds that it is not *necessary:* "no dramatic interest or object is gained by its introduction," says this egregious editor, whose notions of dramatic interest are as scientific as his prosody—scientific, that is, only in the sense of being bluntly indifferent to art.

temptation is the most devilish possible: what Macbeth dare not even desire is suddenly and awfully made to *appear* as the thing fated for him: all he has to do is to act accordingly.—Of course! Once induce him to act, and the thing *is* thereby fated: it has been done! —All falls out as the witches prophesied. Macbeth acts, and has his ambition: but the witches did not tell him what he now finds out—that this is to descend alive into hell. Egged on by his wife, his first atrocious treachery, the murder of the king, gives him the vulgar aggrandisement he desires; but a whole series of crimes must maintain it, each more futile than the last, each more patently ignoble in its motive. And when at last his own destruction stares at him, his life is not merely drencht in wickedness; it has ceased to have any meaning; it has become a phantasmagoria of horrible nonsense: a tale told by an idiot.

This is the process of evil in the tragedy: and it is wholly in Macbeth. The killing of Duncan, and the other murders, are evil in themselves, certainly; but it is with the evil they are to Macbeth that the tragedy is concerned and our interest engaged. And not merely with the evil they are to Macbeth: the evil has become Macbeth himself, the very life of him. And in so doing it has provided itself with a perfect counterpart of good. For note how the two partners in crime react to their guilt. It is (with profound psychological truth) the hard calculating realist, the unimaginative matter-of-fact businesslike instigator—it is Lady Macbeth, who shatters and gives in to the strain of horror and danger she has brought upon herself. But Macbeth goes on enduring to the last: the sensitive highly-strung Macbeth, the fearfully imaginative man, who can see the whole infamy of his crime as soon as he has thought of it, and anticipates all the possibility of its failure; the man who sees visionary emblems of intended crime and the ghosts of crime committed, as clearly as if they were commonplace reality; the man who instantly translates the witches' greeting into the thought of murder, instantly begins devising, has it all complete in his mind, and then has to be forced on to do the thing he has pledged himself to do: and as he goes out on his hideous business, looks on at himself, as if he were watching a figure in a drama, moving "with Tarquin's ravishing strides" towards his victim, while he feels the very earth he treads on repudiate its complicity: this is the person who stands up to the end, who grandly looks despair in the face, and dies fighting, unsubdued. It is not merely that he becomes more daring and resolute in action, the more desperate his affairs become: the whole vitality of the man becomes incandescent. Infinitely keener than Lady Macbeth's is his suffering; and the more he suffers, the more capable of suffering he becomes; and the more he steels himself to endure: *that* is what the singular ability of his personal life has become. And when Lady Macbeth dies, and he realises that he is alone in the dreadful world he has created for himself, the unspeakable abyss suddenly opens beneath him. He has staked everything and lost; he has damned himself for nothing; his world suddenly turns into a blank of imbecile futility. And he seizes on the appalling moment and masters even this: he masters it by *knowing* it absolutely and completely, and by forcing even this quintessence of all possible evil to live before him with the zest and terrible splendour of his own unquenchable mind:

> To-morrow, and to-morrow, and to-morrow,
> Creeps in this petty pace from day to day
> To the last syllable of recorded time,
> And all our yesterdays have lighted fools
> The way to dusty death. Out, out, brief candle!
> Life's but a walking shadow, a poor player
> That struts and frets his hour upon the stage
> And then is heard no more: it is a tale
> Told by an idiot, full of sound and fury,
> Signifying nothing.

There is no depth below that; that is the bottom. Tragedy can lay hold of no evil worse than the conviction that life is an affair of absolute inconsequence. There is no meaning anywhere: that is the final disaster; death is nothing after that. And precisely by laying hold of this and relishing its fearfulness to the utmost, Macbeth's personality towers into its loftiest grandeur. Misfortune and personality have been until this a continual discord: but now each has reached its perfection, and they unite. And the whole tragic action which is thus incarnate in the life of Macbeth— what is it but the very polar opposite to the thing he proclaims? For we see not only what he feels, but the personality that feels it; and in the very act of proclaiming that life is "a tale told by an idiot, *signifying nothing,*" personal life announces its virtue, and superbly *signifies itself*. That, so far as it can be reduced to abstract words, is the action of *Macbeth*. But it is no abstract meaning, but the poem as an actual whole, that lives in our minds: *there* is the shapely order and intense connexion of things that can absorb even Macbeth's "tale told by an idiot" in the sense of a final significance. And what is this significance? Nothing but the completely organised and focussed unity of the poem's total impression; and that is nothing but the figure and person of Macbeth himself: in him the whole poem lives and has its meaning. In his unanalysable quality as an individual we recognise a symbol of life itself, creating and enduring—yes, and dreadfully relishing—its own tragic destiny.

I have taken *Macbeth* as the type of Shakespeare's method in tragedy; and we see how the success of that method has made *Macbeth* a type also of the poetry which the world acknowledges as supremely great—the poetry which collects itself into figures unique in personal force and universal in significance. If there is any such figure more famous than Macbeth, it is Hamlet; but I can only glance at him. Macbeth's tragedy is in the failure of his world: it could not have been avoided, and his agonised triumph over it lasts but a moment. But Hamlet has to face the failure of himself; it is an affair dreadfully prolonged, and he is always telling himself that it might have been avoided—if he had not been Hamlet! Macbeth suffers a metaphysical disaster, Hamlet a psychological disaster; and the latter, no doubt, is the more familiar to our sympathies. Nowadays, at any rate, where metaphysic claims its hundreds, psychology claims its tens of thousands.

What is this disaster, then? We see Hamlet as he sees himself; and we also see him as the living harmony of an immense complexity of events. Every one knows how Hamlet sees himself:

> I do not know
> Why yet I live to say "this thing's to do."

He bitterly despises himself for his failure to act: he can but think and talk about acting, and return again and again to his self-contempt. And the critics, innocently taking him at his own valuation, have held him up to reprobation as the man who could not kill his uncle. He is, they say, the very figure of moral vacillation: and Hamlet himself agrees with them.

This hardly accounts for his extraordinary prestige: it is certainly not as a contemptible figure that Hamlet has impressed the world. What no one can mistake, at any rate, is the fact that he is very vividly alive: he has that inexplicably individual force which is the essence of personality, and which can make itself consistently felt through all the contradictions of thought and action—contradictions, which, because of that unique force inspiring them, we always feel to be, as we say, *in character*. It is a force for which no formula can ever be found; any attempt to describe it will leave out something vital. But it is odd that the critics, in their attempts to describe Hamlet's personality, should have so often left out that most unmistakable, though certainly very indefinable, thing, his heroism.

Very indefinable indeed, someone will say: the heroism of moral vacillation! Well, let us look at this vacillation a little; and as I said just now, we must see it not merely as it appears to Hamlet himself, but as it appears in the play as a whole. Hamlet, we may agree, has made up his mind that he ought to kill the king. That has not been an easy decision to arrive at. He might very well *want* to kill Claudius: he has terrible motives for hating him. But such a decision must have not merely desire, but a conviction of duty, at the back of it. Hamlet knows well enough that desire is easily mistaken for duty. But his long anguish of self-contempt would be without meaning, unless he were convinced that justice, as well as his own desire, demanded the death of Claudius: he must, that is, be convinced that Claudius killed his father. The evidence for that is, to say the least, very dubious: the eloquence of a ghost, and the king's behaviour at the play. Either might be explained away, as Hamlet can see. They certainly do not form a body of evidence on which the king might be publicly impeacht. Still, Hamlet at length is convinced, though by a somewhat insecure and uneasy process: he feels, rather than knows, the king's guilt: a species of conviction which he cannot share with any one. The king must die, however; even though Hamlet can have nothing to rely on but his own ingenuity, and assassination plots in palaces are not lightly brought off. He makes a beginning by feigning madness: but he gets no further. What else ought he to have done?

Anything, say the moralists, rather than deplore his own faculty for delaying action. But they can say nothing so contemptuous of his pitiable introspection as what Hamlet says himself. And what of the play all this while? What *are* these delays which Hamlet so loathes himself for making, or, at least, allowing? As the action unfolds itself, we watch Hamlet continually upbraiding himself for delay which—simply does not exist! There is no delay at all: there is no moment in the play in which we see Hamlet failing to kill the king, no moment of which he could have taken any conceivable advantage, except that single one in which he catches the king at his prayers: a moment which he rejects precisely because it is the *wrong* moment for his revenge— it is too favourable to the king's hereafter. Those contemptible delays, those moral vacillations, for which Hamlet is so notorious, exist wholly in Hamlet's own mind. They are, for him, none the less real and disastrous. They form the tragic harmony of his personal life and the events to which it belongs: none other was possible.

Hamlet, already deeply injured in his emotions by his mother's indecent marriage, becomes possessed by a terrible desire, which must be, to his wounded mind, as corrosive as vitriol, unless he can get rid of it. And it is not a mere personal craving, this desire; it is the thing in which he has come profoundly to believe: the thing, he says, that ought to happen, that must happen.

And this desire, as a matter of practical fact, never has a chance of happening. Eventually, it might have found or made its opportunity; but as long as Hamlet knows it, circumstances are adamant against it. Indeed, it is a desire that could only proceed into action most gradually and delicately: but its possessor cannot meanwhile endure to nurse it privately as the mere inaction of desire. The whole world is out of tune while it remains ineffective: for it is justice, this desire. *Why* is justice less able than the brute process of events? There must be some reason! And the baffled desire returns upon its possessor, and curdles his life, "like eager droppings into milk"; it becomes his poison, and his poisoned life looks in on itself, and knows itself incurably vitiated by the fierce desire it can never get rid of. The poisoned introspection of a noble mind hates itself and despises itself. The fearful conclusion leaps at him. *He himself* is the reason why his desire remains unacted: he is *unworthy* of it. Justice would have been done, had not his cowardice *delayed* it! This is the famous delay we hear about in Hamlet's soliloquies; it is the tragic invention of his own wounded mind.

I have nothing to say of the inferiority complex; I will only remind you that as long ago as Homer's *Odyssey* a character exactly similar to Hamlet took its place in literature. I mean the character of Telemachus. In him we see a desire, a just and noble desire, which is, by the very nature of things, unable to realise itself in action. Events are not merely unfavourable to it: it never has the least chance of insinuating itself into the actuality of events. It can only be thought about and cherisht in day-dreams. And it turns back on itself, detesting its own futility; and becomes its possessor's self-contempt and self-loathing. And that is the profound significance of Hamlet: that is what gives him his prestige, as an individual person capable of representing human nature itself. He is the most unflinching exposure that has ever been made of the trapt anguish of human nature when it finds itself pitifully weaker than events; but in Hamlet it is a weakness inextricably involved with human nature's finest strength. As usual in Shakespeare, the tragedy of the events consists wholly in their transformation into the very stuff of the personal life around which they organise themselves. The *evil* of Hamlet's tragedy is that the only harmony he can find, to resolve the discord of what he desires and what is possible, is bitter self-contempt. But the harmony *we*, the onlookers, find is in that same character's concentration of the whole order of the poem into itself; and how can we find harmony there unless we can find good there to match the evil? But who can miss the good in Hamlet's character? For it is a character which can keep its distinction, even in the midst of its horrible secret disaster: which can be nice and courteous, kindly and amiable, wittily fastidious and greatly indignant, urbanely ironical and serenely disillusioned, even when it privately despises and detests the very nature of its own existence. That is the *good* of Hamlet's tragedy: and heroism is not too strong a word for it. It is, perhaps, a stouter heroism even than Macbeth's.

LECTURE V

POETIC PERSONALITY. THE POET HIMSELF

§ 1

I HAVE never professed, in these lectures, to make great poetry into a *species* of poetry There are, as I have said, infinite degrees of greatness; if we could set up any kind of a scale for poetry in respect of it, we should never be able to mark exactly where greatness begins, any more than we can draw the line on the thermometer where *heat* begins. But put your hand into hot water, and you know it is hot, right enough; enter into great poetry, and you feel, just as unmistakably, the greatness. The analysis of this feeling which I have been attempting has been designed to show that we can, nevertheless, say with some precision what it is we are acknowledging when we admit the greatness of poetry; and that, in consequence, we can also say, without pretending to anything so futile as a nice measurement of greatness, why some poems strike us as greater than others. Poetry being always a harmony of experience, its greatness will depend both on the scope and variety of the experience, and on the completeness and intensity of the harmony of this. *Prometheus Unbound* is not so great a poem as *Paradise Lost*, because the ex-

perience Shelley made into his poem has neither the
scope nor the variety of Milton's. But neither is *Faust*
as great a poem as *Paradise Lost*, though the range of
Goethe's matter is not unequal to, and not altogether unlike, Milton's; the thing here is, that Goethe could effect nothing like Milton's harmony. For Milton centred his harmony deep in the peculiarly personal life of
a character; Goethe's harmony began as a character,
slackened into the easier harmony of an idea, and then
dissipated into the mere juxtaposition of variety.

There are some poems which the world seems agreed
to place in a class above all others, so far as greatness
is concerned. They may not be above all others in the
scope of their experience—not decisively, at any rate;
for once that can be taken as fairly and fully representative of the whole fact of life, its sorrow and its joy,
its power and its ruin, we have reached a height which
will not be notably affected by more or less detail in the
substantiation. There is still, however, the possibility
of a further and decisive step upward towards supreme
greatness; and we found that this step upward is taken
when the poet's art raises the harmony of its matter to
the highest degree of command and intensity, by making it live in our minds as the personality of a character
manifestly symbolic—a Satan, an Achilles, a Hamlet.
We saw also why this personified harmony must have
such a superiority of command over our minds and such
an intensity of concentration. For no mere idea can excite us so profoundly, or draw us to live in it so keenly,
as the fortune of a character whose similarity to our-

The Idea of Great Poetry

selves cannot but provoke our sympathy; and there can be no such unification of diversity—yes, and of opposites and contradictions—as that mysterious, not-to-be-formulated power of personality can effect, simply by uttering these diverse things out of the depth of its fund of nameless power, and thereby charging them all, however they may differ, with the unique savour of its quality: thus giving us underneath our sense of diversity, and even of contradiction, a still deeper sense of connexion—the sense, namely, of an originating personal life.

But so far I have simply taken for granted the fact of this symbolic characterisation. How a poet can create an imaginary character in our minds—and a character which is not only absolutely individual but at the same time a symbol of the poet's intention—is a question we should, perhaps, leave to the psychologists. Is it due to the poet's observation of life? But observation will not give us a Macbeth, any more than a Satan. Is it then the poet expressing himself? But Milton is not Satan; and if Shakespeare is Macbeth, how can he be also his other characters—Cleopatra and Benedick, Isabella and Prospero? We find a similar problem in the art of landskip. If it is merely observation, it is nothing; but, in the nature of it, it is something else than the artist himself. If we cannot expect to meet with Falstaffs and Hamlets in actual life, neither can we expect to see in the open air what Turner or Crome put on canvas: the artist is there, as well as the scene of the earth.

Poetic Personality

So with poetic characterisation. The poet has lived in the world of men, and has come to know that world through and through, delighting in it. But his observation comes to us completely impregnated by his peculiar spirit and by the purpose of his art. Observation will never account for creation; it will not even account for the materials of creation, unless we take it in a sense large enough to include introspection. Milton is neither Satan nor Christ; but it was almost wholly on his knowledge of himself that he drew for the materials out of which he created the characters of Satan and Christ. It may, indeed, be said, and justly, that observation itself is always in some sort creative; for it does not merely consist in noticing traits of behaviour, it goes on to the distinctly imaginative act, not merely of *combining* them (which would be nothing), but of *supposing* a character capable of *producing* such behaviour. Even so, this imaginative character-drawing which we call observation of life is conditioned solely by what we know. The poet's character-drawing, however, is conditioned not only by what he knows, but also by what he requires—for the accomplishment of an artistic purpose to which all his characterization is subordinate. Realism is not the standard by which we can judge of his success; and when we say that his characters are *true to life,* all we mean is that they are *intelligible.* And intelligible they must be, if they are to serve his purpose; they must be characters into whose thoughts and moods and actions we can readily enter, and feel them as our own. But if they are intelligible, we do not trouble to ask whether they are true to life in the realistic sense; we are not disturbed by the fact that every moment of their speech and language is distinctly significant—a thing we scarcely find in the persons of actual life: nor that these imaginary characters, as if it was the most natural thing in the world, continually reveal the very inmost secrets of their beings and their deep reaction to the events and persons round about them: nor—and this is equally unlike what actually happens—that they are presented to us absolutely and wholly conditioned by one single process of things, altogether concerned in that and in that only. In a word, our belief in these characters is not in the least affected by the fact that they, their thoughts and feelings and personalities, are as much the expressive technique of the poet's purpose as his phrases and his rhythms.

But what do we mean by the *personality* of a fictitious character? What gives us the sense of a personality existing in its own right—and not merely the poet's— in an imaginary spectacle of human behaviour? The poet, we must remember, is severely limited in the means of his art; he works, moreover, under the strict self-imposed conditions of his artistic purpose; and yet he compels us to imagine a series of thoughts, feelings, actions, in such a way that an individual person, and an apparently independent person, comes into life within them, as convincingly as if he had actually lived before us with all the freedom and infinite subtlety of real acquaintance. How is it done? We talk, rather portentously, of *analysis* and *psychology* in poetry. But these are rarities—I might say, oddities—in poetry. Indeed, I know of only one genuinely psychological poem—that amazing and, to me, thrilling thing, *Peter Bell*. Where else does poetry concern itself with *the way the mind works?* Except in such a *bravura*-piece as *Peter Bell*, what the poets are interested in, when they portray human nature, is *the result of a mind's working*. And this must be so. It is necessary to their purpose to make their characters, as far as possible, proclaim themselves; this is true of epic as well as of dramatic poetry; for it is the only way these characters can be made to come to life in us in their own unmistakable style. And that must be done intelligibly: that is to say, these characters must live in the same sort of consciousness in which we ourselves live. But what is it we are conscious of? Of our thoughts and our moods; but not of the obscurely conflicting forces which make our minds what they are, not of the mystery out of which these thoughts and moods emerge. That mystery is what Wordsworth was concerned with in *Peter Bell;* and it is the topic of psychology. The core of the topic is personality; and the method of its science is analysis. But the method of poetry is not analysis: it is exhibition. Poetry, even when we can speak of its revelation of the inmost secrecies of a character, is still showing us *what* a mind has produced, not *how* this mind has produced it.

Perhaps an analogy, rough as it must be, will make this clearer. We are watching, let us suppose, a tarn in a pocket of the hills; we are noting the play of the breezes on the surface of the waters. The curves of the rippling pattern are enough to engage our attention. Unless we are very determined scientists, we do not trouble to think of, much less think out, the complicated dynamics of the moving airs which that ripple results from. We could draw, if we had the right skill, the effect of wind on water; and I daresay also, if again we had the right skill, we could make out the mathematical equations of the forces in the air and their friction on the water. Well: there is no more similarity between the poet's and the psychologist's account of character than there is between a picture of ruffled water and the mathematics of its cause. In a *tour de force,* one might make poetry of mathematics; in a *tour de force,* poetry has been made of psychology—in *Peter Bell.*

But normally poetry simply exhibits *behaviour,* whether inner or outer: not trying to account for those forces which make their appearance in behaviour, as breezes make their appearance in troubled water. Yet, if we truly portray the trouble of the water, we give the sense of invisible wind by its effect on that which is, in all its motions, visible. Just so the poet in his exhibition of human behaviour must convey the sense of that which cannot be exhibited—personality. Once more, how is it done? How does a colossal, a superhuman character, a Satan or a Prometheus, to say nothing of a Macbeth or an Achilles, become credible to us as a personality, even though its symbolic function must live in it as clearly as its individual force?

I put these questions more for the purpose of show-

Poetic Personality

ing where their solution lies, than of solving them. Up
to a point, it is not difficult to see how the sense of a
personality may emerge out of a mass of *characterization:* for the two are by no means identical. Who does
not know how common it is in literature, to have elaborate characterization which never begins to impress us
as the authentic life of a person? Yet how simply and
obviously the great poets seem to effect that impression!
They bring in, perhaps, some sharply individualizing
trait; and with one stroke the character has personality
in him. Richard Crookback, the man born to "snarl and
bite and play the dog," has no grudge against his own
deformity: on the contrary, he is quite good-natured
about it; he is actually amused at it. This is much more
convincing than the obvious thing. If he had railed at
it, we should have accepted that as very natural; that is
what we might have expected, and it would have given
him a very possible character. But the malignant who
can quite genuinely see and enjoy nature's joke against
him—that is not only a character: that is a person. Such
traits are the better in effect the more they are unexpected. One of the best in the world is the rejection of
Falstaff by his beloved Prince Hal. At last Falstaff's
great moment has come; his prince is on his way to be
crowned King of England; and—"I know thee not, old
man!" That is the end of Falstaff, the most loveable,
and certainly one of the most admirable, of immortal
men: "Master Shallow, I owe you a thousand pound."
And it is the beginning of Henry as a person—an admirable, but not a very loveable person. Who has not been

shockt by this catastrophe of all Falstaff's hopes? No
dramatic surprise could be more complete; none more
convincing.[1] Instantly, what has hitherto been the mere
characterisation of Henry becomes the inexplicable, the
irresistible force of a person: now we know just *who* it
is that has been so long sharing in Falstaff's disreputable
gusto. He is the man who can steep himself in wickedness because he knows that nothing can soil him. He
can touch pitch and not be defiled: the filth of the world
has no more power over his mind than dust has to sully
white-hot iron. This is the man to succeed in the world:
this is the *person* inside that dazzling behaviour called
Harry the Fift.

The man is more than his actions. However much
of his character is shown us—doing, thinking, feeling or
what not—that is not all; something still lies behind:
for all this comes out of an inexhaustible, incalculable
fund of spiritual energy: and all, however contradictory
it may seem, has its unity and its origin out of this
deeply concealed yet unmistakably divined source.
That is what it is to feel *personality* within, behind, and
always informing, *character*. If it does convince us at
all, it convinces us the more, the more inexplicable it
is. For personality is not a thing we can explain; and

---

[1] The catastrophe has, indeed, been prepared: there have been
clear hints that something of this kind was like to happen. But it
is safe to say that no one, on a first reading, was ever prepared for
it to happen in this manner. It is the manner of it that is so
shocking, and so convincing. It reveals Henry to us as formidably
as Odysseus was revealed to the suitors when he stript off his rags
and shot Antinoos.

to feel it most, that is the quality of it we must feel the most. When Richard woos and wins the Lady Anne, his preposterous success is the very thing on which we base our belief in his personality: for what else could succeed in this style but sheer personal force? But the deepest sense of personality springs from something much less localised and definitely characteristic than this. Who can explain our love for Falstaff? He does nothing we do not know we ought to reprobate; and he does nothing we do not love him for doing. And when virtue at last rejects him, all our feelings side with him against virtue. Why? There is no rational answer; throughout the whole of his characterisation, his personality irrationally shows, infinitely transcending all the manner of its appearance, and quite unmistakable. It is the person we love, let the character—the manifestation of the person—be what it will.

In fact, the distinctly appreciable moments, in which the soul of personality shines through its vesture of character, would seldom make their effect unless the personal force we there so noticeably feel had been implicit throughout. When Satan, in that magnificent moment at the beginning of his enterprise against man's innocence, is suddenly seized by a desire to repent, in his appalled realisation of the doom he has brought on himself; and then grandly recovers the only secure mood for him: we feel that the symbolic behaviour of a character has become, as it were, transparent, and we see through the character into the depths of a personality:

Me miserable! Which way shall I flie
Infinite wrauth, and infinite despaire?
Which way I flie is Hell; my self am Hell;
And in the lowest deep a lower deep
Still threatning to devour me opens wide. . . .
So farwel Hope, and with Hope farwel Fear,
Farwel Remorse: all Good to me is lost;
Evil be thou my Good. . . .

Yet the possibility of this prodigious moment of tragic emotion has been implicit in Satan from the start. He has been throughout a character symbolising a paradox, the pride of individual rebellion against almighty destiny, the very figure of the absolute antinomy—fixt fate, free will. Now this antinomy appears as something more than the behaviour we watch or the character we understand; it comes on us now with irresistible inexplicable certainty as the very life of personal being. But what we have now, only confirms what we hitherto could but feel: the character could scarcely have lived in our minds at all unless we had been able to feel what we can now see so clearly. Obviously, then, it will not do simply to compound, however skilfully, the ingredients of a character, if we are to feel the life of the person out of which character emerges. The personality must have been living in the poet's mind, with perfect distinction of its unique and unaccountable quality, before he committed it to his art; and the pressure of its personal quality makes itself felt in the poet's technique by an infinity of minute strokes of which he himself, probably, is hardly aware, and which no critical analysis will ever quite reckon up. The real problem is, then,

Poetic Personality

how a poet's purpose can transform itself in his mind into the form and the authority of a living independent personality. I can do no more than indicate the place of the problem in that mystery of *how the mind works,* which poetry willingly leaves to psychology.

And the problem lies deep in that mystery, possibly below the reach of rational apprehension. Once more, analogy may help us to understand its nature. An exactly similar problem meets us in the case of that kind of imagery which is called *apocalyptic.* Swedenborg is the classic instance. He lived in visions which presented themselves to his mind vividly and involuntarily; but, however fantastically irresponsible they might seem, they always had a meaning for him. There was always what he darkly called some "correspondence" in them. His conscious mind, by means of them, was telling itself of things that had taken place profoundly underneath its consciousness: they were the pattern of ripples in his mind produced by an incalculable wind. The most he could do towards understanding them was to infer the presence of the wind of the spirit, and something of its direction. Thus, Swedenborg sees some clergy entering heaven: "as they ascended together, they appeared at a distance like calves. On their entrance into heaven they were received with civility by the angels, but when they conversed with them, they were seized with trembling, afterwards with horror, and at last as if with the agonies of death, upon which they cast themselves headlong, and in their descent they appeared like dead horses." The "correspondence" of this is as surprising as the

317

imagery; for "from correspondence the understanding
of truth has the appearance of a horse, and the non-understanding of truth that of a dead horse." Understanding of truth—non-understanding of truth—what
does that mean? Who knows? Certainly not Swedenborg; the terms are but his labels for obscure disturbances in the depths of his being. But he has seen these
disturbances take visible form in his mind—form unaccountable, and yet charged with importance: he has seen
the horses and the dead horses which are to him symbolic.

But we do not have to be Swedenborgs, nor mystical
eccentrics of any kind, in order to experience the imagery which is lived in as something charged with "correspondence." We need be merely what every one
must be at one time or another—*dreamers*. Something
happens to us, or within us, while we are asleep. We do
not know what is happening; but it is presented to us in
an involuntary symbolism, it is translated into a train
of imagery, an experience of events as clear as anything
actual can be, and instinct with singular importance.
Knocking on the door, for example, becomes an adven-
ture with demons in a thundering factory. The insistent summons, joined by an ambush of lurking emotions,
is something our sleeping consciousness can only know
as the inexplicable air of *meaning* which the vision of
the dream carries with it. And just so works the mind
of a poet when a mass of profoundly obscure disturbance is presented to his mind in the figure of a personality unaccountably and vividly alive, yet charged with

symbolic significance: such a personality, for example,
as the Prometheus of Æschylus. What was it which
the power, known to most of us only in dreams, presented to Æschylus' mind as the sublime behaviour and
person of Prometheus? I necessarily give it the spurious definition of *thought:* it was not thought, but indefinable spiritual energy, which dramatised itself in
the figure of the crucified Titan. It was something of
this kind.

Man is in the current of a divinely implacable destiny; but he is made of free will, and he can only live by
asserting his will against his destiny, which is the power
of God. God resents this and will avenge it. Progress
is evil and to be punished. To God the force of the
world is just because it is His own; to man it must be
unjust because it is against him. And as destiny must
accept man's will, but will nevertheless punish it; so
man's will must accept destiny, but is nevertheless un-
conquerable. And as the triumphant force of the world
belongs to a god of immitigable justice, so the passion
of man's life becomes an opposite god of unmerited suffering. Only as gods can both justice and injustice be
endured: and both must be endured. But it is intelligence, and not strength, which will rule in the long run.

If this is not guessed aright, it was at any rate something of this nature; probably the elements were vaguer,
more massively intangible, more mutually incompatible,
and also much more insistent.

What, for example, I have put down as "Progress
is evil," would more likely be a shadowy relic of loyalty

to the tribe—the vague and infinitely serious feeling that, since the only safety is the tribe, everything new is unsafe, since it may loosen or at least unsettle the elaborately strict complexity of tribal society: and the rest of my hypothetical statement could be similarly expanded.

How could such a congeries ever be imagined in that unity of experience which alone can inspire a poem? Not by any intellectual organization, but by some irrational process of fusion that could only occur in the unconscious depth of the poet's being, precisely on the analogy of a dream. But this having occurred, the life of it could only be known—again on the analogy of a dream—in some kind of involuntary dramatisation, an image inexplicably symbolising its origin. The poet's useful possession of this power in his waking hours, as well as in the useless fantasies of sleep, is one of the privileges of what we call genius; and if he is a great poet, and the impulses stirring in him are vigorous and important enough, the dramatic symbolism whereby his mind presents to him their obscure unification will be not merely the spectacle and behaviour of human character, but the distinct energy of a person. This is not a phenomenon of the ages of mythology only. Precisely the same process which gave Æschylus his Prometheus gave, to add modern instances to those already mentioned, Ibsen his Brand and Nietzsche his Zarathustra. Was it not also a mere modification of this process which enabled Walt Whitman to create, out of the wealth of his noble experience, that vividly personal figure which is surely one of the few supremely great things in modern poetry—the figure of himself? But of this kind of symbolic personality there is an instance even more remarkable, which may well be taken as its type; and with some account of this, my argument must conclude.

§ 2

The things which seem to us most inevitable are, for that very reason, as soon as we begin to look into them, the most mysterious things. Nothing could seem more inevitable than the imaginary personalities in which the power of the greatest poetry lives. Far from trying to explain them, I have been endeavouring to show how mysterious they are: and I have been fortunate indeed if I have succeeded merely in making it plain what the mystery is, which lies behind not only Prometheus and his analogues—Job, Satan, Faustus—but also behind Hamlet and Macbeth, Achilles and Hector: behind any character which lives in our minds both as unique personality, and also as poetic technique—the symbolic expression of the poet's sense of the significance of things.

Any such character may be the means of the supremely great in poetry: his large symbolic virtue is the scope, and the intensifying virtue of his personality is the harmony, which we require for poetic greatness: the harmony, namely, which comes of the issue of everything the symbolism includes or can suggest out of a single fund of energy, imagined as a personal existence. But are such characters as those I have just named the

The Idea of Great Poetry

only kind of personified harmony? Are they the only ones to be reckoned with, in our account of what the world has accepted as great, and supremely great, in poetry? That can hardly be: for reflect only, that we have not yet taken account of Lucretius and Dante. If they are not great, and supremely great, poets, who is? There is still, therefore, something to be said: we have still to consider the poetry in which the greatness lives in the symbolic personality of the *poet himself*. I will take Dante as the type of this; and it would not be difficult to justify the choice of him rather than of Lucretius. I could never sufficiently express my admiration for Lucretius; and his motives command my sympathies more than Dante's can ever do. But Dante the theological man is the focus of a far larger, though perhaps not deeper, experience than Lucretius the intellectual man; and assuredly Dante's personality is the more potent and imposing of the two. Do I, by taking Dante's achievement last, mean to suggest that it is the greatest of those which I have discussed? That is possible. It is at any rate certain that the pyramid of poetic qualities, narrowing as they rise until we stand on the apex of supremely great achievement, is nowhere so clear as in the poetry of Dante: I mean, of course, in his *Divine Comedy*.

But have we not already had the poet who expresses himself? Wordsworth and Leopardi, for instance, have their ideas of life; but is not our real interest directed, by means of these ideas, on the personal life of the poets themselves? That is partly true, no doubt: though not, of course, in the sense that we require biography in order to appreciate, or even to improve our appreciation of, these poets. But however true it may be, we yet merely *infer*, as best we may, the personalities behind the poems, with no assurance either of completeness of knowledge or even of certainty in it. No such inference is needed in the case of the poets of whom I take Dante as the grand type. These poets create in their works the figure of their own personal lives as certainly as Shakespeare creates Hamlet or Milton creates Satan; and they do it in precisely the same manner—not by *truth to life* in the realistic sense, but by concentration and enhancement. Every moment of the vitality they portray is intensely significant of the peculiar personality behind it; and it is a personality which reveals the inmost motion of its being to our delighted and assured clairvoyance; and finally it is a personality of which the impression is complete and whole—a *unity* of personal life. In a word, it is a personality poetically created; and created for a poetical purpose. It is the focus of the matter, and the governance of the form, of the poem. In the manner of the life it assumes in our imaginations, the poet has made a symbol of his purpose; and there is really, at the back of this impersonation of a poet's sense of life, the same mystery which we have found in the case of such objective characters as Prometheus or Macbeth.

Whether Lucretius or Dante would have admitted this central concern of their art with their own personal lives is a question scarcely pertinent. I have no doubt

The Idea of Great Poetry

Lucretius would have said his theme was the philosophy of Epicurus; Dante might have said his theme was Holy Church revealing the destiny of man. The fact remains that the poetic symbol of Epicurus' philosophy is the majestic intellectual experience of Lucretius himself—an intellectual experience always charged with the force of a unique and noble personality: and a symbol, moreover, not merely of a particular philosophy, but of the whole sublime ambition of human intellect: namely, to conceive the sum of experience as a rational harmony. And as for Dante—but that is what must now engage my endeavours.

There are many recognized indications of insanity: none more reliable, I suppose, than the conviction of having something new to say about Dante. You will not, I hope, think I am qualifying for the attentions of the alienists now. What I have to say about *The Divine Comedy* is not offered as anything new, but simply in the interests of my argument, which would be left flagrantly incomplete without some notice of that astonishing poem. It is obvious, from what has been said, that *The Divine Comedy* can only be taken as an instance of greatness in poetry, if it is taken in its quality *as a whole*. It happens that this quality has been denied the right to any poetic existence at all by the most eminent of living critics, the man to whom æsthetic theory owes a quite incalculable debt, Benedetto Croce. There would be some excuse, therefore, for considering afresh at least one aspect of Dante's achievement, apart from the fact that it is the aspect our topic requires us

Poetic Personality

to consider. We must face and, if we can, counter the notion, that it is not *The Divine Comedy* as a whole which is poetry, but merely certain moments and episodes in it: the so-called poem as a whole being really a "theological novel," which has poetic merit only in so far as it provides fitting occasions for poetry—that is, for momentary poetry. In that case, not only is *The Divine Comedy* not great as poetry (however great it may be as a monument of theology at a certain stage), but there is no such thing as poetic greatness at all, in the sense these lectures have been supposing.

We shall certainly not disagree with Croce and his followers in their estimate of the momentary poetry of *The Divine Comedy*. We cannot admire it enough; yet even so we may admire it chiefly as the means whereby the poem as a whole comes into existence, as successive layers building up the pyramid of supreme poetic greatness. I merely allude therefore, in the most cursory manner possible, to those qualities for which Dante is, no doubt, most easily praised; for my concern is with that poetic achievement which exists, if it exists at all, as superstructure resting on these.

No greater mastery of words has ever been shown than in *The Divine Comedy;* and I think it would be safe to say of some parts of *Paradiso,* that such an *incantation* as Dante there effects out of the sound and meaning of language can nowhere else be found. Words take on a new being in Dante's poetry: they have more force and more delicacy of force than we could ever have suspected. He is the standing example

The Idea of Great Poetry

of the First Law of Poetics, that the greater the inspiration, the more art is required. Such fierce pressure of personal life as Dante's, such white-hot condensation of manifold experience into instantaneous self-consciousness, could never have reacht our minds without the skill which can use with miraculous precision every possible power of language in simultaneous complexity of effect. And it is interesting to compare the subtle faculty of suggestion which his early poetry has, with the complete domination he can exert over us in *The Divine Comedy*. No poet takes such absolute possession of our minds as he does there.

But as to what he does with this masterful enchantment of our minds, there is no end to the praise of that. I mention only those things which obviously serve to build up our pyramid towards its apex. We may note first the air of sharp lucid realism which he makes his imaginary experience assume: as, for example, in those many strokes which bring home to us the living man alone among ghosts: only he can cast a shadow in this spectral world, and his disembodied companions are amazed to see once more that familiar sign of earthly life; only he, when he is to be ferried across the Styx, makes the boat dip in the water as he steps aboard. This is the power, too, which, in a few lines, brands upon our memories the living attitude and inmost personal force of such figures as Francesca, Ulysses, Sordello; and which makes the progress of the poem a series of unforgettably impressive and minutely precise incidents. I merely hazard one or two specimens: the

Poetic Personality

indifferent angel who comes down to hell to give orders to the furies, walking over Styx "con le piante asciutte," and waving away the foul air,

> menando la sinistra innanzi spesso;

the grotesque solemnity of the escort of demons, and their suddenly flaring quarrel; the descent of the two angels in Antipurgatorio, and the blinding beauty of their faces; "Casella mio" and his song,

> che la dolcezza ancor dentro mi suona;

Filippo Argenti, "pien di fango," and Dante's immortal hatred:

> con piangere e con lutto,
> Spirito maladetto, ti rimani!

Still more astonishing are those unaccountable visions, which we are made to see as distinctly as if we were looking at a landskip, which we know are pregnant with meaning, but out of which we can never separate the meaning: for that reason, no doubt, commonly quoted (I think loosely) as instances of Dante's mysticism. They certainly, in a way we can hardly explain, concentrate into their imagery significances vital to the whole force of the poem: I mean, of course, such visions as the eagle in the Sixth Heaven, delineated by the incandescent souls of the just; or the river of light,

> dipinte di mirabil primavera,

and the living jewels which issue from it and, for all their dazzling colour,

son di lor vero umbriferi prefazii;

and, above all, the White Rose made of the Blest:

In forma dunque di candida rosa
mi si mostrava la milizia santa
che nel suo sangue Cristo fece sposa.

These are the things we can most easily refer to, if we are talking of Dante's characteristic eminence. Without these things, he could not be a great poet; but neither could he be a great poet if these detachable things made up the whole account of his poetic achievement. And clearly not one of these things is present for its own sake in *The Divine Comedy;* not one of them but is brought in by Dante most unmistakably for the sake of something which transcends the sum of their separable virtues. Dante is obviously using them in the interest of his whole intention in the poem. Would it not therefore seem the natural thing, to go on with our account of Dante's achievement in the same way as we have begun, and from the organizing of language and imagery into characters, incidents, visions, to pass on to the organizing of these into Hell, Purgatory, Heaven, and so into the divine method of continual justice; and from this into the still closer unity, the living experience of the whole scheme of man's destiny as a thing personally seen and known, and thence to the very apex of

Poetic Personality

the pyramid, the intense personality of Dante himself, the man who is capable of this experience?

But it is just this continuation, this quite natural continuation, of poetic purpose, which recent criticism has declined to allow. The pyramid must be truncated; there is a stage of its elevation at which poetry ceases to exist. I do not know why this stage should be placed at one point rather than another. It seems to me that if you once begin the poetic ascent you must, except by a quite arbitrary limitation, go on as far as it will take you; and the poetic ascent has certainly begun when out of the meaning of words you allow a character, an incident, to form itself as poetry. But Croce and his followers decline to allow Dante any poetry except these momentary occurrences of it: and each moment occurs, they say, in its own right only: there is no continuity and accumulation of poetic effect in the series of the moments. Instead of allowing the obvious thing, that Dante is using each moment of his poem for the purpose of gradually establishing his whole intention; this whole intention is regarded as a ready-made frame of carpentry into which poetic moments are fitted and let off like fireworks.

I doubt if theoretical ingenuity could be more surprisingly obtuse. Of course, when the poem is complete in our minds, we can see that it has a structure: but it is a structure which exists wholly by means of these moments, and has the same right to the name of poetry as they have. Suppose it true that the theme of *The Divine Comedy* is Catholic eschatology; it is not half true and not a quarter true; but if it was the whole truth, why should not this theme become poetry? To expound an argument as such, is, no question of it, to fall from poetry. But if a poet gives us his vivid intuition of his argument and of all it means to him, if he expresses it as an experience, with a technique which can convey his exultation of reason, emotion, and spirit in living in the sense of truth, and the labour and delight of attaining this, he is giving us what must, by any workable definition, be accepted as poetry. That is what Lucretius gives us. And that, with much more completeness and in a much more intricate harmony, is what *The Divine Comedy* gives us: not the system of Catholic theology, but the individual passion of experience in which, by means of that system, a man feels he understands and can love the inmost reality of things and the purpose of the world. That is permanent, however transitory the vehicle of it may be. Dante lived in his theology like the electric current in a metal wire. The energy was so intense that it became radiant: and it is a conscious energy, and sees the globe of its own illumination round about it. He is living at the centre of spiritual reality; he becomes in his most personal quality the symbol of man knowing and enjoying his destiny. And there is absolutely no theoretical difference between Dante's imaginary meeting with Farinata in Hell, and his whole vision of Hell, Purgatory, and Heaven, along with the sense of the order of divine justice the vision implies. The one is as unmistakably an experience as the other. No one has ever ventured to question the superb poetic quality of the Farinata incident: and the criticism which denies the poetic quality of *The Divine Comedy* as a whole is simply criticism which is not capacious enough to contain it.

§ 3

Croce is a distinguisht authority; but I have on my side an authority to whom I attribute greater importance—that of Dante himself: I mean Dante the constructive critic, the profound and meticulous theorist of poetry. He liked to hinge his principles on his own work: as he did in the *Convivio*, and the celebrated letter to Can Grande. And his main concern always was to show how a poem exists by reason of its whole intention; it is the single result of the organisation of all its detail, detail which exists for no other purpose than to combine in a single result. He would have been amused at the criticism which thinks it has done its duty in discriminating the quality of the detail in a work of art; and he would have asked, in that formidable determination to get to the bottom of things which we call *medieval*, how mere detail as such can give existence to a work of art at all.

Dante distinguishes two senses in a poem: what he calls the literal sense and the allegorical sense. On this hint, amazing and preposterous interpretations have been foisted into *The Divine Comedy*—interpretations which are allegorical in our sense of the word—political, philosophical, and what not. What Dante says himself is clear enough.[1] The literal sense of *The Divine Comedy* is the fortunes of certain souls after death. The allegorical sense is the destiny of man and the idea of perfect justice. "Allegorical" has come to be a somewhat misleading term. But assuredly it is true that there must be always two meanings in poetry, though there is, of course, no distinct line between them: "literal" will do as the name of the one, but the other we had better call "symbolic." A poet, we say, exists as a poet by expressing his experience. But whether this be an experience of everyday matter of fact, or a purely visionary experience as strange and lofty as Dante's, one thing is certain: the experience itself will be incommunicable. The skill of the poet is to make, out of language and the effects of language, a reliable symbol of his experience; and the symbol is understood, when the provocations of its imagery reverberate in emotions and allusions through our minds, in such a way that they finally collect themselves into an imaginary experience exactly corresponding to the original experience in the poet's mind.

But what impels a poet to express himself is the importance a thing has for him; and that is nothing but the whole pattern of connexion and relation it has with other things—including, of course, the poet's own feelings. The poet is the man who sees in things an unusual degree of significance, an unusual complexity of fine and strong relationship with things far and near. Now Dante is the type of poet who finds nothing but

[1] Letter to Can Grande (XIII, *Test. Crit.*).

this in the whole manner of his own life; he is therefore typically the poet who is moved to express simply *himself:* not moods and moments of himself, but the whole scope and style of his personal experience, the whole stature and attitude of his personal existence. He had lived in experience as full and as varied as his time could offer; and everything in it was a metaphor of all the rest. The most significant of all his experiences was so simply because it was the most intense, and because it came just when the characteristic habit of his life was beginning to establish itself. This was, of course, his early love for Beatrice. He spent the rest of his life celebrating it, for it became the centre round which everything else must organise itself. And it is easy to see why, with such a man as Dante. There was, raised to its highest power, all that we usually mean by the passion of love in this experience; but also something which we do not usually expect to find in a love-affair. It had that significance for him which involves every faculty he can live in. Love, for Dante, could not but be an intellectual, as well as an emotional and a sensuous experience: his love of Beatrice saw in her not only the perfection of beauty but the perfection of understanding as well. It was, for him, impossible that the delight of the man who sees and feels could occur without the illumination of the man who knows. He loves Beatrice; and that means that he understands the world: or at least has seen himself understanding the world. For to love her is to be aware of life's perfection.

The Idea of Great Poetry

That Beatrice is the perfection of life is merely confirmed in him by her early death: the angels have petitioned for her presence in the only society that is worthy of her. Henceforth she must live on earth only in Dante's imagination. But this is a life for her of continually increasing activity; she lives, that is, by being idealised: until nothing can command his mind that is not a mode of her. And so, when, after her death, he plunges himself in philosophy for consolation, intellectual joys mean the revived presence of Beatrice. As he could not love her during her earthly life without a kindling of intellect as well as of emotion, so now he cannot have an intellectual ardour that does not recall the image of her beauty.

But philosophy was not his only consolation. He plunged also into fierce and gross passions, which inspired some of the best of his early poetry. He emerged bitterly repentant, rebuked by philosophy as an attribute of Beatrice, and by the vision of Beatrice with all the understanding of the world in her eyes. Yet it was only in idea that this hateful sin was punisht. He had turned traitor to what he knew was the best—to all that the image of Beatrice meant to him, to the service of the vision of perfection. He had proved faithless to this: and no actual punishment had followed. But also he had served most faithfully his country, as soldier and statesman; and he knew the merits of his service. And what followed here? Ignominy and disgrace. His wages were, to be a condemned man begging his way through exile. He had grievously sinned, and all the result was, a sense that he deserved punishment. He had done nobly, and the result was punishment that was bitterly real.

Henceforth he devotes himself to the vindication of the idea of justice. The more unjust these temporal realities are, the more triumphant becomes his belief in a justice ideal and eternal, making these bewildering moments of earthly life a necessary stage of its method. He recreates the affairs of this world under the evident law of an ultimate and unmistakable justice, which lets nothing wrong go unpunisht, nothing good go unrewarded. He portrays Hell, Purgatory, Heaven; and the whole range of life on the earth contributes to the vision. And over all his experience of this ideal world presides as his especial director—at first through a delegate and afterwards in person—the spirit of Beatrice, the image of the love which is also understanding—the image of that exalted experience which loves its own destiny because it can understand it. Need it be said, that Beatrice is Dante's image of his own profound desire? Or that the theology of the poem is his symbol of the satisfaction of his desire?

For this theological scheme of Hell, Purgatory, Heaven, and the superbly vivid substance in which it lives, is, of course, Dante's literal meaning in *The Divine Comedy*. If I had to stay there, the poem would be, for all the marvel of its verbal technique, a repellent curiosity. The literal meaning of *Inferno* is to me the most abominable superstition that has ever pestered humanity: pass from it to the religion of the Homeric

The Idea of Great Poetry

Hymns, and you pass from barbarity into civilisation.

But who ever thought of staying in the literal meaning of *The Divine Comedy?* No one, certainly, who reads it as poetry. Beyond, but by means of, this literal meaning, we see the symbolic meaning: we see the spirit of man placed in a world of implacable process, yet determined to create for itself its own sense of its destiny. And this, it has resolved, shall be in accordance with the most sublime faculty it has, the love of justice. Dante gives us this as it works itself out through the whole fate of man, and with a concentrated propriety of detail and lucidity of significance that make it more intensely our own than anything the actual world can offer. And at the climax of this story of eternal justice told in terms of earthly life, comes the vindication even of this. It is the nature of man to insist on justice: and we are made to feel that absolute reliance on justice will at last bring man's mind into perfect accord with the unspeakable inmost reality of things. We live, therefore, the whole possibility of this world in one great coherence. From the depths of lewd and detestable crime up to the height of indescribable ecstasy, the whole conceivable range of human faculty—rebellion and submission, torment and delight—becomes a single harmony of impression, when Hell, Purgatory, and Heaven have finally organized their sequence.

That is the very thing we have found to be required for greatness in poetry. But for the supremely great, something more than this, we found, was needed: namely, the concentration of this in a figure of vividly

336

personal life. And here is the acme of the symbolic meaning of *The Divine Comedy*. The figure of Dante himself is the immortal, unchangeable thing that steps out of his poem: the intensely individual figure, with all its resentments and abasements, indignations and pities, its pride and its love, its generous glorying in the good and ferocious scorn of the evil. Symbolic personality is, from the very nature of the poem's form, the thing which *The Divine Comedy* gives us more remarkably than any other poem. For the whole process of events in the poem is the process of the spiritual experience of Dante himself: and out of it all emerges the personal man, who takes on himself the demand that destiny shall be just, and satisfies the demand by *understanding* the act of destiny as the act of justice. Dante is not only the type of the grand style in poetry, but of the grand style in man's commerce with his destiny.

Let me, in conclusion, just say that the instances of great poetry which I have given you have not been meant to represent anything like a complete series. I have said nothing of Sophocles or Pindar or Virgil, Tasso or Calderon or Racine. I have made but trifling references to Chaucer, to Æschylus, and other poets only less important than these. But I merely brought those poets in who would, I thought, make my argument clear. If they have not done that, they have at least, I hope, directed your thoughts to an aspect of poetry which, it seems to me, needs some emphasis to-day. I do not mean merely the quality of greatness; but that which makes the quality of greatness possible. I have indicated it often enough, and perhaps too often, by the distinction between *poetry* and *poems*. *Form—coherence—unity*—these are well-worn terms; and just because they are, I thought it a fitting topic for such a course as this to argue in favour of their unchangeable importance, by considering poems which cannot rightly be appreciated at all, unless these terms have some meaning for us.